# THEY TOOK MY CHILDREN AND I FOUGHT BACK

A FATHER'S 10 YEAR EFFORT TO REGAIN CUSTODY OF HIS CHILDREN

WILLIAM O'CONNELL

# CONTENTS

First Edition published 2021

ISBN: 978-1-63795-054-8 (print)
ISBN: 978-1-63795-055-5 (ebook)

Cover design: Erin Ewasko Black, Bellia Print & Design
Book design: Fiona M. Jardine
Typeface: Crimson Text

# DEDICATION

*I dedicate this book and my efforts in this decade-long cause to my children and to all fathers who are denied equal justice in any family court. I would be the first to acknowledge a loving relationship is the best environment for raising one's children. It is a love of life to watch your children grow, one that requires a monumental effort by both parents if it is to be done well. But if that is not the circumstance in any family then the law is correct, the best interest of the children must prevail. If the court fails in its decision, then the best-qualified parent must do what is right, what is needed to protect the children. Fathers have a right to be a part of that effort and family courts should not impose the barriers they do against any fathers' rights and obligations in that endeavor.*

# INTRODUCTION

The United States Constitution provides legal rights and protections to all who live in this great country. We are taught these unalienable rights accrue to all in America. Most movies and television dramas rather simplistically imply that justice for all wins the day in America's courts. We are taught to trust the system, that the laws, judges, juries, police, and good legal representation will provide that promised justice.

Not to disappoint anyone, but one must participate in this legal system to discover for themselves just how this notion, belief in justice for all, is or is not applied. The beloved Constitution, laws, judges, Appellate Courts, the Supreme Court, lawyers, juries, facts, evidence, questions, and answers are all but building blocks in this search for justice. I suggest our legal system does not guarantee you justice but merely provides you the option to fight for it.

This literary effort recants the many legal promises due to a father seeking justice and custody of his young children in a family court. I was that father, accused of domestic violence, I was removed from my children and home. I sought my rightful place back with my children. All six lawyers I consulted told me my hope to regain custody of my children was not a reasonable one. I believed the laws promised, mandated equal justice for all, a fair hearing of the facts. No, I was told it was best to just concede, that justice was not available to me in this circumstance and that fact should just be accepted. Lawyers told me it was not worth the effort to seek the promised justice for all.

Chiseled into the marble façade above the entrance to the U.S. Supreme Court building is the preamble "Equal Justice Under Law." To assume such a broad declaration of justice in the United States applies to the New Jersey Family Court is a mistake. As a father, one enters into this system of justice at your own risk. Local attorneys told me that and my time in this justice system proved them correct. My children and I waited for the promised justice that this court would never deliver.

It was the promised justice for all that carried me for ten-plus years through this case seeking that which was denied to me and my children in family court. Did I ever expect this effort would consume so many years of my life? No, but that is the distance traveled in this case. Not a love story but about a father's love for his children held hostage to a system of injustice that cared little for the children's welfare and even less for his. This is a true accounting of those years of four judges; nine lawyers; numerous complaints, motions, and responses; three appeals; lawsuits; four arrests; a bail hearing; three trials; two custody evaluations, and whatever else they could throw at me.

This is not a story of family court justice, but a story of justice denied in family court. I was guilty of one thing in this family court, I was a father.

# A GREAT START TO LIFE

My life followed the script as I wrote it for myself. I grew up in a blue-collar, refinery town of 8,000, that sat on the Delaware River just across from Philadelphia. I got along, had a great time as a kid doing all sorts of things kids should do; did some dumb things too but survived those and learned a lesson or two, and moved on with life. I left South Jersey and went across the country to a national university to experience more of life's opportunities and challenges, majoring in accounting and finance. Upon graduation, I took a job in NYC with a major international corporation. After a six-month stay in the city, I asked for the opportunity to hit the road as they say. I would travel a good part of the world for the next six years auditing the myriad functions of the corporate entity.

In my first three years auditing the company's facilities, I traversed the US; worked in Calgary, Alberta for several months, and spent several weeks working in Puerto Rico before being offered the opportunity to travel internationally off the continent. I jumped at the chance to see more of the world. My first international assignment in March 1977 took me to the west coast of Africa working in the various former French colonies of Senegal, Togo, Mali, Upper Volta (now Burkina Faso), Niger, Ivory Coast, Cameroon, and Burundi.

Typically, our team of two would stay in any country for at least three weeks but we would spend eight weeks or more in both Senegal and the Ivory Coast. Who would have thought my two years of high school French would ever have paid off? I knew enough French to converse at a basic level in the offices, and I could easily count to one hundred. I wandered the local streets and felt confident enough to ask general questions. Although many in the offices and community spoke English well enough, I reveled in practicing the French I knew. I also took a weekend trip to Banjul, The Gambia, home of the wildly popular Alex Haley novel and TV series Roots. Leaving Africa in late November 1977 my next assignment took me to London before I was to start a new eighteen-month assignment tour to South America, Panama, and the Caribbean.

My father passed away while I was working in Abidjan, Ivory Coast. Advised father had but days to live, I rushed home to South Jersey, but he hung on. I returned to Abidjan in ten days where I received another call two weeks later advising father had passed. I again flew back and forth to New Jersey. For some unknown reason, I vowed to remain out on the road after these two quick trips home and would not again return to the States for more than eighteen months.

I left London after a few weeks and arrived in Trinidad and Tobago, the island nation off the northeast coast of South America. The company owned a large compound some thirty miles south of the capital city of Port of Spain. This company facility was not only home to its largest refinery operation outside the U.S., but it was also home to all the British and American expatriates that managed the plant and the company's local oil production, onshore and offshore. The compound provided family housing, apartments for visitors, a country club that hosted many weekends and holiday social gatherings, a large swimming pool, tennis courts, and a K-12 school. A town itself that supported a community of perhaps 2,000 senior staff and family members. We also had easy access to beautiful Caribbean beaches on the weekends. Life after work on the compound was relaxing and entertaining. After an abbreviated stay of just a few months, it was on to South America.

I arrived in Bogota, the capital of Colombia on March 27, 1978, to join up with two other American auditors with whom I would make this assigned tour through South America. I was advised that at least three prior company auditors had not made it out of Colombia on these assignments without being married. We were warned the women were beautiful, most spoke English, and they liked Americans. The Colombian audit was relatively large in that it entailed reviews of the accounting, marketing, and oil production operations within the country. We would be in Bogota for six months. I moved from a week's stay at the International Hotel in downtown Bogota into an efficiency apartment in the north of the city. Taxis made travel easy within this bustling capital city of some seven million people that was sprawled along a deep valley 8,500 feet up in the Andes mountains.

Bogota and Colombia were in a state of distress as international drug cartels and other criminal networks held much control and influence over all aspects of Colombian life. Security was a constant concern and being an easily identifiable American did not improve matters. Upon my arrival in Bogota, I was taken to meet the manager of the company's business, a well-placed Colombian. After a cordial welcome, we got down to work. This manager would slip out to lunch two weeks later, without his usual and required security entourage, and was abducted in broad daylight. He was never seen alive again.

My new apartment was in a micro-hotel of just eight efficiency units and I settled into a third-floor unit for what was to be my home for the next six months. I typically returned to the apartment at about 6:00 PM. One evening upon entering the lobby I immediately noticed a new, young, and attractive hostess. Waiting for my turn at the small front desk, this young woman smiled easily and was somewhat nervous at her new job. As I approached, I slowly spoke in English not knowing her abilities in the language. She immediately advised she was bilingual and she spoke English well, and surely much better than the French I hammered out in Africa. I introduced myself and she told me the hotel owner had advised her of the two American guests who worked for the well-known American company.

I found myself looking forward to my nightly return from work so

I could meet up with this young woman, Paula. Just twenty-one-years-old, she was in college taking courses for education in the hospitality industry. This job sufficed for the course-required internship in the industry. Although Paula lived with her parents and younger sister within a mile of this apartment building, her parents and culture frowned on this young woman being in college and out at night, much less working. She did not know how to drive a car. Her father dropped her off at 4:00 PM and picked her up at 8:00 PM each day she worked. Paula's family had some financial standing as compared to the vast majority of the country. Her father's grandfather was a former President of Colombia in the 1920s. Typical of much of Latin American society, there was a great disparity between those at the top levels of society who owned a significant percentage of the country's wealth as compared to most of the indigenous population who scraped by for whatever they could get. But Paula's family lived modestly compared to others within her extended family of uncles, aunts, and cousins. I would find out later that both Paula and her sister, six years younger, were adopted. Paula was found living with an elderly grandmother at age one as her parents reportedly died in an auto accident. The younger sister was adopted at age seven having been abandoned by her father after her mother's death.

After a week of chatting in the lobby, I asked Paula out on a date. She had to ask her parents but her family was excited that they would get to meet this American, college-educated, working for this well-known American company, paid in dollars, Catholic. What could be better? Paula's mother advised her to be ready for the 7:00 PM date as "gringos" were notoriously prompt compared to local customs. The company provided me twice-weekly at-home Spanish lessons so I felt even more comfortable practicing my new language in the office and with Paula's family and friends. I eventually dropped these lessons, explaining to the American college-educated tutor, Paula would teach me all the Spanish I would need to know. Paula would subsequently advise my apartment was used as a model in that I kept it so neat.

I had to leave Colombia in late June to renew the ninety-day visa I was given upon entry into the country in March. As these visas expired, those of us on the audit team would travel to Panama for a long weekend, secure another ninety-day visa at the Colombian Consulate, and return to Bogota. I bought Paula a Spanish guitar and gave it to her as a gift upon my return. After more of this courtship, I asked this young lady to marry me in late July. We were married in early September 1978. Paula was over thirty minutes late for the 8:00 PM wedding mass. Paula's family was excited by the prospects and good fortunes of this young woman who was married to an American, would travel more of the world, and then live in the U.S., something most could only hope to do.

My mother, several siblings, a brother-in-law, and an aunt traveled to Bogota for the wedding. I will forever remember my mother's insightful quote, "when the heart is on fire, smoke gets in your eyes." The courtship was fast for sure, but I was twenty-six and ready to begin to plan our future lives together. Traveling as a married couple to the Caribbean, Panama, Ecuador, and Brazil was exciting for me, and Paula looked forward to new horizons of unknown cultures and new-found freedoms. It was an opportunity of a lifetime for this young woman, now considered best-married in her extended family. Yes, I was to be yet another auditor to leave Colombia married after an assignment of just months. It must be the water, or maybe the thin air. We took a ten-day honeymoon to Cartagena, Colombia, and then to Aruba and Curacao.

My first assignment after Bogota took us to the Dominican Republic for three weeks of hotel living before heading back to the continent to Panama. Here we would spend the next three months and enjoyed access to middle America that was the canal zone, and saw the disparity of wealth from what existed just across the street in Panama City. The Canal treaty was getting kicked around in Congress at the time and the local officials did not appreciate much of what was said in the states as to the abilities of the Panamanians to manage the canal. Upon arrival in Panama, I was booted to the end of the immigration line a few times and Paula, traveling on her Colombian passport, was accused of being a prostitute. Both our passports were seized and local company personnel took us the next day to clear matters up and regain possession of our documents. On to Quito, Ecuador for an assignment that would last four months. Here is where reality fogged the married life of two cultures having been wed together on such short notice.

Paula's parents did not work and the family enjoyed daily full-time maid service that catered to the family's every whim. The maid was a young, married mother of two children who traveled by bus for an hour from the south of Bogota to work in their home in the north of Bogota. She arrived at the house by 7:00 AM and did not leave most days until 7:00 PM to take the long bus ride back home. This maid prepared all meals, carried breakfast up to the parent's bedroom every morning, set and cleared the dining table, did the dishes, cleaned the home, washed and hung the laundry, ironed the clothes, and put them away. You name it, she did. A very pleasant woman of humble means with a difficult job that required her to answer to every beck and call from the family.

I was the eighth of nine children and we had no maid service in our struggling middle-class American household. We each had assigned chores by day and week. Besides my morning paper route through high school, I had to scrub the kitchen floor every Saturday before I could leave the house for the local basketball court. For three summers during college, I drove an ice cream truck twelve hours a day, six days a week, for the opportunity to make good money. I continued in the paperboy business but worked on a truck route from 4:30 to 7:00 AM before heading out to work the ice cream route at 9:00 AM. My mother would greet me most nights with a hot meal upon my return home from the route near 10 PM. Both my parents worked and all my siblings planned futures working outside the home. The cultural contrasts were startling. After meals in Bogota, I readily took my dishes to the kitchen; offered to help do things only the maid did. I was told you can't do these things, although everyone appreciated it was quite American. I taught Paula to drive their family car much to the chagrin of her mother. I always left a generous tip for the maid after any of our visits to Bogota. It was not a lot of money but the mother-in-law certainly frowned upon this as my tips would be considered significant relative to the local wage scale. I bought uniforms and supplies for her young children just starting school.

Our most significant experience of cultural clash surfaced in Quito. In the new apartment, I advised Paula we should look to eat more dinner meals at the apartment as it was more relaxing than restaurant dining every night. A good home-cooked meal was to be relished. Never having cooked anything in her life, Paula struggled for ideas for meals and how to prepare them. She settled on a local version of a heavy pasta-like spaghetti and after a couple of weeks of nothing but spaghetti I told Paula I could not eat any more spaghetti; the sight of it ruined any thought of a home-cooked meal. I did not eat spaghetti for several years after this stay in Ecuador.

We moved to Rio de Janeiro after Quito. We rented a furnished apartment and enjoyed the beaches and weekend tours in and around Rio for the next six months. The company provided a chauffeured car as it was considered too risky to expose the company or ourselves to any involvement in a local car accident. Paula enjoyed her newfound freedoms and was quite capable in the big city. We also traveled to Sau Paulo for my weeks' work there. Paula mastered the local bus routes and taxis extended her reach throughout much of the city. Paula enjoyed learning Portuguese whereas I struggled as I would mix the little French I knew with the little Spanish I knew while filling in the gaps with English. Paula joined a social club affiliated with the many Americans that lived abroad in most of these foreign cities. Life was good!

After Rio, it was on to Port-a-Prince, Haiti for four weeks where Paula became friends with the Colombian ambassador. We were invited to his residence for a well-cooked meal. Then back to Trinidad for a six-month assignment. Not too bad for all of my first twenty-eight years of life, now happily married for two of them.

While I looked forward to this return trip to Trinidad it seemed to have burst Paula's enthusiasm for travel. Although she enjoyed several trips back to Bogota to visit family and friends as we traversed South America, the compound's location limited Paula's access to the preferred city life of Port of Spain. After several months in Trinidad,

Paula asked us to plan our return to the United States and settle down. I contacted headquarters and within a month or two we were headed back to the States. I was content with a life of continued travel but was agreeable to return home and begin real family life in the United States.

# 2

# HEADING HOME TO REALITY

Not wanting to return to the NYC environment, I accepted a
position at the company's regional accounting offices located
in Cherry Hill, NJ. We were back in my home roots of Gloucester
County, just twenty-five miles southeast of Philadelphia. We
purchased a home in a suburban community and I carpooled thirty
minutes to work. We purchased a second car so Paula could get about
and discover the area and find what opportunities she wanted to
pursue as to continuing her schooling or finding work.

I soon sought a transfer from the accounting function to the credit
department which was looking for someone with my financial background. This regional credit office managed all the company's billions
of dollars of retail, distributor, and industrial product sales from
Maine to Georgia. Upon my transfer to the credit department, I was
asked to look over a contentious credit file. The company was sued
for $500,000 by a gas station operator located in upstate New York.
The retailer's suit alleged he suffered "mental anguish" trying to deci-
pher our business records for his three businesses. The file was many
inches thick and documented over three years of transactions
commingled on the monthly statements to such a degree no one could
vouch for the company's records for any of the three businesses.

I took the file home and over the next two weeks, I unraveled this accounting mess. All transactions documented, we headed to an arbitration hearing in Syracuse, NY. Within a few hours we had proven our case and the customer's complaint was dismissed. I was received back at the office to some acclaim having salvaged a win from a seemingly no-win situation. I remained in the credit function and progressed through the ranks as I understood credit and had a knack for getting things done. I would be a witness in two other trials with another employer years later. I loved credit management and it would be my career until I retired thirty-five years later.

Unable to conceive children, we worked with the fertility clinic at the University of Pennsylvania in Philadelphia (UPenn) for the next three years with no success. We had even chosen names for both a boy and a girl child that just did not happen. We went through the usual rigorous testing to identify the fertility issues but no definitive issue was ever disclosed. I came from a large family that had already accumulated fifteen nieces and nephews to date, but while we remained hopeful, we were resigned to the infertility issue.

In 1981 the company announced this local office was to close and be consolidated in Houston with other regional offices from across the country, and my job was transferred there in 1982. To avoid this transfer, I took another job within the company, again in Africa, managing the budget for an offshore oil drilling operation in Luanda, Angola. The work schedule was twenty-eight days working in Luanda and twenty-eight days off work to do what you wanted to do. It was a two-day trip each way to get to and from Luanda through either Rio de Janeiro or Paris. This twenty-eight-day work schedule allowed Paula to take additional trips back to Bogota while I was working in Angola for the month. This job and its travel demand would further delay any resolution of our desire for children. I returned home through Rio three times, which allowed me to meet up with Paula in Bogota. On another return trip home from Angola, I met Paula in London and we toured through Europe for two weeks. Again, life was good. But the inevitable was only deferred; after eighteen months of offshore dry holes the operation was closed down and my position ended. We moved to Houston in 1983.

As it became obvious there were undefined fertility issues in our relationship, the thought of maybe not having children was disappointing. We decided not to continue the fertility treatment in Houston as it was emotionally draining. Like most couples, you plan to have your kids to raise, to teach them, and to watch them grow. When we floated the idea of adopting children I was cautioned by my family about possible hidden issues when adopting children. Then too, in the U.S. at the time there was the relatively new theory of open adoptions. I can recall discussing those issues with the Catholic Charities staff in Houston who we worked with as we considered adoption. The last thing I wanted was a birth mother having a presence, an influence in raising a baby we adopted from her. No, this would be our child to raise, our responsibility. Then too there was the cost of adopting a child. This was well before there were company benefits or federal tax credits available to reduce the cost of adopting children. I remember broaching the subject of the cost of adopting a child through Catholic Charities. Their fee for services was ten percent of the family's income plus legal expenses. My only question was that at gross or net income. It was gross income.

Having little success with our efforts, and the anticipated long delays with available American adoption programs in Houston, we reached out to adoption agencies in Bogota. While visiting Paula's family we visited a public adoption agency in Bogota. I can remember leaving that visit in shock at the condition of the physical building and seeing babies and young children all over the place. We then visited a private adoption agency Paula's mother knew. Here, we entered a very organized, clean facility with a foyer that had two small rooms off the entrance, one decorated in pink the other in blue. My level of anxiety dropped immediately. What difference money makes. We were welcomed by the managing staff and were walked through the adoption process. Being an adoption that would take the child overseas, we were educated as to the rules and requirements to bring a baby into the United States as an immigrant. Ok, let's do it. We were given a timetable of up to eighteen months as to when we could expect a call from this agency that a baby would be available for us to adopt.

Several months later in February 1984 the adoption agency called Paula to announced our little girl had been born. We were soon on a flight to Bogota and took possession of Michelle at five days old. Paula was subsequently visiting her family the Christmas of 1985 and went to the agency to visit with Michelle and to drop off our application for a second baby. The agency reported they had many babies in the house and asked Paula if she would help them out and take home and care for an infant girl born Christmas day while she was visiting at her parent's home. She did and two days later the agency called Paula and said we could keep this Christmas baby as our own if we wanted. Paula called to question me on this option and I said "take the baby." I had to complete the extensive immigration paperwork from Houston before our new baby Adriana could arrive as an immigrant on U.S. soil. The process took time and finally Paula and now our two children arrived home to Houston in late April 1986. I made a promise to care for and protect these babies, give them the best opportunities in life.

Finally, a miracle of sorts, while I was serving on a jury trial in Houston, Paula and the babies picked me up at the courthouse, and Paula told me she was pregnant. The miracle of life came when Katie was born in April 1987 four years after we had abandoned all fertility treatments. These little girls now consumed our lives. Katie's delivery was very difficult and this infant was held in the hospital's ICU for a week before we could bring her home. I can still picture the delivery nurse whisking Katie away as I was assured everything would be alright. And then another miracle four years later when Molly was born. Why these two births after so many years are not known but our fertility specialist at UPenn declared them to be his miracles although we had left his services years ago. Having six sisters, including a twin sister, I seemed destined to raise a family of little girls. I loved those babies. We did pig-piles on the living room floor; I would tackle any one of them as they tried to sneak past me. It was great and I loved those girls.

During our five-years in Houston, several subtle issues became more apparent as Paula seemed to struggle. She became withdrawn both socially and physically and was hostile to the Texas culture, not willing to even take the children outside to play in the yard. I carpooled with four others from the office so Paula had almost daily access to our car. She made friends with two older women with roots in Latin America. Paula's family visited just once from Bogota while Paula and the kids traveled back there yearly. I took on more and more responsibilities around the home as Paula struggled to keep up with caring for the children and the home. I did the housework as Paula noted: "you can do in an hour what would take me all day to do." We put in an inground pool hoping it would lure Paula outside with the kids, but they only went out to play when I returned home. Michelle swam like a shark at an early age; Adriana was content to sit on the pool steps; I carried Katie in my arms in the pool. Otherwise, with Paula, they were either in the car or in the house with little in between. Life became stressful as nothing seemed to appease Paula. She loathed housework, she did not like to cook and was not good at it, she did not like Houston's heat and humidity, and seemed most content riding around with the children in the car. We were even sued for $100,000 when Paula's car struck a young worker walking across a McDonald's parking lot. It was always something.

Paula mentioned to me a comment made by a young mother, Rose, another transplant from New Jersey, who lived at the end of our street. Seeing Adriana always clinging to me, this neighbor asked Paula if she was jealous that this baby was so attached to her father. Paula replied "no" she saw no problem with the bond this child had developed with her father. I was the fun parent the kids loved to play with; while Paula struggled day-to-day getting along. I helped put the girls to bed each night; I had to sneak out of the bedroom most nights trying for up to an hour to get Adriana to sleep.

Now two-years-old, Adriana woke us one-night screaming. I rushed to her dark bedroom at 2 AM and took hold of the child in the crib. She was shaking violently. I yelled for Paula to come and help. The doctor on call that evening was by chance our pediatrician who told us to rush the child to the children's hospital in downtown Houston. Fortunately, it was early in the morning, and we raced across twenty miles of empty interstate. Upon our arrival, Adriana was rushed into the ER. I was an emotional wreck and upon the doctor entering the room he ordered me out as the child was prepped for a spinal tap. Adriana screamed for me and all I could do was cry outside the door. Paula was pretty calm and collected throughout this episode. I didn't know if it was her nature or that she had so detached from this child. Adriana had suffered a seizure but she did not suffer any long-term effects.

Then there was the incident of Paula having been caught shoplifting items totaling about $40 with the three children in tow. The youngest, Katie, just three months old was in a stroller. I returned from work that day to an empty house and soon a phone call from Paula. She was at a local department store and said she had been taken into police custody. I made my way to the store and seeing the sheriff's car parked at the door, I entered fearing the worst. The store refused to drop the charges. Paula had the money, why not pay? Was it a case of postpartum depression? I asked the police to allow me to take the children out of the store so they did not see their mother ushered into the police car. Paula was taken to Houston's Harris County jail some twenty-five miles downtown while I took the children home. I arranged to leave the two oldest children, now aged four and two years old, with a friend uttering an excuse we had to take three-month-old Katie to the doctor. We would pick the children up in the morning. I held Katie in my arms as I waited outside the major city jail until Paula was released on $600 bail near midnight that day in July 1987. Within two months we had found a lawyer, participated in a pre-trial hearing, paid fines and legal fees totaling $1,500, and pleaded for an adjudicated sentence of six months' probation.

This experience did little to improve the home situation. Having questioned a prior "purchase", Paula assured me it must have been the children who had picked it up and brought it home. I told Paula she had to be aware of what the children picked up while in a store. I soon assumed Paula was the one who had collected these items and not the children. Paula would later concede she used the children to facilitate her shoplifting habits.

Paula's six-month probation required her not to leave Texas and report biweekly to her Probation Officer, a Hispanic woman. Paula hated those meetings as she felt this woman was very condescending. Upon completion of her probation, Paula demanded we return to New Jersey after these five years in Houston. If need be, she would take the girls and go back to New Jersey without me. She wanted out of Texas; she hated the place. She complained that with so many Hispanics in Texas, she was presumed to be Mexican. No, she was Colombian! Some South American nationalism here. I was quite content in Houston and saw many career opportunities at work in the credit function. Also, the Texas university system would provide many options for the girls' college education.

Despite my best wishes, and not wanting to lose my family, I went into the office and told management of my wife's demand to take the children and return to New Jersey. I made no mention of Paula's recent legal circumstances other than to say she did not like living in Texas. I took a week off to go to New Jersey in the hopes of finding a job. I called a former manager I had worked with at the Cherry Hill office who did not make the move to Houston. Did he know of any local job prospects? He said the owner of a family-owned business had called just that morning asking if he knew of someone for a credit manager position. I interviewed two days later and was offered the job. I returned to Houston and advised my employer I had found a new job in New Jersey. I was offered other job options with the company in downtown Houston and Atlanta but noted there were no opportunities with them in New Jersey. I thanked them for their efforts but I had to leave if I wanted to be with my children. It was not the company or the location, it was Paula's demand we leave Texas. I was processed out of this job that same day upon my return and walked away from a fourteen-year career with this major multinational corporation.

With Paula's threat to take the children and leave, we arranged for the sale of our home, put our furnishings in storage, and returned to New Jersey in the Spring of 1988. We moved into my mother's home I had left some sixteen years ago. We accepted some responsibility for caring for my mother who was suffering from Lupus while we looked for more permanent housing. Paula soon found a two-acre lot, ten miles away in a growing rural community. We contracted to build a two-story colonial home and after a year at my mother's home, we moved into our new home in April 1989. Paula stayed home to raise the children while planning her goals of continuing her college education.

Unbeknownst to me, my sisters decided to move my mother from the home we shared with her, in the latter part of our year-long stay. I was told a few years later that the women hired to provide day time in-home care for my mother refused to continue services while having to work around Paula. Three different aides felt Paula looked to use them as a maid service, asked them to do our laundry, asked to watch the kids from time-to-time, etc. They complained to my sisters and eventually, over several months, all three aides had left the care of my mother. Not wanting to create another issue for me to deal with, the decision was made to move my mother from her home. She passed away a few months later at my sister's home in Poughkeepsie, NY. Told of my mother's immediate failing health, I rushed 150 miles to visit her only to find she had passed away an hour before my arrival. It was during the next two to three years that issues with Paula became even more obvious and onerous as she struggled to care for a family of three children, providing meals, and managing a home. Having been raised in Bogota with daily maid service, she had little passion to learn parts of the American way. She knew little of day-to-day home tasks such as entertaining the children, preparing meals, cleaning, laundry, or how to iron clothes. Paula took my dress shirts to my elderly aunt to be ironed. I mistakenly thought all immigrants adapted to American ways and means as we had all the conveniences one would need to facilitate most day-to-day functions within the home. Three of the four known auditors' marriages to women from Bogota ended in divorce.

Having left Houston and the girls just entering their early school years, our attention turned to educating these budding blooms of life. Michelle grasped everything quickly; Adriana struggled more so, but then most would when compared to Michelle. At Michelle's sixth grade graduation she walked away with most individual subject awards and the top academic award. A parent approached me at the end and noted it seemed to be the Michelle awards banquet. The school instituted changes that dispersed all awards more evenly amongst girls and boys in future years. As I recall, the new policy was no child could take more than two awards in any year. Katie, who loved math and thrived academically, only wanted the math award. Four years later at her graduation, Katie would receive the Spanish language and the top academic honors awards but not the math award. Much to my dismay, none of the children learned to speak Spanish in the home. I believed Paula just could not focus enough even for that task.

Tensions continued to rise within the home as Paula struggled day-to-day, and we entered marriage counseling in 1989 with an older priest, Father John, who was resident at the Catholic diocesan center located in Blackwood, NJ. Father had a Ph.D. in psychology and ran the Diocesan Counseling Services. We met with Father bi-weekly over several months. We discussed many issues that were bothering me, those that were bothering Paula, and those that both-ered us both. Issues of responsibilities at home; demands on time; demands of the children; and Paula's demands for more freedom from all that was the family. I suggest Paula loved the idea of children but lacked much or any of the mental and physical stamina needed to raise children. She relished dressing the little girls up to take them out but struggled to manage the day-to-day care and concerns of young children within the home.

After many of these counseling sessions with Father over several months, he pointed across the room to Paula one evening and said "I believe you are bipolar." He suggested she seek confirmation of his diagnosis and any needed treatment at the Mood Clinic at the University of Pennsylvania in Philadelphia. Not much more was said of this "diagnosis." The family problem having been diagnosed, we stopped these counseling sessions. I only knew of bipolar disorder by the more colloquial name, manic depression. I finally had a label for what I saw to be Paula's behavior and why she "fled" the home and all its responsibilities so many times. Bipolar disorder is defined as a serious mental illness as those afflicted struggle to manage their lives as they rotate in and out of states of mania and depression. The euphoric high is equated to that of an addictive drug high that so many crave. The lows, depression, sucks the life out of them and they don't function well at all. Paula struggled to accept responsibilities around the home; preferring to be anywhere but in the home. She would eventually concede she found the home a "prison."

# 3

# THE PROBLEM SOLVED; MAYBE NOT?

Paula eventually took some evening courses at the community college but never settled into any one program. She then initiated a two-year program to secure certification in Montessori education at a college located an hour away in a western Philadelphia suburb. Two years later this effort ended as Paula never completed the final project required for program certification. A six-month extension was granted and still the project was not completed and Paula was dropped from the program. I wanted Paula to complete this program, complete something. While Paula went off two nights a week to Pennsylvania, I had the children at home to feed, bathe, help with school work, and get them into bed. Likewise, Paula took several day-job opportunities including two where she worked as a bilingual interpreter in local municipal and county courts but quit those too. Paula would later acknowledge she hated sitting around courtrooms for hours waiting to be called to translate a document or what someone said in Spanish.

In February 1991 we were blessed with our fourth child, another little girl, Molly. No treatments, just nature taking its course. This joyous time was subsequently fraught with added issues. I was to learn casually from Paula one morning that her day's plans included a scheduled blood test. Anxious, I asked why? To monitor the levels of the drug Lithium that the Mood Clinic had prescribed she take for treatment for their confirmed diagnosis of bipolar disorder. This was the first and only indication I knew of Paula seeking any treatment relative to Father's suggestion of more than a year ago. Anxious to learn more and get involved in this effort, I was shut out in every way. Paula told me the clinic had tried several months of cognitive therapy only to determine that it did not work for her. Cognitive therapy is centered on identifying and changing inaccurate and distorted thinking patterns and behaviors. Maintenance of the drug Lithium was the prescribed treatment in Paula's case. I would never hear about the Mood Clinic again. I was never advised what was being done or when; never invited to participate in any visits or discussions with the clinic's staff, and I was never told when Paula elected to stop the treatment of her own volition.

Paula was crying upon her return from a pediatrician appointment with Molly, now two years old. I asked what happened? The pediatrician had scolded her for continuing to nurse this child. I found it a reasonable question but no answers were ever provided to me. The first two adopted children were not nursed, and Katie, the first natural-born child, was only nursed a few months. Nursing a child was not a cultural issue as women from the "haves" of Colombian society frowned on any nursing of infants and babies as something only the poor peasants would subscribe to doing. My sisters all found it unusual that Paula continued to nurse Molly well past two years of age. I later learned that Paula was advised by doctors at the Mood Clinic that if taking the powerful and toxic drug Lithium she could not nurse a child as the baby would absorb the toxic drug through the breast milk. Nursing this child provided Paula the excuse needed to not take the prescribed Lithium which regulated both the depressive lows and manic highs a bipolar personality would experience. Paula would later concede to me her decision to stop the Lithium medication. She said, "I don't miss the lows but I sure miss the highs." I later called the Mood Clinic in an attempt to get some input from them. I told them Paula had been a patient there; been diagnosed bipolar; that cognitive therapy reportedly did not work with her; prescribed Lithium, she stopped taking the medication. The staff member merely said they could not confirm any of what I said due to issues of a patient's medical privacy but conceded I was in a difficult situation.

I continued to function around Paula's acknowledged mental illness not knowing anything of what to expect day-to-day. Paula fled the house at every opportunity while contributing little to maintain any structure within the home. Laundry was all over the place; meals were limited at best; cleaning was not her thing. She refused to participate in our local Catholic parish just four miles away, instead choosing one located fifteen miles away. Eventually, Paula left that parish and settled into yet another, a Hispanic-dominated parish, in Camden, NJ, some thirty miles from the home. Camden was a perennial leader on any list of the most economically, socially, and criminally challenged cities in New Jersey and nationally. Camden's title at the time was "murder capital of New Jersey" and well known for its illicit drug trade. Paula traveled into Camden two nights a week for the parish's bible study and prayer groups and again for Sunday mass. I questioned the young parish priest if he saw any issues with this young mother of four children driving 30 miles one-way, two nights a week into Camden? He answered no, he saw no issues. I asked if he thought it was safe that this mother of four children traveled deep into Camden alone at night? The priest noted Paula was chaperoned back to the interstate after services. I questioned who chaperoned her into the city to get to this parish? No answer.

The effects of the unmedicated mental illness became more evident over time and stress levels within the home rose steadily. I, working full time, was many times left in full care of the children as Paula dropped the kids off at the Deptford office as she headed to evenings out for school, or church groups. I maintained the home inside and out. On other nights I was met at the pantry door upon my return home from work as Paula headed out to Camden. One evening, pregnant with Molly, racing to Camden in the pouring rain, Paula crashed our second car as it jumped a curb and it was totaled. Fortunately, just some bumps and bruises. Now with just one car, Paula's nights of running out did not abate. Paula would have four auto accidents in five years, totaling two cars.

# YET ANOTHER SOLUTION

Paula eventually conceded she continued to shoplift upon our return to South Jersey. Horrified at this revelation, I asked my brother, a Catholic priest, to come to the house to address the issue with us in the hopes of getting Paula pointed in the right direction. We did not need a repeat of the Houston episode and all that emotional and financial distress. My brother visited on a Saturday while we were still living at my mother's home and the three of us drove around the neighborhood as we discussed Paula's continued shoplifting. Paula, having discontinued treatment at the Mood Clinic, admitted she had again engaged in shoplifting and my brother advised she had serious issues that needed attention. Ironically, Paula's favorite target was reportedly a small religious store run by an older couple. As this couple doted over the children, Paula had all the time needed to pick through the rack of children's cassettes and videotapes that she would play while driving with the children in the car. In response to our concerns, Paula approached the pastor of the parish she was attending fifteen miles from our home. This older parish priest advised he had little background counseling on the subject matter but referred Paula to a friend, a Catholic nun.

This nun, Sister Catherine, was the Director of Pastoral Care at a local Catholic facility that provided daycare and rehabilitative services to handicapped children and young adults. Paula was being counseled by Sister Catherine weekly beginning August 1992. Months into these sessions, Sister Catherine insisted on meeting with me. I finally agreed to meet Sister Catherine over two lunch breaks in February 1993.

My two hour-long conversations with Sister Catherine ranged far afield and she wanted to focus on my family's history. I questioned what did that have to do with her counseling Paula for her compulsive shoplifting habit? Upon leaving my second, and what I deemed to be my last visit with Sister Catherine, she stated, as I approached the door to leave her office, "I could support divorce in this case." I turned to her and said "a divorce? I'm not looking for any divorce. We have four children at home." Paula would later advise me Sister Catherine had diagnosed me, after just these two hour-long meetings, as a dry alcoholic. Both knew I did not drink any alcohol. It would appear Sister had convinced Paula her problem was not her shoplifting but rather me, her husband.

With stress levels high, we entered into yet another Catholic-sponsored marriage counseling effort in the early Fall of 1992. Father Fred, a diocesan and professionally trained family counselor, worked out of the Gibbstown parish just seven miles from our home. All the old issues and some new ones were brought to the discussion table as we tried to regain control of the marriage from an unmedicated bipolar personality. Fingers were pointed, claims made and denied, frustrations expressed, and demands noted. All this while Paula continued counseling with Sister Catherine for her shoplifting habit. Father Fred admitted to knowing nothing of Sister Catherine or her counseling services. Sister had no credentials for counseling on any subject.

The counseling effort with Father Fred was coming to a head after several months of bi-weekly sessions as I believed he began to see Paula's true personality and what damage it was inflicting on the family. Financially, emotionally she was a drain on the family. Then there was Paula's demand we replace the second car that she totaled last year on that rainy evening racing to Camden. We had just then purchased a new seven-passenger van that would allow Paula to comfortably and safely carry the four children whereas I would take the second car to work. Having totaled the second car, our new van registered 33,000 miles in just one year.

Our bi-weekly counseling sessions with Father Fred were on Wednesday nights. A current topic of discussion was Paula having drained the joint checking account of $3,000 in January 1993, writing some twenty checks to "cash" for amounts of $25 to $250. I had not noticed these many checks hitting the bank account until check #1325, dated January 29, 1993, written for $2,050 cash was drawn from the account. Paula claimed she was repaying a debt she owed to an aunt in Bogota. I took Paula off the joint-checking account as she provided no accounting for all this cash she had taken or any payment to the aunt. Father Fred was not enamored with Paula's callous abuse of the family's finances at this point.

After another counseling session in late February 1993, I telephoned Father Fred the following Monday to advise he need not plan the week's discussion relative to Paula's demand for a second car. She had purchased a used car on Friday, February 26, and charged it to the credit card for $6,000. Father Fred was shocked. I took Paula off the joint credit card accounts. We met with Father Fred just twice again and the discussions were very contentious. As we left the last week's session Father Fred told Paula "we will talk about you next session."

Two days later, on a Friday, March 26 I arrived home from work at 6:30 PM, and our lives as a family were to be forever changed.

# WELCOME TO NEW JERSEY FAMILY COURT

I routinely called home every evening before leaving the office to ask Paula if anything was needed at the house: food, school supplies, etc. This Friday, March 26, just minutes before I was to make my usual call home, Paula called me to ask when would I be home. Surprised by the call knowing our routine, I acknowledged I was just about to call her as I was packing up and expected to be on the road within minutes. Nothing is needed at the house, I would be home by 6:30 PM. I arrived home and entered the house from the garage through the pantry door. I did not notice the second car being there or not, but upon entering the kitchen I did notice my four little girls were not there for the usual welcome at the door. I dropped my briefcase and headed upstairs and hearing no noise, I again called out to announce my arrival, but again to no answer. I did notice some clothes folded in the master bedroom and my only thought was some laundry got done today. I headed back down the stairs continuing to call out that I was home to what now seemed to be an empty house. Strange, Paula had just called asking when I would be home? I opened the door to the basement but it too was dark. I returned to the kitchen and noticed an envelope on the counter addressed to me. I opened it and as I read, I was struck with sheer panic.

Bill, I wished there had been a better way. I have thought this much more than you will ever believe me. I know that what I am doing is the only way I know to protect myself and the girls. I cannot stand and allow more threats, accusations, attacks, name-calling, and angry outbursts from you. I am afraid of you and what you might do to me and the girls. I know in my mind and my heart that I have tried everything to make this marriage work. I hope you will understand that I had no choice. I know this is very painful for all of us because I share the pain. God bless you. Paula.

I called my brother in sheer fright. My brother noted we knew Paula was a troubled person and I agreed, but this? Could she have called from the Philadelphia airport, maybe even Miami, and already be on a plane back to Colombia? I soon saw a car coming up the dark driveway and suggested that perhaps this was them, someone who had an answer. A knock on the door came and I opened it to the local Police Chief and another officer. I asked: "where are my children?" The chief advised "they were safe" and I questioned "safe from what?" The chief advised he had a family court order to remove me from the premise; that a domestic violence (DV) complaint was signed against me by my wife. I was advised I had ten minutes to collect my things and vacate the home, not to return until the court approved of my being on the property. If I violated the order I would be arrested.

The two officers followed me upstairs and the clothes laid out on the bed was what I was allowed to take, nothing else could leave the house. If not on the bed, I could not take it, not even shoes under the bed. Within these ten minutes, one small suitcase packed, I was escorted out of my home to my vehicle and warned against any unauthorized return. I would leave my home, my children that night not to return and regain custody and possession for ten years.

What was the basis of Paula's claim that had me, her husband of fourteen years, removed from the marital home? Katie, now six years old, and I were sick at home with flu-like symptoms on March 22 and 23, 1993. Paula was out of the house both days, doing what I had no clue about. On Tuesday evening March 23, I told Paula that I planned to leave early the next morning to catch up on work at the office. I was in the kitchen Wednesday morning about to leave for the office at 6:30 AM. Paula came downstairs and asked me not to leave until she had the chance to take a shower before any of the children woke up. I said "ok, but hurry." At 7:10 AM Paula returned to the kitchen dressed and seemingly headed out the door. I asked, "Where are you going?" She said she had missed her Monday night swim class at the YMCA in Woodbury and if she left now, she could hopefully make it up with this early morning class. I told her "go."

Paula told me I needed to drop Molly off at some unknown sitter's address in South Woodbury as that person also had a young child who regularly played with Molly. Paula then left the home. I proceeded to get the three older children up and ready for school, fed them breakfast, made them lunches, and got them onto the school bus at 8:30 AM. I then headed into Woodbury to drop Molly off at this sitter's home. Just two blocks from this address Molly vomited, suffering the same flu symptoms Katie and I had endured. I told Molly, "we are headed to the Y to get your mother out of the pool" to take care of her.

We arrived at the Y near 9 AM. I entered the pool area and not seeing Paula in the pool, I asked the instructor if she was about. No, they had not seen Paula that morning. I stopped at the CVS across the street, bought wet ones in an attempt to clean up Molly, and I returned to the south of Woodbury. I approached this unknown rowhome and a young mother greeted Molly as someone well known to her. I said I was the father; the child was sick and I did not know the whereabouts of the mother. This woman willingly took Molly from me and welcomed her into her home. I did not get to work that morning until 10 AM. Paula called the office at 11 AM to acknowledge Molly was sick. I merely asked "where were you; the baby is sick? I was very late to work and you were not at the Y." Paula explained in her rush to get out of the house that morning "I forgot my bathing suit and decided to go to church in Camden." I hung up the phone in disgust.

Upon my return home that evening Paula all but ran me over as she was rushing out the pantry door to the garage as I entered the kitchen. Very bothered and angry from the morning's episode of her non-swimming event at the Y, I asked: "where are you going?" Paula said she was headed to the Camden parish for a bible study function. I then said "stop" as I put my briefcase down on the kitchen counter, some ten feet from where she stood near the pantry door. The children were in the area. I told Paula "she was crazy if she thought she would get everything in a divorce, the house, the kids. I would burn the house before I gave it to you." With that, Paula left for Camden not to return until nearly 10:30 PM. Nothing more was said or thought of this exchange. Two nights later I was escorted from my home by the police.

This story takes you inside such a private affair, a divorce, and looks to tell the story of this father's efforts to seek custody of his little girls in New Jersey Family Court. Is this father given a fair chance for a hearing of the facts of the case? Will lawyers even suggest he has a reasonable means to the desired end, custody of his children? Is justice served? As both the husband and father in this case, as much as I saw my cherished family being shredded, I endured yet another concern. The legal system didn't give much consideration as to how it ripped my family from me in the process; as it systematically instituted efforts to disenfranchise me from my children. There was a legitimate concern that the legal system did not afford this father, most fathers, an equal right to legal equity, justice. I would soon learn that in this system of "equal" justice I was not considered equal, but in fact, the system considered me a threat to the process.

I rode the public service bus nine miles home every day from a Catholic high school. It turned towards my hometown at the main intersection in the county seat, Woodbury, where this most usual of courthouses occupied the corner. Unbeknownst to me, this building housed Gloucester County Family Court. I saw those who looked to be lawyers outside, milling on the sidewalk or crossing the street. I'm sure I imagined what might go on in that courthouse but never knew that years later it would hold my destiny and that of my yet unborn children.

An old cliché claims "nobody ever said life was fair." I believe that much of our lives are predicated upon factors that we have little control over. Born into wealth; one's innate IQ; your physical size and abilities are genetically predetermined to a great degree. Even being in the wrong place at the wrong time can determine your fate in surviving an accident or even being a victim of a random crime. Living with these factors we can't control; we do have the means to control many other circumstances that impact our daily lives. Then there is the law, which implies, dictates all are to be treated equally, fairly; the law protects all of us.

I too believed the law protected us all. But then one only needs to be a minority, of a disadvantaged group in this country to know that the law is not equal; it does not protect all; it is not fairly applied. The law and those that work in the trade have their prejudice and bias that can add yet another factor that determines the outcome of any legal experience. The legal cliché "justice is blind" is but a hope in that it implies justice is impartial and objective in seeking the promised justice for all. It is not! A glance up from the textbooks will confirm the reality that the law is not always fair, not equally applied in all cases for all people in our society. History details the legal abuses against many that go back decades and continue to the present day. How laws are enforced and by whom and where dictates much of the promised justice that is denied to individuals and groups. These injustices today are found in statistics, on police lapel videos, smartphones, dash cameras, and on appeal.

The adverb fair implies a set of rules applied equally. All sports are played with a set of defined rules; balls and strikes; what actions constitute a penalty or a foul, and all these rules are administered by referees and umpires. We now rely on instant replay to best decide calls the human eye can't discern without a doubt. The law too has its codes, even a Bill of Rights, rules of conduct, statutes, case law, appeals, and countless arguments that are employed in that search for the promised justice for all.

As the father of four little girls, then just two to nine years of age, I was escorted out of my home and ordered into this system of justice. I was forcefully removed from the lives of my children and summoned into New Jersey Family Court to contest a complaint of alleged domestic violence that was filed against me by my wife of fourteen years. Blindsided by this assault on me and the children, I sought legal representation. The pending charge and the Temporary Restraining Order (TRO) denied me any chance of direct contact with Paula to resolve this matter amicably. No, this would have to be resolved through the legal process, the law. Surely, there would be a hearing, a mediation, a trial of some definition, a presentation of facts, and this issue would be resolved. Justice would be exercised. I trusted I would soon return to my children, my home, and my wife. I soon concluded that justice, as defined by New Jersey Family Court law and practices, was not fair to fathers.

Early in this process, I began to doubt the touted virtues of family court law and systems. I decided I would need to enter the fray with an earnest effort if I was to right the wrongs brought against me and my children. I would wade into this hell on earth, to experience first-hand the justice promised to all in America. My experiences as a father seeking custody of his children, would prove that justice is not fair, and surely not for this father or his children, in this family court system. It was soon exposed for what it was; a court, a system, a process that cared only about one thing, one person; that being to protect the mother. "Family Court" was the biggest misnomer of them all, perhaps best described as a lie, a fraud, a gross misrepresentation. In all my numerous appearances in these court proceedings over those many years, I can honestly say I never once heard a reference to the family. No, there was nothing in these proceedings about preserving my family. At best I would suggest this institution formally known as the family court could best be described as divorce court; war court; women's court; liars court; anything but a court of justice with any concerns for my family.

Laws were enacted after the civil war in late nineteenth-century America to account for the newfound freedoms of the negro slave. The war solved but a few of the slavery issues in the country. Some states, unwilling to concede that former slaves now had a legal status equivalent to white citizens, enacted Jim Crow laws. Yes, the law said the black man was equal but others agreed he must be separated from whites in many, if not all, venues of society. New Jersey Family Court established its own unwritten Jim Crow law in its divorce courts. Men and women in divorce cases were to be separated, but they were not considered equal. The mother was the preferred custodial parent of children. The father had no standing in this court.

What I found in this family court was the legalized practice of discrimination. The law defines the essence of discrimination as formulating opinions about others not based on their merits but rather on their membership in a group with similar characteristics. I was the father; I was the male and New Jersey Family Court law and practices were rife with discrimination against me and all fathers.

Most family court proceedings function behind closed doors. Although the hearings are almost always open to the public, few ventures inside to listen, watch as a family's private affairs are washed in the public domain. There are no news reporters in any of these court sessions looking to garner a story for local consumption. This was not about a public celebrity but a middle-class family of six that lived their lives as inconspicuous as most. There are few salacious stories of marital affairs or stories of criminal behavior embedded in these typical family court hearings. No, most are just considered private, family matters. Sad for sure as families are dissolved by agreement or torn apart by animus and few have the stomach for that under most circumstances. The children of these failed unions, if any, are rarely mentioned although some legal text suggests the welfare of the children is what these exercises are about. Others believe it is all about money: the house; the cars; the bank account, the retirement savings, and child support. Judges acknowledge these issues early in this process but choose to ignore the existence of the children for the most part; most attention is directed to the other "assets" of the failed union. The public generally knows of these cases only in statistics; the number of divorces; the divorce rate; the issues of the single-parent families. The basis for most of these statistics is heard, considered, and resolved in the local county family court.

Most of us go through life day-by-day, planning for those things we can foresee, life as we know it. It is the unknown that trips most of us up. We get through these events, planned or not, as best as possible. Most people don't plan for adversity and even fewer people plan for how to deal with it. Hopefully, our acquired skills and instincts allow us to cope and endure should such events occur. Some succeed more so than others in each phase of life, but a general goal for most is to get through life with a degree of personal achievement for ourselves and to provide a level of security for our children that allow them to carry on the torch. All families experience unwanted events, accidents, health concerns, or financial issues. The best we can hope for is to survive and live life.

As the father of these four young children, I learned quickly that the New Jersey Family Court justice system was not at all interested in me or my concerns. Paula has declared me *persona non grata* and the system will do all it can to dispose of me; deny me an equal standing in the process that is supposed to determine who is the better parent to raise these children; what is in the best interest of these children.

# 6

# THE COURT TAKES CONTROL OF MY FAMILY

I was taken from my children, my home, on a statement filed against me by my unmedicated mentally ill wife who accepted no responsibility to the family. Paula now had the freedom she craved with no one to question her day-to-day activities. Unfortunately, there were now four young children left in her care. I was scared of the legal process; angry at such an irresponsible person; fearful for the children and who was to care for them. Paula now had her desired life of manic states of mind while she suffered the consequences of her bouts of depression and no one to question what was going on?

This is the heart of what this story is about. How does a husband, father survive, and hope to recover from a situation where he finds his children in a threatened state under the control of a wife who refused to medicate her mental illness? At the same time, he is thrown into legal jeopardy facing a family court system that is very hostile to fathers. I suggest it is the equivalent of a soldier in war; a police officer at a crime scene shootout; a lost child in the family. I had never previously had any contact with the police but for a traffic stop or parking ticket. The two officers who escorted me from the home that evening, while somewhat apologetic, explained they had to execute the court's order. I was advised my court date was the following

Friday, April 2, 1993, in Woodbury, for a "final hearing" at the family court in the county courthouse. I was in a state of mental and emotional shock that evening as my worst fears of what Paula was capable of doing came to fruition, actions I could only describe as evil.

I headed to my sister's in Alexandria, VA for the weekend as my extended family began to comprehend what had happened. Several siblings had previously expressed concern for the future of this marriage but I would not have left it; we had four children and I had weathered most of what had been thrown at me to date. But this was different, Paula now sought sanctuary in the law, in family court, something I knew nothing about. I returned from the weekend in Virginia and spent the next two weeks at my twin sister's home in Woodbury, the county seat and home to the family court that now had taken custody of my life and controlled my access to my children.

I returned to work Monday morning an emotional wreck and the people in the office rallied around me with support. They saw the children with me so many times and knew of my love and affection for them; that the children were attached to me. Too, the office was only four miles from the courthouse that would prove to be my home away from home for years to come.

The following Monday I called Father Fred to tell him that Paula had signed a domestic violence complaint against me and had me removed from our home the preceding Friday evening, March 26. The court ordered that I not return to the home property until this complaint was adjudicated. Father said he could not counsel a married couple not living together in the same home. We would never hear from Father Fred again. I was on my own.

The next week, I met with three local attorneys who practiced family law and picked one almost randomly to represent me in this legal effort. All three advised I was in a very difficult situation while one questioned the validity of the domestic violence charge suggesting the situation was but an argument. A mistake was made in my choice of attorney that I would question years later, but that was history to be learned. For now, I had to go on instinct, bad judgment, and the imposed herd mentally as fathers are ushered through family court.

I placed a call to the Philadelphia offices of the ACLU thinking they, the most ardent defenders of any person's rights, would offer some advice, direction. The older gentlemen who answered that call, upon hearing my summary of my legal jeopardy, questioned the call and said that this was not a legal issue that concerned the ACLU. Convicted murderers on death row; the civil rights of minorities; discrimination across many spectrums of life in America; but a father's right to custody of his children was not a legal concern of the ACLU. Perhaps the ACLU knew family law better than most.

What was not to be believed was Paula's claim that she felt threatened by the argument that fateful Wednesday night as she headed out for yet another evening. She was not threatened after her Houston arrest and its ramifications; I had not threatened her after her demands I quit my career job and return to New Jersey; I had not threatened her upon her admitting she again continued to shoplift upon our return to New Jersey; I had not threatened her after the many evenings she left the home to go into Camden; I had not threatened her after finding she had drained the bank account and purchased a car on a credit card; I had not threatened her as she left for the swimming class that morning; why would she be so threatened that night when I finally said enough; and challenged her on her continued erratic behavior? What most aggravated me was that she was not there to care for the sick child that morning.

No, she was not threatened. But the system required a certain reaction by me that would be sufficient for her to initiate a domestic violence complaint. This was a planned, calculated, and executed effort to provoke a reaction from me that would suffice as the basis for a complaint against me. Looking back, Paula's purchase of the car; her taking $3,000 from the checking account were all planned and executed steps in a strategic divorce process. The filing of this complaint would remove me from the home and secure her position as the custodial parent of the children. The complaint process at the court did not ask what might have precipitated such an argument; my "threat" to her? No, it was never about any argument or threat; the system now had what it needed to begin the process of trashing this man and to begin the divorce process on a woman's terms.

Months later Paula acknowledged her plan to go swimming at the Y that morning was a lie. Her only intention was to go to the parish in Camden despite any claim to care about the children; that she even wanted to participate in their care; or had any concern for their well-being. She was mad that I continued to question her every action in these later months; even after the credit card purchase of a car and the many checks written to drain the bank account. Based on her record to date, I would have thought a reasonable person would have made it their business to question the moves of this unmedicated bipolar personality who would now claim in court she was the most respon-sible adult to care for the same children she routinely denied. But that was yet more lies from a pathetic liar who cared nothing for the truth.

I learned from Paula that she routinely dropped the kids off at a church in Woodbury that provided free summer daycare as she left them to go do whatever she wanted to do. This situation only became a concern when she questioned my brother if she needed to worry that the children were being taught religion while at this protestant church daycare. Advised that might be a legitimate concern she stopped taking the children to this daycare. Then too, we met a grandmother, a friend of my mother's, after mass one Sunday while living temporarily at my mother's home. This grandmother mentioned she watched a few of her grandchildren from time to time and suggested Paula bring our girls by someday to play. Always searching for a place to dump the children, this too turned into yet another opportunity to leave the children in the care of someone else so she could take off. I apologized too many times as I had to pick my children up on my way home from work as Paula never returned for the children. The beleaguered grandmother advised she could no longer have my children visit. There were others. Paula had picked a co-worker friend and her husband to be godparents to Molly. I ques-tioned this choice as these "friends" were not family. Within time this godmother wrote Paula demanding she not come by to visit; do not ask any more favors; to leave them alone. Molly would never know these godparents. Upset by this response from these godparents, her friends, I advised Paula she had a habit of sucking the life out of friendships with her abusive ways of using people, asking for much while giving little in return.

So here we are and how we got here as best that can be documented by my years of compiled records that stand five feet tall. The DV complaint, filed March 23, 1993, by Paula alleged "shaking fist in front of her face" and stated he "would burn the house down." But Paula was standing at the pantry door and I was at the kitchen counter, ten feet apart. I was far from her face. Too, the children were in the area. But the truth was never a factor in this case. I might add no such referenced physical threats were claimed in our meetings with Father Fred. Paula's complaint also alleged "the last six months of harassment." I'm left to assume she found the long-running counseling sessions with Father Fred as harassment.

The battle of my life was just beginning and if I had known what the future was to hold, I'm not sure what I would have done. There are few institutions as embedded in bias, discrimination as New Jersey Family Court. Statistically, New Jersey Family Courts only granted fathers custody of their children seven percent of the time as of 1993 statistics. State statutes, judges, and lawyers supported the mother as the preferred caretaker of children. The highly touted and dated "tender-years doctrine" was now supplanted with the more recent doctrine of the "best interest of the child." No more was the mother to be considered the preferred custodial parent, best able to care for children. The law now called for a formal process to determine who was the best custodial parent for the children. But legal doctrines, like laws, are worthless words if not implemented by the courts. In New Jersey Family Court this father's capabilities were never considered. He was some foreign alien who seemingly had no means, abilities, or desires to care for his children; the father was but the featured non-custodial parent at best, suited only to provide mandated financial support. Yes, the father could get visitation on some calendar schedule but he was prejudiced against as incapable of possessing the means to have care or concern, or even the ability to raise his children. This level of legal bias was so ingrained in practice and statistics in New Jersey that a father was hard-pressed to find a local lawyer in 1993 who took his effort seriously to fight this court's bias. But I was to learn this law and all its bias first-hand, the hard way. I decided I would fight the system; I believed I was the preferred custodial parent for the children in this case.

What was the origin of this engrained legal bias against fathers? History traces the genesis of family law to early English common law that ruled fathers retained custody of their children in a divorce. Father's rights were equal to his property rights. In the early part of the 19th century, a prominent British feminist, journalist, and social reformer, who had lost custody of her children in a divorce, began a campaign for women's rights. These proposed rights included the belief women should be given custody of their children in a divorce as they were best suited to care for young children in early 1800 England. Working with politicians, she convinced the British Parliament to pass a law that established a mother's right to the custody of children in a divorce.

This early English lobbying effort resulted in the passage of the Custody of Infants Act of 1839. This Act gave judges a level of discretion in child custody cases that initiated the presumption of the mother's right to custody of her young children aged seven and under. Subsequently, in 1873, the British Parliament extended the mother's presumption of child custody to the age of sixteen. This Tender Years Doctrine was to become the standard of family law for much of the world that traced its legal roots back to common law established in the British Empire.

Many, including father's rights groups, found the Tender Years Doctrine biased against fathers. To secure custody of their child, fathers had to prove the mother unfit, yet mothers did not have to prove the father unfit as a custodial parent; mothers merely had to be in a divorce proceeding and the court presumed the mother to be the best custodial parent. This legal presumption ran contrary to the equal protection clause of the Fourteenth Amendment of the U.S.

Constitution. Despite this legal contradiction family courts continued to value mothers as the custodial parent of choice for decades, well into the late twentieth century. I experienced this known bias in interviewing seven lawyers who practiced family law in New Jersey in the decade of the 1990s.

Finally, in 1974, Ohio became the first state to formally abolish the Tender Years Doctrine in considering child custody cases. The Divorce Reform Act (Ohio Revised Code Section 3109.04) established the "Best Interest of the Child" doctrine to be the sole test for determining which parent should have custody of children in a divorce in Ohio. This Ohio law detailed ten factors to be considered by the court in determining the best interest of the child(s), including the mental and physical health of the parent seeking custody of the child.

Now understand, in all but the most egregious of cases, the court presumes both parents have a right to joint custody of the children; the issue always comes down to which parent should have residential custody of the children. The parent with residential custody acquires the mandate to make all day-to-day decisions about the child's welfare; accrued all the rights of the "loving" parent who is resident every day with the child; as opposed to the non-custodial parent who generally only participates in non-essential decisions and who is only allowed visits on a scheduled weekend if not less based on the court's ruling as to a visitation schedule, and always subject to change. The non-custodial parent is also obligated to financially support the children and by default the custodial parent.

In 1993, forty percent of divorce cases in New Jersey were predicated on a filing of a domestic violence complaint. Such complaints asked the court to consider the husband a threat to the immediate family. In too many cases, false filings of domestic violence complaints are the initial step in any divorce action as it leads to the husband, father being forcefully removed from the marital home and branded a threat, violent. The father having been removed from the marital home; the mother is declared the preferred, custodial parent of the children. Such efforts are as well-executed as any Osama Bin Laden assassination.

The best interest of the child doctrine refers to the parents' physical, mental, and emotional well-being relative to being able to raise children. Unless proven otherwise, it is assumed by the court that children benefit from having both parents play an active role in their lives. I sat through many case hearings in family court and can attest to the court having concerns with any parent(s) dealing with an issue of drug or alcohol abuse, and subjected them to random testing. These parents were most times ordered by the court to seek professional help so they might be better able to contribute to the wellbeing of their children. In all my many hearings with this same court system over ten years, never once was Paula questioned by the court as to her acknowledged mental illness. In these ten years in New Jersey Family Court, the elephant in the room was Paula's mental fitness. The legal doctrine of the best interest of these children was moot in New Jersey Family Court.

The best interest of the child doctrine requires the court to search for that answer. Who is the parent best suited to provide for the well-being of the child? The court most times relies on professional experts to evaluate the parents and children in making this judgment. My family court efforts fell victim to professional incompetence and corruption.

New Jersey's version of the best interest of the child, Statute 9:2-4, spells out the rights of both parents relative to custody issues. Specifically, the statute states it is in the public policy of this State to assure minor children of frequent and continuing contact with both parents after the parents have separated or dissolved their marriage; it is in the public interest to encourage parents to share the rights and responsibilities of child-rearing to affect this policy. The rights of both parents shall be equal and the court shall enter an order which may include: joint custody of a minor child; sole custody to one parent with appropriate parenting time for the non-custodial parent; or any other custody arrangement as the court may determine to be in the best interests of the child; any custody arrangement is agreed to by both parents unless it is contrary to the best interests of the child; and in any case in which the parents cannot agree to a custody arrangement, the court may require each parent to submit a custody plan which the court shall consider in awarding custody.

Numerous court opinions in New Jersey case law say much about the welfare of children caught up in a divorce action. Many of these legal opinions are quite eloquent in their choice of words, but provide little for the welfare of the children of divorce. And surely not in this case. Like the ubiquitous speed limit signs that litter any street or highway in the state, most such opinions are ignored to a great degree. The often-quoted case law ruling, Beck v. Beck 86 N.J. 480, 497 (1981) acknowledged courts had broad discretion in custody determinations in divorce proceedings. The paramount consideration in any child custody determination is to foster the best interest of the children involved. This standard accounts for the child's "safety, happiness, physical, mental and moral welfare." These fine words, like many quoted in other cases of New Jersey family law, were never a consideration of this divorce and custody case. These lauded and many-times quoted opinions of family law were more like myths; perhaps read for inspiration but not seemingly applicable for the dynamics of the real world of family court. Knowing these basic tenets of New Jersey child custody law, perhaps best described as mere insights, I approached this effort, and these proceedings with open eyes and a belief, hope that justice was at hand. But my cherished hopes and beliefs for justice due were to be dashed as much by the legal profession as by the court itself.

# 7

# THE FIGHT FOR JUSTICE BEGINS

I made an appointment to meet with the lawyer I decided to contract with for this legal response to the DV complaint and resolve all issues in the hope to preserve my family. Meet Marty, an established divorce attorney who had three decades of practice in family court under his belt. I met Marty on March 30, 1993, at his Woodbury office and we sat and discussed the circumstances that prompted Paula's filing of the DV complaint. I noted the many months of family counseling with two different professional counselors of the Catholic church, Paula's acknowledged diagnosis of bipolar disorder, and the prescribed Lithium medication. I referenced Paula's prior arrest in Houston for shoplifting, and that she acknowledged shoplifting even upon our return to New Jersey; I referenced the weekly schedule where Paula was either at an evening class or going to the Y; bible and prayer groups at the Camden parish. I told Marty about Paula's inability to accept employment opportunities; I referenced Paula's irresponsible financial transactions of buying a car on a credit card and draining the bank account. I thought I had built up a pretty good case of evidence and facts that would support my contention Paula was not a viable participant in the parenting function but rather a risk, threat to the children, the family. We soon learned facts and truth were not a requisite in this family court. I was looking to hopefully return to my family; Marty's professional experience told me this was the beginning of the end of my marriage.

Marty advised that my case was assigned to Judge Herman. We need to add a comment here about Judge Herman and the many fathers' public complaints about his court. I asked Marty, having been assigned to Herman's docket, should we not ask him to recuse himself from this case based on the current public information and discourse in the local media about this judge? Marty said, "that was not an option." Gloucester County was one of the smaller counties in New Jersey, considered rural by state standards as compared to North Jersey's population base. There were maybe five judges assigned to family court in the county. I was quite concerned after reading the many recent headlines of the local newspapers that reported and debated this judge's court demeanor. Judge Herman was denied tenure after his initial seven-year appointment to the bench, only the second judge in New Jersey history to be denied tenure. The State Judiciary was reviewing and weighing the numerous fathers' complaints of this judge's reported biased court conduct. A public hearing was to be held at the state capital, Trenton, to address the judge's courtroom demeanor and many fathers and rights groups participated. I got Judge Herman by alphabet draw and I was stuck with him.

We would need to contest the claim of domestic violence, but was this just the prelude to a divorce? I'm sure Marty had seen this play-book too many times to doubt it. Marty tried to enlighten me on the challenges of contesting a mother's claim to custody of the children in New Jersey and that Judge Herman "was the least of your worries." To prove any mother "unfit" was difficult if not a near-impossible task. Surely, there were issues, complaints, and even questions about what Paula was doing and what prior and current damage she had wrought on the family unit but that did not necessarily make her "unfit as a mother." To be clear, the benefit of any doubt was with the mother, not me, the father. But the need to find this mother "unfit" was the old law, the mechanics of the tender years' doctrine, right? There was no definition in New Jersey statutes that defined a parent as unfit; it was by definition an unknown, at best a vague subjective "conduct that has a substantial adverse impact on the child." What did the unfit issue have to do with the current day doctrine of "what was in the best interest of the child?." But this was New Jersey Family law practiced even in 1993. The law of the day considered fathers unfit parents by gender.

This early work session was in preparation for the scheduled "final hearing" of April 2, 1993, 1:30 PM, to address the immediate issue of Paula's filing of the DV complaint against me alleging "six months of harassment" and "shaking fist in front of plaintiff's face" and stated he "would burn the house down." I was forever to be known as the defendant, the one accused, never husband or father in this case. Paula was the plaintiff, the accuser, the protected entity of this court system; she was the mother. I considered Paula's long-running history the threat to the family more so than I ever was. Marty agreed to subpoena Father Fred to this hearing to hopefully testify to what I alleged were family issues being addressed in the ongoing counseling sessions; Father's expressed concerns for Paula's purchase of the car on the credit card and other dealings that put continued stress on the family. If need be, I told Marty, I wanted a custody trial to determine which parent was best qualified to care for these four children; what was in the best interest of the children.

Ironically, some thirty years later we now routinely see ads on television extolling the virtues of drug therapy that help the bipolar personality manage the effects of this disorder. Take a pill and the condition is manageable; don't take the pill and they are all over the place. I would suggest even today, had those ads been on television, so public, in 1993 nothing would have become of that medical knowledge either.

The afternoon hearing of April 2, 1993, was to address Paula's DV complaint against me and proceeded with opposing counsel stating my words were of threatening behavior. Marty countered that I was frustrated and angry with Paula's actions and questioned whether Paula had been prescribed Laetrile and she correctly responded "no."

The drug she was prescribed and acknowledged taking and tested for its toxicity was Lithium, not Laetrile. Marty got this wrong. The judge questioned me about what I had said relative to the "argument" and I repeated in detail my frustration with the lie about the morning YMCA swim class, the purchase of the car on a credit card, the funds taken from the joint bank account, and in the same tone of that infamous evening "that she was getting some bad advice if she thought she would get the kids, the house, everything; that I would burn the house before I give it to you."

The hearing, now more than an hour-long and into the mid-afternoon, was abruptly stopped as Judge Herman was told of a family emergency and he had to leave the court. The competing lawyers were instructed to draw up a continuation of the temporary restraining order (TRO) for a subsequent hearing. The lawyers each pushed their client's agenda in drafting this continuing order and the process of bartering my life away began in earnest. I insisted on daily phone contact with the children at 5:30 every evening; I insisted on extended contact with the children and was granted visitation every Wednesday from 6-9 PM; every other Friday from 6-9 PM; every Saturday from 9 AM to 5 PM; and every other Sunday from 9 AM to 5 PM; all visitations were to be in the marital home. Paula would vacate the property during my scheduled visits. I was responsible for paying all utility expenses at the home; all insurance expenses; the mortgage and taxes, plus providing $125 of weekly cash child support. This continuation order noted we would return to court on April 29 to resolve the issue of the DV Complaint. The written version of this day's order detailing this temporary agreement, as simple as it was, would not be finalized in writing by the lawyers until November 4, 1993, seven months later.

It was at this initial court hearing that Marty turned to me to ask "who was Sister Catherine?" Opposing counsel noted she was Paula's mentor in this divorce action. How Sister Catherine went from counseling Paula for compulsive shoplifting to advocating for divorce from an "abusive husband" was beyond me.

Marty and I left the court and returned to his office. There we continued to argue the merits of my case and the prospects of me getting custody of the children. Marty continued to state it was next to impossible to unseat this mother as the custodial parent; in light of this DV complaint, that I was the one behind the eight ball. Marty argued I would be unable to maintain the marital home in light of my pending obligations for child support and alimony and hope to have some financial resources to maintain my living standard. No, I was adamant, the house could not be sold as that would expose the children to Paula's financial issues and allow her to move them away from me. I wanted a custody trial. Marty and I didn't make it to a second hearing. I could not, would not accept his advice; I needed a more aggressive defense than the one he could offer. Perhaps when Marty suggested "you need to move to California;" that I was "too involved in this case" did I realize he did not represent my best interest or that of my children. Marty and I parted ways after just this one hearing as he would not fight for me or my agenda; to contest the common rule that fathers had little right to custody of their children in New Jersey and that the mother, the system must be appeased. Paula soon announced her plan to file for divorce.

# 8

# NEW LAWYER, SAME OLD ADVICE

I n the meantime, opposing counsel, seeing me legally exposed with no legal representation after having dismissed Marty, applied to the court to enforce the litigant's rights on April 13, 1993. This new filing alleged I called Paula a name, followed her to the YMCA, and told the children not to call her mother. Such a legal effort was to incite an already stressed process and looked to pile on charges against me when those of the initial hearing of just two weeks ago had yet to be adjudicated. And the "final hearing" of April 2 was now rescheduled from April 29 to June 8. These delays further dislodged me from the marital home and my children.

On April 28, 1993, I hired a second attorney to represent me in this effort. Out with Marty and in with Gerry. I was referred to Gerry by an aunt who used his services for miscellaneous legal advice. Gerry was described to me "as a family man" and I interpreted that to mean he cared about a father's desire to maintain his family and would fight for those rights. Only time would tell. I met with Gerry and told him I wanted a custody trial that would expose Paula's many issues and that I deserved a hearing of the facts. But I was dealing with lawyers that practice in New Jersey Family Court with all its rules, case law, statutes, and whims. Gerry again subpoenaed Father Fred on June 1 for the pending hearing continued to June 8 which was again deferred until July 1. Maybe Father Fred didn't get the phone message or even the subpoena. Surely this second effort would elicit a response if not his appearance in my defense. As previously noted, we would never hear from Father Fred again; he took all his knowledge of this case to his grave when he passed away in 2013.

With a change of attorney and awaiting a response from Father Fred, we entered the June 8 hearing. This hearing was reintroduced by Gerry to Judge Herman as the one where "the plaintiff bought the car on the credit card." Judge Herman responded, "I remember that." Again, nothing was resolved, issues disputed, Father Fred again absent, the case was deferred again to July 1 as the court gave the parties time to implement the agreement to date and to deal with Paula's announced plan to file for divorce. My visitation schedule with the children was maintained but with all visitations now ordered to be outside the marital home; our home was to be listed for sale, my remaining personal possessions were to be surrendered to me, I was responsible for payment of the mortgage and taxes, all utilities, all insurance policies, weekly child support of $125 by wage execution, the IRA was to remain frozen, the DV complaint that initiated my removal from my home and children was summarily dismissed without prejudice.

The June 8 hearing ordered I would have no contact with Paula in person, by phone, or email; my daily phone call with the children was to be maintained; child support payments would be made through payroll deductions managed by the county Probation Department. The DV charge was dismissed without prejudice-I was found neither guilty nor not guilty of domestic violence, yet this charge was subject to perpetual recall at any time. There was no trial of facts, just an hour of court banter that decided my fate. Akin to a hangman's noose around your neck and they reserved the right to pull on it at will. Not innocent; not guilty; they just wanted me removed from the marital home on Paula's terms, so they could establish her as the preferred custodial parent. But the more immediate question that begged to be answered was what prompted this filing by Paula while we were still in marriage counseling with Father Fred for several months.

Sister Catherine was Paula's acknowledged mentor in this divorce. I soon contacted the director of the facility where Sister worked, Brother Edward. I asked Brother Edward if he knew that Sister Catherine was counseling my wife, a diagnosed bipolar personality, for her compulsion to shoplift? I told Brother Edward that Paula's lawyer identified Sister Catherine as the mentor who supported and advocated for this divorce. I also mentioned Sister Catherine's comment to me some weeks ago, "she could support divorce in this case."

No, he knew of no such counseling being performed at that facility but did admit I had a very difficult situation if what I said was true, and he wished me well. Sister Catherine was immediately pulled from all counseling services, and Paula was advised that Sister Catherine was placed on leave. Paula was furious and this matter was addressed in a subsequent hearing alleging I had interfered with her counseling services. I told the court I had every legal right to address my concerns with the State and this facility relative to what I believed to be unprofessional, if not illegal counseling services performed by this nun.

I filed a complaint on August 9, 1993, with the New Jersey State Board of Psychological Examiners alleging Sister Catherine was providing psychological services without any qualifications. The State's response dated September 29, 1993, noted examples of your wife's conduct may, indeed, be consistent with the diagnosis given by the specialists. The conduct, as described (including repeated violations of law threatening potential imprisonment and removal from her family), might even be found to pose significant problems for your wife's welfare as well as your children. In summary, the letter stated the Board would not be able to address your concerns because the provisions of the Practicing Psychology Licensing Act specifically exclude members of the clergy from a requirement of licensure. The best they could suggest, based on my complaint, was "seeking review of your serious concerns with her supervisors." That I did with my call to Brother Edward and Sister Catherine was put out of the business counseling those diagnosed with a serious mental illness. I then wrote to the Bishop of the Diocese of Camden to advise him of the counseling being performed by this nun who advocated for divorce. Sister Catherine and the priest from Paula's Camden parish would subsequently come to court a year later to testify against me at a hearing.

Before the DV complaint, I was taking our daughter, Adriana, to the local library on Saturday mornings for a couple of hours to help her with schoolwork on various subjects. The library provided quiet time and a one-on-one effort that was not available at the house on a Saturday. Adriana and I enjoyed this personal time together without the other girls pulling me in all directions. As it was with all kids, what subjects one liked the other did not. So, we worked with Adriana on those subjects.

This Saturday morning library time ended abruptly when I was removed from the marital home on March 26. Our lives were shattered and we were all in much distress. I was no longer living at home, and any interaction with Paula was fraught with tension. She now controlled the scene; I was very threatened by her willingness to manage any interaction with a threat to call the police or threaten more court action. Over the many years of this divorce, I was arrested four times on complaints filed by Paula. Of these four arrests, and many more threatened, the children were in my custody at my home for three such arrests. The children were quite distraught as the local police came to my residence to enforce a complaint filed by Paula.

Three times I was taken from the home in the presence of the children and taken to the local police station and processed for these complaints. I was then returned home to the children who surely must have worried about what happens next? The complaints would be answered in court weeks later. These complaints were all about violations of the restraining order that strictly defined my limited actions around the marital home. All depended on Paula's mood at that moment or day. In each instance, I was found not guilty of the charge or it was just dismissed. But this was a weapon Paula was willing to employ to exercise control as this divorce played out in family court. Long term, I believe, the children saw these efforts as bad in that they placed me in jeopardy when they depended on me and wanted to be with me. I was not the threat to them, the mother was, in that she threatened me, their father.

I decided to learn more about this system I was now mired in. Early into this divorce action, I took part in two group meetings at the Cherry Hill Library sponsored by a fathers' rights group known as FACE (Fathers' and Children's Equality). FACE staff advised that the New Jersey Family Court system was very biased against the father's rights. Fathers were thrown into divorce and custody issues and lawyers advised they had little to no chance of gaining custody of their children in New Jersey. Likewise, FACE noted that lawyers would do little for your benefit and cost a small fortune relative to what little financial assets one might retain after the divorce. Their advice was that if you had it within you then your best option would be to represent yourself. The group offered limited legal support as they were not lawyers but several of the men knew the system and laws well enough, as they had lived through it for some years themselves. In the weeks to come, I went to two other local FACE meetings hosted by a father who lived near me in Mullica Hill. At both meetings, I met as many as fifteen fathers and other supporting family members. I listened to stories of claims and actions and court orders issued against these men. I could not believe what I was hearing. I was distraught by stories of contempt for what I presumed was a legitimate legal option. I left and never returned to another FACE meeting.

I was reminded of an old movie I watched as a kid. A classic and reportedly true cowboy tale in every sense; good vs bad; justice vs injustice; law vs vigilantism. The opening scene of *The Ox-Bow Incident* told the story of a dusty town in 1885 Nevada where a posse was being raised by an angry bully, a retired Army Major, as rumor reported a favored local rancher had been murdered and his cattle rustled. The posse headed out of town in full gallop in search of the villains with no facts other than what the rumor allowed. The posse came upon three sleeping cowpokes herding cattle a distance outside town, at a landmark known as the Ox-Bow. The cowboys acknowledged they had purchased cattle from this local rancher but knew nothing of any murder, the rancher was alive when they left him hours ago. The Major took command of these proceedings, what was to pass for a jury trial, and the majority of the posse condemned the three cowboys to be hung for the murder of their friend. The accused pleaded for their lives; a chance to prove their case; demanded a trial outside of the grasp of this posse, this mob. No, the Major demanded swift justice, death by hanging.

One of the detained cowboys pleaded for his life; that he had a wife and two children who needed him. "Take it like a man" he was told. The posse swung into action and final preparations were made to lynch the cowpokes now sentenced by this mob. The Major told this accused, distraught father of two children, "other men with families have had to die for this sort of thing. It's too bad, but it's justice." This father shouted back "what do you care about justice?" The three cowboys were surrounded by this mob, their jury. Their hands were tied behind their backs, and they were saddled on their horses. Nooses were crafted and pulled around their necks and the three ropes slung over a nearby low-lying branch. Any last words were requested? None would suffice. A shot was soon fired, and the horses raced out from under the "guilty" and their bodies swung from the ropes. The town's sheriff passing nearby heard the shot and approached the posse as the three lifeless bodies hung from the branch. Questioning what had happened, the posse shouted and exalted in their claim they had found those who had murdered their friend. The sheriff announced the local rancher was not dead, that he had been wounded but that he had caught the person who had robbed their friend. Here, the posse had murdered three innocent men with their brand of justice. The sheriff ushered the posse back into town to face the justice they denied these three cowboys.

Eventually filmed in 1943, *The Ox-Bow Incident* won a nomination for Best Picture Oscar and entered cowboy film lore. My understanding of what I was told and would learn of family court justice in New Jersey brought me back to the story, the justice of *The Ox-Bow*

*Incident.* The analogy was clear, a rabid posse of prosecuting divorce lawyers; court personnel issuing orders based on the word, rumor of one person; judges and the law hostile to the accused before any hearing of fact or reason; much less all the testimony and evidence that would or should be presented by the accused. The system tells a father he has no chance; there is no justice for him in New Jersey Family Court. Take what little they give you and run; go to California; no sense fighting the mob rule of this court. A prerelease screening of this film was received with a muted response from the audience. The audience did not believe such cowboy justice was a realistic portrayal of the American system of justice. They did not know family court justice.

Gerry and I would meet once more in his office to discuss the case and strategy. Again, I wanted a custody trial, a hearing of the facts. And although pressured to sell the marital home, I did not want to sell the house. I agreed to a realtor, but there was no discussion of a listing price, and I never met or spoke with anyone from that entity. Paula announced in April she would file for divorce, so I asked in August where was that divorce filing? She had the kids, the home, I was paying all the bills, what was I getting from this effort and not yet guilty of anything? The attorneys both pushed for the sale of the home as that was their collateral for payment of fees, especially for opposing counsel. It was also suggested that any equity I had in the home be escrowed for future child support.

I continued to write Gerry outlining my agenda. In an earlier office visit, I offered to buy out Paula's equity in the home valued at $165,000; but I would not list the home for sale for less than $180,000.

I picked up the children for the regular Saturday visitation in early September 1993. Everyone seated in the van, we left the property generally within ten minutes. We returned to the house at 5 PM that day only to find a realtor's "for sale" sign on the front lawn of the property. The children started to cry and asked why the house was for sale? I told them I knew nothing of it. Two of the girls left the van as I parked in the driveway, approached the sign, and started to kick it.

They returned to the home in distress and I assured them I would work to stop this sale. I didn't even know the listing price for my own home. I asked a friend to call the realtor's office on Monday. It was listed for $164,900. I called Gerry and asked how the home was listed as I had not signed any listing agreement and did not even know of the listing price. Gerry advised that I had agreed to a $165,000 price in our prior discussions. I said the $165,000 was my offer to buy out Paula's interest in the home; but that $180,000 was the minimum selling price I would agree to. He faxed over the listing agreement and asked me to sign it. Gerry and the opposing counsel agreed on the listing price and arranged for the realtor to take the listing. There was no meeting with the chosen realtor or to get a professional assessment of the home's value.

I still had not been given my remaining personal effects from the home, some seventeen weeks after the June 8 hearing that ordered the same. I asked if Gerry had filed the motion on my behalf demanding the custody trial, which by New Jersey law had to be held within three months of such a filing. Furthermore, there had been no documentation of any income earned by Paula, whose earnings could be used to offset some of all the expenses I was paying since being removed from the home on March 26.

In a letter dated October 19, 1993, I informed Gerry that Paula had agreed the eight-year-old daughter Adriana could live with me, as this child had always expressed that desire. I asked Gerry to pursue this option with opposing counsel. Then too there was the charge that alleged I had failed to pay the homeowners and auto insurance installments. Need it to be said the policy billings were sent to the marital home and Paula never forwarded them to me for payment? After much insistence, I again told Gerry we needed to file for divorce, that Paula was living life with no financial responsibilities and I was paying all the bills. Their mentioned filing for divorce in April and again at the June hearing had yet to materialize now six months later. My complaint seeking a divorce was filed on November 12, 1993, and among other things, I demanded custody of the four children.

That same day I received notice of an offer on the sale of our home. This offer hit me like few things, as I now felt my agenda for the children was seriously threatened. I faxed a letter to Gerry demanding answers. What had become of my offer to buy out Paula's equity? What had become of Paula's agreement to allow Adriana to live with me? Where were the records of Paula's income as that would reduce my level of required child support? Where were my remaining personal possessions? As for the pending custody trial, had any effort been made to secure Paula's medical records, as ordered by the court, relative to the acknowledged mental illness issue? I told Gerry not to respond until he had all of my issues answered.

An initial offer of $153,000 was received on November 12 and Gerry advised the realtor I had rejected the offer. Gerry questioned this decision. A second offer from the same perspective buyer was presented a week later for $158,000. I rejected it. I was up $5,000 ignoring his advice. Our attorney-client relationship was failing fast. Finally, within a couple of weeks, I received a call from the realtor at my office and this individual noted they had received a full cash offer of the $164,900 listing price. I advised this agent, still unknown to me, that what he had was a buyer; what he lacked was a seller in this transaction. The realtor then told me he "had a court order to sell this home." I told him in no uncertain terms he had no such order and to never call me again.

A November 18 letter from Gerry was his best if the only effort to date to address my concerns. He again questioned my means to maintain the marital home assuming I lost the requested custody fight and he questioned my characterization of opposing counsel as something that served to exacerbate the hostility I felt. The opposing counsel has done me no favors and did nothing to protect my children. I could care less about the feelings of opposing counsel. Gerry said Paula would not now agree to allow Adriana to live with me. He then expressed concern for the future based on my level of frustration and anger at the current situation. Although ruled by law, there were no assurances a custody trial could be held within the mandated three-month period. And no, he had not secured any of Paula's medical records from the Mood Clinic or from the psychiatrist who had billed Paula $1,700 for the prior year's psychotherapy treatments.

Gerry then questioned the "tone" of my letter. He claimed not to be a "hired gun" to execute whatever instructions I gave him. If that was my perception of his job then he suggested I seek another attorney. Gerry also advised the summary of the court order from last July had finally been resolved with opposing counsel, and the scheduled December 2 hearing to address such resolution was not needed. Five months later and finally the two lawyers had resolved in writing what was agreed to in court in July. Gerry asked me to digest the contents of his letter and give him a callback.

Digest his letter; it made me sick, it made me contemptuous of him and this legal system. It was more of the same just months later and from a different lawyer, even a "family-type guy." Nothing changed: you had no chance for custody; you won't get your kids back; issues relative to Paula's mental health had yet to be addressed; sell the marital home to save yourself. At $125 an hour, I surely assumed Gerry was a "hired gun" working for me and my interests. And at those rates, he damn well better shoot straight.

Every letter deserves a response and I formulated one late into the evening of November 19, 1993. To say this was a turning point in my life was an understatement. I was emotionally wired like never before, threatened for myself and the children. This decision was one I contemplated and there was but one answer. My response to Gerry follows.

I received your faxed correspondence late yesterday and distressed as I am with "more of the same," I mulled a response into the night to give me a chance to adequately formulate it. This letter is as much a response to the "system" as it is to you.

My bitterness and resentment of the system and my "ex" is real, and hopefully, I will learn to live with it if I am unable to overcome it. But I want a hearing of the facts that the legal profession so eloquently espouses to deal with, but that the system so brutally denies. But it is a system designed by lawyers, run by lawyers, and profited only by lawyers. This is why our system fails so miserably. Just ask the victims, not their lawyers.

I was never given the courtesy of a written offer from (realtor) but merely a phone call... I will demand my rights as an owner. I will advise...the offer is rejected. Many grounds are obvious to me. We are already up to $5,000 in five days. Not bad for a "nut."

A child's love is to be earned, unless, of course, the "system" now mandates that fathers alone must earn this treasure; mothers get it by birth-right. Adriana never said she did not love her mother. Paula has said, "she can't cope with this child." All this child wants is to live with the parent whom she has found to be much more responsive to her and her needs...

I must also challenge your opinion of Paula as the long-lasting mother who will always be there. She is not there today, wasn't there yesterday, and assuredly will not be there in the future.

Why is there no custody hearing within the mandated three-month time period? If you listen to everybody within the system you get the impression that the true concerns are for the benefit of the kids. Yet in typical legalese, what should be is not and what can't happen does. This is why we have the system we have, run by lawyers. What a system! But if you tolerate it then you deserve it. I just won't tolerate it anymore. This is America! I will address the custody issue.

Your only answer to justice on the issue of reduced support is to sell the family home out from under the children. Were Paula's payroll records ever requested? I went into court in March with my financial records fully exposed and dissected. Yet eight months later we still know nothing about her financial standing, at my expense. Perhaps presumptuously, I read your remarks that you have not yet secured the medical records from the University of Pennsylvania or her psychiatrist as having not even requested them. After eight months of my ranting that we are dealing with a person with a mental illness, a problem that drives all other aspects of this case, the system has again failed to seek justice through truth, preferring to deal with innuendo and hearsay of the mentally ill. But opposing counsel did dodge this bullet to his credit and my detriment. All the smoke, in this case, comes from opposing counsel, not from any house fire.

As for the final issue, as a paying client, I believed you were there to represent me and my agenda. Yes, you are entitled to your opinion based on your judgment, and your advice is considered. But it is my life and that of my children that is at stake here and being ripped apart. I prefer to listen to an opinion but to make my own decisions. I have seen little within the system that makes me believe that only lawyers have the answers. Since you seem unwilling to adequately address my agenda, get issues handled in a timely fashion, then we must end this relationship.

Please forward the final bill for services rendered. I, as responsible as I am presumably guilty of dastardly deeds, will see you are paid. I will represent myself, pro se, in the future. I was foolish to trust my future and that of my children to anyone else. For the record, I have no faith in any justice in this great country, but I relish the right to fight for it.

This letter allowed me to vent against my legal representation; Paula's actions and the family court system that now controlled much of my life and threatened my children. I sat up into the early morning hours and composed the following poem that came from my soul and told who I was and what I stood for in the looming battles I could not yet foresee. But this was my life and those of my children at stake and I was willing to fight as I had never had before.

*DADDY, PRO SE*

> *I am Pro se*
> *I did it my way*
> *I'm so sad, so sad*
> *But I am still their Dad*
>
> *What is claimed as a Mother's birthright*

*A Father must make a stand for and fight*
*Of sorts a moral defeat*
*But never will they know me to be a deadbeat*

*I stood for truth and the facts*
*Yet there is something the process still lacks*
*Is it fairness, surely not lawyers*
*Any visit will witness they jam the halls and foyer*

*I am their Father for life*
*We will carry each other through this strife*
*It is but this once I have failed my little girls*
*But I will do much to restore the luster to these precious pearls*

*Surely the facts will confirm I am no liar*
*But nor do I aspire to be an esquire*
*Of all the labels we affix this day*
*I am adamant, I am first Daddy and then pro se*

I soon told the court that I had dismissed my attorney and would be representing myself and my children in this case. My response was faxed to Gerry; I was overwhelmed with doubt. Could I do this; speak publicly, take on the family court system, lawyers, and the law? I had but one answer, I had to if I was to save the children; save the home for them and salvage our fortunes and futures.

Abraham Lincoln said, "He who represents himself has a fool for a client." I was somewhat aware of the challenges a pro se litigant faced in any legal process. Then too, I was even more aware that a father could not get good legal representation in his fight for custody of his children. The two lawyers I employed to date argued against my efforts; argued I had little to no chance of winning anything; argued I should submit to the system and desert my children as amicably as possible and move on. It was that inability to just walk away from my children that provoked me to continue on my own, and prepare for the battles that were to come. Did I anticipate all that was to come my way? No, but I was determined to surrender to no one until justice served these children. I would demand justice from this family court.

Again, upon notice of my pro se representation, opposing counsel immediately filed an order to show cause on November 23 alleging numerous violations of prior court orders in a six-page certification. A hearing was scheduled for December 2, 1993. Things move fast when they want them to. This filing alleged among many things that I had disparaged the mother to the children; failed to pay child support; blocked Paula from exiting the driveway; and demanded the court incarcerate me and order I undergo psychiatric counseling. A subsequent supplemental certification added yet another five pages of similar fodder to the dunghills of justice. This supplemental, filed December 1, claimed I, among many things, would not obey any court order; disputed the proposed wording of the order relative to the June 8 hearing; complained of my letters to the Diocesan Bishop and the Rector relative to Sister Catherine's counseling of Paula; called opposing counsel's office to complain bitterly as to the wording of the drafted order of the June 8 and July 1 hearings that had yet to be finalized five months later; then too, they argued I defied the agreement to sell the marital home after an offer had been made at the listing price.

I approached this December 2 hearing with much trepidation. Could I defend all they alleged in a complaint now totaling thirteen pages? Plus, the original DV complaint was still perpetually pending; subject to disposition at any time they chose. I was filled with anxiety; my hands were soaking wet with perspiration. In the hearing I contested all of their alleged characterizations but noted my level of frustration with Paula; in dealing with lawyers who got nothing done in months at my expense; that the order from the June 8 hearing had yet to be filed five months later. I told the court "I was representing myself pro se because the prior attorney did not represent my interest or that of my children. The sale of the marital home was not in my interest or that of my children; that we had just built the home in 1988 and it was situated in a good community with a great school;" and "if the mother didn't like it, she should move, the children stay in the home." Judge Herman agreed the home need not be sold.

Opposing counsel then contested my right to the daily phone calls with my children as they claimed these calls interfered with Paula's ability to manage her day. The Judge turned to me for a response and I answered "ask him if he talks to his kids every day? If he says yes then I want the same." Opposing counsel merely rolled his eyes. My daily phone calls with the children would remain in place.

While visiting my sister in Alexandria over Thanksgiving, the parish bulletin published an article styled *Violence*. This article noted that there was a difference between violence and anger. In a society that demanded more of its participants, people were frustrated at getting those demands met. There would be a rise in anger if these demands remained unresolved. Getting those frustrations addressed would go a long way to reducing that anger. I distributed copies of this article to the court and opposing counsel who objected to this mailing. Judge Herman asked what I was doing. I noted, "the article addressed the differences between violence and anger; that I was surely angry at what was happening to myself and my children at the hands of the mother, but I was not violent." The court was obligated to address my frustrations. The judge ordered me not to send any more articles.

Another issue was to be addressed. Paula's parents lived in Bogota and after fifteen years of marriage had only visited our home once; and came to Florida but once where Paula took the children to visit these grandparents. No birthday gifts were ever sent to the children; no Christmas gifts were ever sent to the children; at best Paula took the children to visit Bogota several times over the years at great expense to ourselves. In November 1993 Paula filed a motion stating that her parent's home in Bogota had been "in a tragic fire" and both parents were in the ICU at the local hospital. Paula asked the court to release the children's passports so she could travel to Bogota with the children to see their dying grandparents.

My response to this issue was factual. I stated there was no proof of any such fire, no pictures, just her spoken word; that Paula was in the throes of a bitterly contested divorce and had no other family here in the U.S.; Paula had no steady job here in the U.S. What hospital would allow such young children into their ICU to visit patients reportedly in the arms of death from a house fire? Colombia, at the time, refused to extradite Colombian drug lords indicted in the U.S., so what chance did this father have to get Colombia to return these children to the U.S. when they had all rights to Colombian citizenship? Plus the U.S. State Department urged all Americans not to travel to Colombia due to security concerns and the level of violence and risk of kidnapping in the country, and after 13 years living in the U.S. Paula had yet to request American citizenship.

The judge asked Paula what guarantees she had to return the children to the U.S. and their father upon a visit to Colombia? Her answer, "I'm very close to my church." The judge ruled that was not sufficient security for the return of the children. He ordered she was allowed to take two children to Bogota and upon return then take the other two to visit the grandparents. No trips were made to visit these grandparents. There was little ever mentioned again of this fire in years to come but we note Paula's mother lived until 2003 and the father passed away in 2012. I asked the court not to allow Paula to take Michelle and Molly together on any such scheduled visit as I feared she would never return for the other two children. The judge seemed offended by my suggestion. As a footnote, I worked in Bogota for six months and made several visits there while traveling through South America. I previously noted to Paula I had only seen two firehouses in all my travels throughout the sprawling city of seven million inhabitants. In the States, every neighborhood in our towns and cities had a firehouse. Paula agreed and stated there were few firehouses in Bogota as everything was built of brick and stone; that nothing ever burns.

We had weathered the first eight months of family court justice. The original threat "to burn down the house" was dismissed "without prejudice" by Judge Herman in the hearing of July 1, 1993. Not convicted of anything but not allowed to return to my home, I could only see my children on a court-mandated schedule. We did manage to void the sale of the house the children called home, and my issue of Paula's unmedicated mental illness had yet to garner a minute's consideration in this court of justice. I was removed from my home and the lives of my children and yet not guilty of anything after eight months and four hearings. This was New Jersey Family Court justice at work.

The children were in a state of shock as they found their lives completely turned around and under threat. I was the one who cared for them so many nights when Paula went out. They now found themselves under the care and control of the mother. Michelle, almost ten years old, would now assume a prominent role within the household. She was very protective of the youngest, Molly, now almost three. Paula continued her many nights out, as the children were left in the care of a bevy of young babysitters from the neighborhood, aged thirteen to eighteen. Meals were limited as Paula was no cook. Breakfast and lunch were now the benefits of government programs as the household qualified for such assistance. In a community of upper incomes, the children felt the stigma of the free meal programs among their friends. Dinners were packaged noodles, rice or the declared "crazy meal" of ice cream. The two middle children, Adriana and Katie, who shared a bedroom, isolated themselves within the home. Paula accused Katie of being so much like her father she called her by my name, Bill. Adriana, always the neglected child, was even further isolated.

Our mandated daily phone calls were my best chance to assure the girls I was around, ready, and able to help. I was there, just not in the home. Our routine scheduled visits gave them some sense that someone cared for them. On our visits I always provided them well-cooked meals of their favorite dinners; questioned them about school work and any other concerns. If they needed something, I made sure they got it. Schoolwork and projects became the lore of many weekends and I insisted they do their best.

In my ten years of scheduled visitation with the girls, I only missed three times. Once I was too sick to visit the girls and did not want to risk getting them sick. Paula offered to bring them to me. Another missed visit was about year three into this effort. My family believed I needed a break from the stress of the situation. My brother convinced me to join him on a week's trip to Florida. I felt so bad having left the girls I cried during our daily phone calls and assured them I would be back. The third missed visit, some years later, was when I felt so threatened by Paula, I dared not go to the home. This established bond, trust between the girls, and I only grew over the years. I was there for them and they were there for me as we traveled this road alone. The girls expected little from their mother and got less.

In the first year of this divorce, I had the children overnight with me for a weekend at my apartment. I doubled over in pain one evening scaring the girls and myself. I called a friend from work who lived in the same complex to please watch the girls and I drove myself to the hospital ER just four miles away. I was diagnosed with kidney stones and was back home hours later. Twice more over these ten years, I would experience kidney stone attacks. By the third time, I made my way to the ER and on my way to the bed, I diagnosed myself with yet another attack of kidney stones. Give me the IV as that was my immediate relief. Meeting with the urologist I was questioned if I drank too much soda, tea, coffee, or smoked, in the usual search for the cause. No. Finally, the doctor asked if I was under a lot of stress? Yes, I was going through a divorce. That will do it, he said. I only had these three attacks but the stress of this divorce never lessened. From start to finish, I would lose thirty pounds, dropping to 120 pounds during these ten years in the search for justice in family court.

# 9

# DON'T TRUST THE PROFESSIONALS

Having made the conscious decision to fight the system, I also decided to hold all parties accountable as myself, as a father was accountable for all sins. On November 29, 1993, I filed a complaint with the County Board of Realtors relative to specific violations of the Board's Code of Ethics and Standards of Practice relative to the listing of the marital home for sale by this local realtor that violated four specific articles of the ethics code when they contracted to sell our house.

The County Board of Realtors responded in January 1994 dismissing my complaint because they had a record of the signed listing agreement (they failed to mention this document was not signed by myself until 12 days after the listing date). They also noted each party to the listing was represented by an attorney and advised: "when clients are represented by an attorney that all legal matters, including offers, are to go through the client's attorney." Again, not to belabor a technicality, but the realtor, in this case, had no record or evidence from me that this attorney represented me in any issues relative to the sale of this property. The lawyer they referenced was representing me in a divorce, not a real estate deal. Also, this attorney they claimed represented me had no signed power of attorney that authorized his participation in this transaction. I had never met the realtor; never advised him I was represented by a lawyer; I was never advised by the realtor as to the listing price negotiated for this sale. The realtor performed no market survey for this pending sale. The listing price was determined by the lawyers. Should we mention the board did not address the question of why my attorney did not sign the listing agreement if he had the legal authority they claimed? There was one party in this transaction with whom the realtor had no relationship, me.

Having been denied a complete and competent review of the facts at the County Board, I forwarded my complaint to the New Jersey Real Estate Commission. Their Chief of Investigations answered in June that the realtor "did not violate any real estate licensing laws or administrative rules." I should probably mention that in a subsequent conversation with Paula's second attorney, the listing realtor was reported to be a cousin of Paula's first attorney. I never confirmed that as fact but it surely suggested to me how this real estate transaction could get so far done when one of the owners never saw the realtor and the attorney had no power of attorney justifying his exclusion from all phases of the transaction.

An article in The Wall Street Journal dated July 26, 1994, was titled *Teacher gives Real-Estate Agents Below-Average Grades on Ethics*. The article opined that perhaps real-estate agents were "getting a bum rap" in people's perceptions of their dealings with the industry. It was noted the American public consistently gives the profession low grades. A 1993 Gallup Poll ranked twenty-six professions for honesty and ethical standards, and real-estate agents placed a dismal 19th - below even lawyers and television talk show hosts. The report noted real-estate agents "ranked just above high school students in their ability to make ethical judgments." You mix divorce court participants and their shenanigans with real estate agents and you get a toxic mix for ethical lapses of judgment, maybe even fraud.

The case proceeded into 1994 with me feeling better having accomplished one thing at best, we saved the home for the children; they did not want to move; I did not want them to be moved. In a letter dated January 12, 1994, I addressed issues with opposing counsel regarding the care of the children in the home. Michelle, ten years old, had been sick and was taken to the ER. Kept from school the next day, Paula took the child to her workplace; and never advised me of the ER visit. I was never allowed to care for the child at my home the next day. Then there was the incident where Katie, aged seven, was left with a sitter and was thought to have contracted chickenpox. Taken to the doctor, it was determined to be flea bites from the sitter's flea-infested home. I received no response from opposing counsel. A filing dated January 20, 1994, advised this lawyer left the case. We won't miss you!

The new opposing counsel representing Paula made me a final written offer to resolve this case before a full-blown custody trial. I was offered maximum visitation in exchange for Paula retaining physical custody of the children and the marital home. The offer was said to spare the children the effects of the pending psychological screening that was typical of any custody trial. I rejected the offer. A February 4 hearing date was to allow the parties to select the custody evaluator and that selection was to be approved by the court.

I received a copy of a "Continuation of Temporary Order" dated January 26, 1994, signed by Judge Herman that summarized the decisions of the April 2, 1993 hearing. Ten months to put to writing what was agreed to in court last April. Among many things, the order noted I was to have no contact with Paula unless provided by the court; I shall have daily phone contact with my children; and detailed the continuation of the same visitation schedule in place since the initial hearing. I was to receive specific personal property and my remaining clothing still at the home. The last of seventeen items referenced in this order noted: "the plaintiff's domestic violence complaint of March 24, 1993, is dismissed without prejudice." The original complaint of domestic violence that initiated my removal from my home and children was dismissed with no judgment of guilt or innocence.

It is my opinion that this DV complaint and many like it issued against fathers are merely a means to an end, a court-sanctioned tool to get fathers out of the marital home with no trial of facts. If anything, the court's refusal to decide this complaint was sufficient evidence that it was never about any threat. It was an accepted tool, a preferred weapon of the divorce process, a court-sanction medium used in filing a false claim against the husband; a legal means to extract him from his home, his children, for the benefit of the mother. I can only assume they call this family court justice. The State of New Jersey participated in this miscarriage of justice and facilitated its misuse disproportionately against fathers.

The court's agreement that the marital home need not be sold was resolved at the hearing of December 2, 1993. The signed court order of the July 1, 1993 hearing reported the marital home was to be sold but it was not signed by the court until January 26, 1994. Unsigned prior court orders of months ago were being negated by current court rulings. These inordinate delays by the lawyers in getting court orders drafted and signed was abusive. Do we call this lawyering?

I wrote to opposing counsel on February 1, 1994, outlining several issues that I suggested needed to be resolved, hopefully amicably, to move this case forward on a more positive footing. I suggested their ignoring my requests and filing frivolous complaints would not produce any benefits for the case. Among the items, I questioned was Paula's prior demand for a separate phone line into the home to facilitate my daily phone calls with the children. Paula now agreed she did not want to monitor the children's use of this "private line." That was now too much responsibility for her. I also asked that the children be allowed to stay overnight at my apartment on weekend visitations. I requested consideration for filing a joint tax return as most advantageous financially; and finally, I addressed the orthodontist treatment that had been considered for the two oldest children before the filing of the DV complaint in March 1993. So much for hope in this case. Again, no response was ever received from opposing counsel. They did not want a resolution.

The signed court order dated February 23, 1994, relative to the December 2, 1993 hearing continued the weekly child support of $125 that was now to be collected electronically through the

Gloucester County Probation Department. The weekly supplemental cash support payment was in addition to my payment of the mortgage and property taxes; all utilities and insurance expenses at the marital home. This December hearing also had the court order the parties to participate in a custody mediation session with the court's mediator. I believed this to be the best and only chance yet afforded the children to express their concerns for matters of this case and what happened within the marital home now under Paula's control. I have no record or recall anything of this mediation effort with the children, it never happened. This written order failed to mention the judge ruled the marital home need not be sold.

Finally, we were moving forward to a custody trial. If the parties could not agree to an evaluator then the court would choose one at this February 4, 1994 hearing. Judge Herman called our case and immediately confronted me as to why I had not answered the opposing counsel's most recent filing, yet another motion to enforce litigant's rights? This latest motion, new opposing counsel's effort to intimidate me, included Paula's nine-page certification alleging numerous instances from the prior two months where it was said I had engaged in negative comments with the children about this case; I disparaged the court; Paula and her lawyers.

I advised the court I knew nothing of any such filing. Judge Herman ordered "swear him in" and I took an oath "to tell the truth, nothing but the truth, so help me God." I again was questioned by the judge why I had not answered this latest motion filed against me? Again, I stated I knew nothing of what he was speaking and held in his hand waving at me from the bench. A copy of the document was handed to me by the court clerk and I was asked to confirm that I had not seen this document. Looking at the document for the first time, I stated I had not seen this document. I did mention my mailing address referenced on the motion was not correct. The judge somewhat chagrined, advised I take this copy home and answer it in time for the February 18 hearing date. The court was dismissed.

Opposing counsel's motion demanded I be held in contempt for discussing the case with the children and failing to pay the auto insurance on Paula's car and requesting I pay her attorney's fees. The motion was supported by their multi-page transcript of conversations Paula gleaned from the children over the prior two months. The complaint was based on what Paula construed to be my comments being in contempt of the court's order not to discuss the case with the children. My response to this motion was to state the affidavit reflected alleged communications that were but a compilation of hearsay and misrepresentations garnered from children aged three to ten years of age; that did not reflect the true context of conversations and were littered with inferences to suit the mother's efforts to discredit me. Somewhat typical of the referenced comments are reported below:

"December 11, 1993, wherein it was reported (father) takes the girls shopping for Paula's Christmas gift, as ordered by the court, and he tells the kids what the mother needed was a new lawyer." I answered, "I was trying to make a game of finding an idea of what to buy the mother for Christmas. Some of the other suggestions included a car, a new lawyer, jewelry, underwear. We settled for expensive perfume."

"December 12, 1993, wherein it was reported: "the father tells the oldest daughter that he had ironed 21 shirts and that (unlike the mother) he can do a lot."" I answered, "I had told my daughter that I had ironed 21 shirts and that I could do anything. I wanted the children to know that I am still standing, full of confidence, despite the circumstances." I have told them regularly "I will always be here for you, never doubt it."

"January 8, 1994, upon their return from a visitation it was reported I said "he is going to drown you and your lawyer."" I answered that I had no recollection of such a comment but noted: "I surely plan to drown them in facts at the divorce and custody hearings." The car insurance was not paid because Paula never gave me the billing.

Opposing counsel wrote the court on February 18, 1994, relative to my sworn statement that, because of a wrong address, I had neither received nor seen a copy of their motion to enforce litigant's rights. I testified the address was not correct and that likely accounted for its non-delivery. Opposing counsel stated that she had initiated an investigation of my answer with the U.S. Post Office in Deptford and the apartment management where I resided. The attorney alleged I lied to the court in my response of not having seen or received the referenced motion. I answered the court on March 1, 1993, disputing their claim that "I was less than candid" on the matter. I agreed I lived at the apartment where the referenced mailbox was assigned to my apartment but I elected not to open that mailbox as I had already established a mailbox at the Post Office next door to the courthouse. I did not want my mail lost by a misfiling at a cluster box of some 20 apartment units per building. I have been on record with prior counsel and the court as recently as December confirming my correct mailing address. Opposing counsel's inability to get my address correct was not my concern.

And in yet another subsequent filing by opposing counsel, they disputed my understanding of the judge's recent ruling that the children were allowed to bring movies, toys, and bikes with them on our visits; the children's items were not to be held hostage by the mother. They argued the court ordered no possessions (mine I suggest) were to leave the home; toys, movies, bikes included. Opposing counsel suggested we both be compelled to listen to the taped hearing of the day to ascertain whose understanding of that day's order was correct. I answered the court's ruling had been made and if they could not get it correct then I should not be required to do double-time to confirm what was an obvious and reasonable ruling. If required to vouch for their lack of attention to details as to the court's rulings then I wanted to be compensated as she was, and at her rate. The issue was dropped. Toys, movies, bikes go with the children.

At the next scheduled hearing on March 18, 1994, opposing counsel opened suggesting the court initiate a plenary (fact-finding) hearing to address their claim that I had committed perjury at the February 4th hearing relative to my mailing address of record. The court's response was a swift "drop it."

I noticed an anomaly of family court proceedings that struck me as odd. In all courtroom proceedings, I had ever seen, mostly limited to old cowboy westerns or current episodes of TV court dramas, the parties are always sworn-in to "tell the truth, nothing but the truth, so help me God." This family court demanded no such allegiance to the truth, but in the most extreme cases. In all my years I was sworn to tell the truth but once; Paula never to my recollection. I came to the conclusion family court had no use for truth or facts in most instances; they had their predetermined bias and opinions well before anyone spoke a word. The truth did not matter in this court as I believed they presumed both parties lied through their teeth. As my poem said, "surely the facts will confirm I am no liar" as I would only, could only deal in truth and facts. Perhaps, my first lawyer, Marty knew too well that a father's sustained effort to seek truth or even justice in family court was fatally flawed. Facts and truth had no bearing on justice in this court.

Yet another letter from opposing counsel dated March 4, 1994, referenced that her client now shared my sentiments that the marital home not be sold. Opposing counsel noted that the realtor might file a claim for damages for the lost sales commission as the contract listing price was offered by a buyer and I had rejected all offers on the property. I advised counsel to tell the realtor, still unbeknownst to me, to "sue me." The realtor made no effort to collect any commissions on this negated sale.

# 10

# THE MUCH-PROMISED CUSTODY TRIAL

As part of all divorce proceedings, the court requires both parties to participate in a Matrimonial Early Settlement Panel (MESP). This is the court's best and last effort to get the warring parties to "see the light," the folly of (my) demand for a custody trial. The court solicits such counseling from local attorneys, as a pro bono service, who are well versed as to the law and practical matters relative to custody trials. Each party meets with a disinterested attorney, who reviews the facts as they are advised of them and weigh in with their best suggestion as to the prospects of pursuing the case to trial rather than coming to some amicable settlement.

To this end, I met with an attorney, a partner from a ranked regional law firm, a graduate from the UPenn Law School, for about forty minutes. Having heard my best case for custody, he advised my hope for custody of the children was dead on arrival. The system was such that I would lose custody of my children; be compelled to pay child support and alimony; get a schedule for visitation with the children. Again, I was told any effort to get the court to determine this mother, any mother, as "unfit" was, at best, a very long-shot. I'm sure Paula heard a summary that instructed her she only needed to claim motherhood and she was set for life. I rejected the recommendation to settle, surrender to the system. I assured all I would pursue justice the old fashion way, in an American courtroom where facts, truth, and reason would prevail and bias, lies, and deceit would be routed out by the process. But again, they are still advising on the old law, the tender years' doctrine. The best interest of the child was the doctrine of the land was it not? Need we remind all this was New Jersey Family Court in 1994.

The March 18 hearing was to deal with the procedures for the pending custody trial. The chosen evaluator was a medical doctor who owned a psychiatric practice in the adjoining county. This candidate was pulled from a hat, the local phonebook. The court outlined the minimum standard for such an evaluation was to include two standard psychological tests to be given to the parents; the children were to be interviewed; the home environment visited, and any other people or records could be reviewed relative to determining the best custodial parent in this case. Also, in addressing my motion, the court ordered Paula's medical records from the Mood Clinic and other psychotherapy sessions were to be made available as part of this custody evaluation in preparation for the trial. I felt good as we were finally making progress. The evaluation report was to be completed and back to the court by June 22 for distribution to both parties to prepare for the custody trial. The court ordered opposing counsel to advise the selected evaluator.

My much-desired custody trial would eventually fall to the brutal inequities of family court justice. Professional evaluators were seemingly bought and sold and attorneys willingly participated in the effort. I interviewed three other local attorneys while considering the custody trial. All acknowledged a father's effort to seek custody of his children was a difficult proposition at best and had very low odds of winning in family court, even with Paula's record as best as I could summarize it in half-hour sessions. They all admitted to working with an evaluator who was best described as "sympathetic" towards their client. But the biggest hurdle all conceded was being a father seeking custody of his children.

I elected to go pro se in the custody trial, as I had lost all faith in any hired legal representation to fight for my agenda. The court laid out a schedule for the exchange of interrogatories each side demanded of the other. The court denied my request to have Sister Catherine answer interrogatories relative to her role as Paula's "spiritual counselor." I demanded Paula's arrest record from Houston. They objected noting, if such a charge existed at all, it may have been adjudicated, as they had found no such record in their search. I argued the record of the shoplifting charge did exist and as for it having been adjudicated, that would need to be determined by fact, not speculation. I called the Harris County Court, Houston, and found the relevant case number and advised all in a subsequent court filing. Upon receipt of the record from Texas, it was confirmed the case had been successfully adjudicated and the court ruled this criminal incident in Paula's past could not be a part of the custody trial. I knew and expected this ruling, but I had planted the seed as Paula claimed there was no such incident. Just another contradiction of facts.

Opposing counsel argued for a protective custody order for Paula's medical records in defense of my demand for access to her records for the pending trial. I argued their effort was not so much to protect Paula's medical records but to hide the truth and facts of her medical history. I had documentation of expenses paid for her psychotherapy and the acknowledged treatment at the Mood Clinic for bipolar disorder. The court ordered her medical records could be accessed but only for purposes of the custody evaluation and trial but that I was not to have access to those records. I would not see those medical records but trusted the custody evaluator would be able to sort through them. I would get the evaluator to confirm certain facts as I knew them.

As was so much an issue with this case, what was to be, did not happen; what should have been was not. I arranged to meet with the professional evaluator for an hour wherein I outlined my claim for custody of the children relative to the issues I knew Paula suffered through. Subsequently, both parents were interviewed in a joint session with this doctor. He asked me if I was open to reconciliation. I stated I believed in that for the first six months only to find it was a false hope. It was during the first joint session he asked me to explain why the mother could not be trusted as the custodial parent in this case? I referenced the mental health issues; the shoplifting issues; her inability to share responsibilities at home in favor of church bible studies and prayer groups; etc. He asked Paula if she continued to shoplift and she responded she "was only caught once." He then asked if she continued to shoplift and she said "no." Paula was not questioned why I could not be the trusted custodial parent.

I was very defensive throughout this joint session as I perceived the evaluator wanted me to concede custody as he surely believed the mother was the preferred custodial parent. Within twenty minutes of initiating his second hour-long joint-session, he declared it over and stated he would write his report. I asked "what about the children?" and he questioned, "where do they live?" I noted some 30 miles south of his office. He said he had not as yet made up his mind to see the children. There was nothing said of the court-mandated two psychological tests that were ordered, the standard for such custody evaluations. Seeing the evaluator's bias against me; he not having seen the children; having not performed the standard psychological tests; not having gotten Paula's medical records from her psychiatrist or the Mood Clinic that would have documented the diagnosis of bipolar disorder and that she had stopped the Lithium medication, I decided to withdraw my motion for a custody trial. Based on what the evaluator had stated and done and did not do in his evaluation, his work product was flawed if not fraudulent. I could not risk a trial that denied me custody of my children.

We returned to court on June 22, 1994, to receive the custody evaluation report that the court had ordered was to have been produced for the pending custody trial. The professional evaluator had not yet filed his evaluation report with the court. Judge Herman acknowledged my decision to withdraw my claim for a custody trial and acceptance of the current non-custodial arrangement. As the hearing progressed, I expressed to put on the record what I had experienced in the evaluation conducted by this court-sanctioned evaluator. I advised the court there were no psychological evaluations performed of any parent; Paula's medical records from the Mood Clinic or her psychiatrist were not accessed; the children had not been interviewed; that the evaluator accused me of being unwilling to reconcile the divorce and had conducted an effort at reconciliation rather than perform the mandated evaluation. Judge Herman was caught off guard by my allegations and questioned opposing counsel on the matter. Opposing counsel acknowledged she was aware of the effort to mediate the differences between the parties and that the evaluator had not done the mandated evaluation. Judge Herman noted he would write to the evaluator questioning what had transpired in his efforts to perform this court-mandated evaluation. The custody issue was settled for the time being to my dismay and misfortune and that of the children, who I believed hoped for a change of custody to my care. We were dealt a devastating setback in our efforts to attain justice in family court.

Judge Herman's letter to the evaluator, dated June 27, 1994, noted "both placed on the record the fact that you had endeavored to initiate mediation services rather than perform the custody evaluation for which you were appointed by this court. (I understand that the mediation effort did not meet with much success). I am very much concerned and would appreciate your written explanation as to what authority you undertook to change the scope of the court's order without prior court approval."

The evaluator answered Judge Herman's letter on July 8, noting "I had just returned from a retreat in Montana and hastened to reply to your letter of June 27." He insisted he "did not initiate mediation services rather than perform the custody evaluation for which he was appointed by the Court." He continued "it is true that I (with your written authority) saw the couple in conjoint sessions on two occasions. On one of those occasions, I advised that the raging conflicts between them were sufficient to harm the children regardless of what the custody award would be, but I did not initiate mediation efforts. There was talk of a mediation effort and in fact, I had discussed it with (Paula's) attorney to see what her response would be to such an effort. She seemed satisfied with this as an approach if it were to occur. However, I did not inaugurate the mediation procedure. The discussion of a possibility was used as an assessment of the parents. My final opinion was that, because of their heated and entrenched positions, it would not be a good idea." He closed by stating "I was making ready to visit with the children when the notice came from (opposing counsel) that the case had been settled and that my report would not be necessary."

I wrote to Judge Herman to contest the evaluator's letter and refute his answers and claims. I requested his review of the facts, as additional information has now become known, as to the conduct of the professionals who were involved in what I allege was not a custody evaluation. The evaluator's letter of July 8 implicated opposing counsel as the one who gave tacit approval of the mediation effort, despite the court's order. I, not represented by any lawyer, was not aware of this substantive change in the scope of the exercise. As I testified in court on June 22, I was questioned by the evaluator about a reconciliation. I was put on the defensive immediately.

My first session with the evaluator was a review of a brief history of the 15-year marriage that I could outline in the ten minutes before meeting with him. We discussed Paula's lifestyle in Colombia and he suggested that Paula was attempting to live that lost lifestyle here in the US. I was questioned if I would entertain maid service in our home, to be paid for by her parents. I told the evaluator I did not think her parents could afford such an expense but questioned why we do not question her lack of responsibility and her history of behavior. I attributed much of her inability to "cope" with the diagnosis from the UPenn Mood Clinic of bipolar disorder. The session ended with my noting I just did not trust the woman.

The first joint session, May 4, was very acrimonious, wherein I questioned Paula's commitment to the family because of her history of irresponsibility.

The second session, May 25, opened with the evaluator stating it was futile to attempt to "reconcile" this relationship. All he wanted to know is why each could not accept joint custody. Paula was all for it. I answered that I was not for it because I knew her to be irresponsible.

It was at this time I questioned him about seeing the children, which is what I believed this whole process was about. He then asked if Mullica Hill was near Medford. I told him it was ten miles south of Woodbury. He then advised he had not yet made up his mind about interviewing the kids. In his letter to the Court, the evaluator states he was just planning to make arrangements to see the children. I doubt this as the evaluation report was due back to the court by June 22.

In the evaluator's final billing to me, received just last week, the invoice noted services for "psychiatric evaluation including custody evaluation." There was none of the above under any stretch of the imagination. By the way, he did conclude after the likes of the two joint sessions I have just described, that the Mood Clinic had made a misdiagnosis of the bipolar disorder condition attributed to Paula. This is a recognized mental illness, difficult for most medical professionals to identify, that involved months of testing at the Mood Clinic. This was discounted by the evaluator and without any other testing to my knowledge, all within a 50-minute session with a very deceiving personality that I still don't know after 15 years.

Needless to say, I reserve the right to seek custody of my four children at a later date, on a more level field where facts and professionalism are all taken into account.

The county sheriff's department manned the courthouse entrance with a large scanner looking for contraband. After any number of appearances in court in just the first three years, the deputies became familiar with me. One deputy acknowledged me as "the nemesis of the court" and I answered I preferred to see myself as the "conscience" of the court in my efforts to seek justice for all. The court and lawyers always reserved the right to contest my constitutional rights to justice. Fortunately, the search at the courthouse entrance did not confiscate my wits or my free will. And for that, this case wore on.

# 11

# THE UNPROFESSIONAL
# PROFESSIONALS

This professional evaluator acknowledged he never sought Paula's medical records from the Mood Clinic. For the record, the evaluator's Curriculum Vitae, dated 1994, listed but two current titles; Adjunct Professor of Sports Science, University of Delaware; and Adjunct Professor of Psychology, University of South Florida. A Wall Street Journal article dated August 23, 1995, noted a growing issue with courts asked to accept the testimony of so-called experts in dealing with issues of psychology. Some judges, frustrated by the shades of gray in psychology, are tossing mental-health experts out of the courtroom. Even psychologists and psychiatrists concede that their field is an inexact science because mental states don't have observable physical symptoms." The Georgia Supreme Court threw out the testimony of a neuropsychologist as "too speculative and incompetent", citing state laws that suggest psychologists aren't qualified "to render an opinion concerning a diagnosis of a mental disorder." These charlatans are sought out, paraded, and sold as experts in custody hearings when many times I would suggest they are participants in civil fraud.

Not to be denied an opportunity to contradict her prior court testimony, opposing counsel filed a certification with the court on

March 27, 1995, to refute my allegations of professional misconduct. The attorney certified "the father alleges that evaluator initiated a mediation effort instead of continuing with custody evaluations after speaking with me. This is not accurate. The role was discussed but rejected by my client. On or about May 9, I related (client's) position to the evaluator. I told him that my client would not agree to participate in mediation and that we wanted him to continue with the custody evaluations but that the parties resolved their differences before he completed the process. The parties settled the issue of child custody on June 22." Opposing counsel did not sit in on any of these evaluation sessions so her claims carried no weight as to what took place in their effort to defraud me.

Now again, I'm no lawyer but the responses by the evaluator and the subsequent certification by opposing counsel were both littered with contradictions of the court testimony given by myself, Paula and this attorney on June 22 wherein I exposed what I knew to be a corrupted evaluation effort. Judge Herman's letter to the evaluator dated June 27 referenced "both placed on the record the fact that you had endeavored to initiate mediation services rather than perform the custody evaluation for which you were appointed by this court." Opposing counsel's certification in response to my letter to the court dated July 14 now claimed her client was made aware of the mediation effort, acknowledged the evaluator's effort to attempt such a mediation while certifying her client rejected such an effort because she could not afford another evaluation should the mediation efforts fail. Judge Herman summed up this entire miscarriage of justice, at my expense, by noting he would make it his business to see that this evaluator never again performed a court-sanctioned custody evaluation in this family court. The court should have reprimanded opposing counsel as well.

As this hearing came to a close, I advised Judge Herman "I'm going to write a book about this case someday." He replied, "I'm sure you will." This is that promised book that details what had transpired to date and the unforeseen that was to come over the next eleven years as a father seeking justice and custody of his four children in New

Jersey Family Court. But this was only the first sixteen months, and now mid-year 1994, and we had much to do just to get through 1994 much less the next eleven years.

New Jersey Statute 9:2-4c detailed the Court's obligation in seeking the "best interest of the child" quoting the following as some factors to be considered:

> In making an award of custody, the court shall consider but not be limited to the following factors: the interaction and relationship of the child with its parents and siblings; the history of domestic violence, if any; the safety of the child and the safety of either parent from physical abuse by the other parent; the preference of the child when of sufficient age and capacity to reason and form an intelligent decision; the stability of the home environment offered; the quality and continuity of the child's education; the fitness of the parents; the extent and quality of the time spent with the child before or after the separation; and the age and number of the children. A parent shall not be deemed unfit unless the parents' conduct has a substantial adverse effect on the child.

A random legal website noted a child custody evaluation is conducted by a psychologist and they will produce a report. The evaluator will interview each party and depending on the age of the child or as defined by the court's order for that particular case. Further, the evaluator may interview other relevant individuals, request psychological, medical, and school records. Said report usually has a large impact on the court's award of custody. The parties can agree on a joint expert or each party could hire their expert. Custody evaluations are expensive. Again, more of the promised mandates of a custody evaluation in New Jersey. My children and I got interference, incompetence, bias, and lies. We got no evaluation.

The court sent me correspondence dated June 28, 1994, and the address label referenced me as "Esquire." I responded to the court on June 30 referencing the erroneous title "Esquire" stating, although offended, "I did not take it personally."

As previously noted, months would lapse before drafted orders of any hearing would be presented by opposing counsel to my attorney or me for review. Many times, there were differences as to what the court had ordered as the resolution of a day's issues as opposed to counsel's draft of the order. Any such differences would have to be reconciled with opposing counsel before agreeing to the final wording of the proposed order, then to be presented to the judge for signature. Weeks or months after a day's hearing these proposed orders would show up in the mail asking if I had any objection to the opposing counsel's scripting of what had been ruled some many weeks or months ago. On many occasions, the answer was yes. Here opposing counsel tried to slip in all kinds of goodies for their client's benefit, and once signed such agreements became the final acknowledgment of that day's court business. The word "may" would become "maybe;" "can" was now "can't;" etc... I read these drafts for every such nuance of change that could impact me.

In one example, the initial hearing of the DV charge against me was heard on April 2, 1993, and it was then continued until June 8 and then deferred until July 1. The order of those day's hearings was not memorialized in writing and signed by Judge Herman until January 26, 1994. In these ten months, I had dismissed two lawyers and Paula was on her second attorney. In the December 2, 1993 hearing, my initial appearance pro se, the judge agreed the marital home need not be sold. Opposing counsel's proposed draft of the order of that hearing failed to acknowledge the court agreed the marital home was not to be sold. Opposing counsel now argued the six-month property listing having expired was sufficient notice of that agreement. I argued no since a prior court order noted the marital home was to be sold a subsequent court order needed to acknowledge that the home was not to be sold. I feared Paula coming back months or a year later to argue the court had ordered the home to be sold if that fit her state of mind. The prior issue of the kid's toys being allowed to go with them on visitations was yet another example of differences that needed to be corrected before any final order was to be signed by the Court.

Another issue of the order drafted from the December 2, 1993 hearing was submitted by opposing counsel on February 2, 1994. The copy of their proposed draft of that day's proceedings was sent to the court and me under the "five-day rule." This rule was a rather punitive effort by one party to get things done promptly when timeliness was never an imperative in this case. The rule states if no objections were made within five days of the filing date of the proposed draft of the order it was assumed there were no objections. The judge hearing no objections signs the order defining the ruling of that day's business.

Unfortunately, opposing counsel, who had recently left this case, sent my copy of his proposed order to an incorrect address and I never saw the proposed draft of this order. Hearing no objection from me, the court signed this order, and it now became part of the permanent court record. I eventually received a copy of the court's order for the December 2 hearing. The order read "the defendant was found in contempt of court relative to his improper contact with the children." Seeing this embedded falsehood, I immediately filed an objection to this order, noting it was a false record of that day's hearing. The new opposing counsel objected to my objection and we were soon back in court.

Opposing counsel again suggested both parties be compelled to listen to the court's taped recording of that day's hearing to confirm whose facts were correct and award her fees for the effort. My response was this was a blatant error and I should not have to pay for lawyers' errors. I knew what the ruling was, that if another instance was confirmed, then the court would hold me in contempt. I answered that if they insisted we listen to the tape, a redundant effort of that day's hearing, then they should compensate me at the counsel's hourly rate. Such an expense would compel counsel to get it right.

Sure enough, in a letter dated May 5, 1994, opposing counsel confirmed to the court the order as drafted by prior counsel relative to the December 2, 1994 hearing was correct; that I was found to be in contempt of court. Again, back to court as I objected that their claim was not correct. The court advised its administrative assistant would listen to the tape of the hearing in question and the court would accept that as the definitive ruling of the day relative to me having been found in contempt of court. The court's clerk returned a memo to the judge noting "the defendant was not found in contempt of court. A warning was issued-if another violation he would be found in contempt." Just as I had testified and in contradiction of what two opposing attorneys had reported to the court three times. This was the reason I scoured every written word from the lawyers. A corrected order was submitted and the record reflected that I was not found in contempt of court. Going forward, I made the effort to draft the proposed orders and file them with the court. This forced opposing counsel to address these court orders promptly and I was sure my summary of the day's hearing would be accurate compared to those prepared by opposing counsel.

Opposing counsel wrote to me on April 28, 1994, requesting Paula be allowed to enjoy the pending Mother's Day weekend with the four children, asking me to give up my scheduled weekend visitation time. I responded in agreement noting "I presumed all days are Mother's Day. It is the fathers that are denied days with their children."

In a letter to this attorney dated May 1, 1994, I tried to impart some sarcasm into this truly life-changing court experience. A portion of the letter is copied below:

Since the system mandates, I cannot be a father today, what better way to pass the time than to write to my adversary about what most people would consider to be useless stuff. I've tried to tell people that in court on Friday I learned a very important lesson, i.e., lawyers only understand things that are in writing. I then telephoned the group, Individuals Devoid of Intellectual Objectivity to be Sane, (IDIOTS) and they confirmed for me that in all those rules of the court, specifically, Rule #2B-4a1.h, says lawyers need only have the capacity to comprehend the written word. I questioned them about all the verbiage between lawyers found outside the courtroom, and how is it possible for such a contradiction in an organized culture as "the law?" They assured me that all that verbosity outside the court was not the practice of law, but something more akin to a pagan sacrifice of the victim (the accused) to the God of all law, the Bill of Rights.

I asked IDIOTS where non-lawyers could find this golden book of court rules and they said they believed it was published by Milton Bradley, on the inside cover of a game called "True Adventure." I quickly ran to Toys-R-Us but they said they would not sell me a copy as I was not a lawyer. I told them I was pro se, and proud of it, but to no avail. I would need a law certificate. Instead of law school, I'm saving box tops and should have a certificate in about three months.

In a continuing effort to hold all parties accountable in this sordid affair, I filed a complaint in Camden County Superior Court-Special Civil Part (Small Claims Court) against the custody evaluator for a refund of the $600 I had prepaid as a down payment for the $1,500 custody evaluation fee. My claim was filed August 16, 1994, and I alleged fraud in that the court-ordered evaluation was not performed as defined by the family court; I referenced Judge Herman's letter wherein he questioned the evaluator as to why he changed the scope of the court order; and that the evaluator had refused to refund this payment upon my prior written request. A few days before the scheduled court date for my claim, the evaluator called me at my office and stated "I can't go into court." My response was "I don't care if you show up or not; I would get my judgment and a sheriff would come to your office to collect it." We settled for a refund of $400.

A Dual Final Judgment of Divorce was signed by Judge Herman on August 8, 1994, formally ending my tumultuous fourteen-year courtship with Paula. My mother had warned me, there was lots of smoke in this proposed union. The judgment outlined all areas of agreement: my scheduled visitation; my obligations for child support and additional billings for health and auto insurance; sharing the four children as tax dependents; rehabilitative alimony for Paula for four years; the marital home would remain the domain of the four children with the mother the designated in-home custodial parent while we shared joint custody of the children; all household furnishings would remain in the home (I did not want to strip the home where the children resided); again, my remaining personal possessions were to be released to me, now 14 months from the original ruling of June 1993; we each retained our respective automobiles and credit card debts; I was ordered to pay $2,500 towards opposing counsel's legal fees and we agreed to participate in divorce counseling to "ease tensions and move forward with their lives." Well, that seemed easy relative to the unforeseen that was to be over the coming years. But we stopped the sale of the house the children called home and prevented or surely delayed any effort by Paula to move the children away from me. I have always counted this as my greatest win if one could presume family court afforded fathers any wins at all. There was no counseling to ease tensions.

Most galling was the court's order that required me to pay $2,500 of legal fees to the opposing attorney. This is the same attorney that contaminated the evaluation procedure; who twice reported to the court I had been found in contempt; who alleged I had lied to the court about my mailing address; who contested the children's right to take their movies, toys, and bikes on visits with their father, and made no good-faith effort to resolve any issues of this case amicably. Opposing counsel contributed nothing to this case but was awarded substantial fees by this court. Counsel then left the case. Thanks for nothing!

We were moving on, albeit slowly and cautiously. I was intent to hold all parties accountable in this madness. The lawyers were hounded by me at every turn to get things right; get things done on a timely basis; address my issues and assume nothing in this case. That said, I cleared my desk and took a more serious look at the evaluator. Yes, I got my $400 refund of his fee but I noted the bias and discrimination this system held against fathers seeking custody of their children. Local lawyers stated the obvious and statistics confirmed mothers were the preferred custodial parent. The State of New Jersey continued to subscribe to the touted "tender years doctrine," a legal principle dating to nineteenth-century law. That doctrine had been ruled obsolete in words but not in deeds. Mothers were still "assumed" to be the better custodial parent short of being declared unfit. Fathers were presumed to still be out on the open range foraging for meat; maybe jousting with the king's enemies; fighting outlaws and Indians, and plowing the field for the next harvest. Fathers were deemed unfit by gender.

Case law confirmed child support is the right of the child and the responsibility of both parents after a divorce, even making the case that each parent paid their fair share of the children's needs. The more recent New Jersey Statute N.J.S.A. 9:2-4 referenced "that it is in the public interest to encourage parents (post-divorce) to share the rights and responsibilities of child-rearing." Just more of that legal verbiage of New Jersey family law. Most times reality was the opposite of this espoused legal utopia and those that dared challenge it did so at their peril.

Statutes and case law defined, in this case, this court refused to consider any circumstances as to the welfare of these children. A subsequent review of this case confirmed the court's bias. Mediators and lawyers, knowing of the case history, still confirmed the father had little to no chance for custody of these children. A confirmed instance of an unmedicated mental illness; a history of financial and other reckless transactions counted for nothing against the mother. What was it that fathers did to deserve this contempt of justice in New Jersey Family Court? The justice meted out by the posse, the mob, in the saga of *The Ox-Bow Incident* continued to haunt me as but a modern-day lynching of fathers by a mob who cared nothing for the facts of the case. They espoused justice for all yet denied it at every opportunity for this father, and the children themselves.

The custody evaluation was my best chance to get a hearing of the facts; get a hearing outside of the court's bias; to get justice. Yet this professional evaluator failed on all levels as he consorted with opposing counsel in performing his assigned task and attacked me in the process. I sought to expose all those who denied me and my children our day in court; a hearing of the facts of this case. The court's order mandated the process to be employed in this evaluation. The first mistake was the court trusting opposing counsel to act as the conduit (an Officer of the Court?) to arrange for the evaluation; to relay the protocol and procedures outlined by the court. The court's instruction was not put in writing to the evaluator but left to the opposing attorney to make an honest approach for the benefit of both parties. That proved too much trust for a case that lacked any trust.

I filed a complaint on August 17, 1994, with the New Jersey Division of Consumer Affairs, Board of Medical Examiners, outlining all of the issues previously alluded to relative to this evaluator's conduct in performing the court-mandated evaluation of this family in anticipation of the custody trial. I also noted my $400 settlement with the evaluator for what I alleged was non-performance of his court-mandated evaluation. The Executive Director's letter of November 14, 1994, acknowledged in the letter below, the Board had completed its review of the submitted complaint.

In your complaint, you indicated that (evaluator), a psychiatrist, was selected under court directive by you and your estranged wife to serve as an expert witness to conduct a custody evaluation in a divorce proceeding relative to your four children. You allege that (evaluator) was unethical in his management of the situation and perceived that he attempted to mediate the marriage rather than evaluate the family. You reported that no psychological testing was administered and your children were not included in the process.

The Board, in reviewing this information, notes that (evaluator) conducted two individual and joint sessions with you and your wife and submitted his report to the court. You were dissatisfied with the report and the settlement which you accepted to preserve a home for your children.

This Board believes that you are attempting to utilize the Board as a means of getting back at (evaluator) after unsuccessfully attempting to have the judge appoint a new expert based on the same allegations. This Board believes that it is not the appropriate entity to address this matter and the Board is, therefore, not in a position to review this matter further.

Seeing the Board's response, I directed a letter to The New Jersey

Attorney General who oversees the various professional Boards aligned under the State's Division of Consumer Affairs. My letter to the Attorney General noted my displeasure with the Board's work product relative to a complaint filed by a consumer. I accused the Board of having lost its ability to be objective in its role of consumer "watchdog." The Board accused me of seeking revenge against this evaluator and I believed my complaint deserved a more professional consideration.

I then sent a response to the Executive Director and copied the State's Attorney General, to refute his claim that I just desired to "get back" at this licensed physician. I accused the Board of slaying the messenger while failing to exercise its mandate to protect the New Jersey consumer from professionals who failed to perform while collecting fees for their services. I reiterated the details of my original complaint against this evaluator relative to the court-ordered custody evaluation protocol; that the judge questioned the evaluator's efforts of mediating this divorce instead of the ordered evaluation; that both parties testified to the evaluator's effort to meditate; that he never sought the medical records from the Mood Clinic, but in fact, refuted the diagnosis of mental illness without any supporting professional work or qualifications for such a rebuttal; that he never timely filed with the family court the required report of his efforts; and I suggested that the "Board has failed in its capacity as 'watchdog' for the consumers of New Jersey. Perhaps even falling into bed with the professionals they were charged to monitor in an effort to maintain the standards of ethics and professionalism on which the citizenry depends."

The Board's new Executive Director acknowledged the former Director's letter contained "an unfortunate choice of words" and "I apologize on behalf of the Attorney General for that." My "request for a further review and based on new information my complaint would again be presented to the Board for consideration." After some six months, I again wrote to the Board to advise them I had sent a copy of my complaint to the Chairman of the State Senate Committee responsible for monitoring the conduct of this Board. I also told them

I had sent a copy of my complaint to the Governor to hold the Board accountable to the citizens of New Jersey.

On June 8, 1995, the Board's Director responded noting that the matter was again reviewed by the Board on April 5, and suggested that the "details of this case be provided to an outside consultant for their advice as to whether or not the professional evaluator acted appropriately in this matter." The Board responded on July 26, 1995, stating:

> It has not been presented with any additional evidence that would alter its previous opinion on this matter, which does not find that (evaluator's) actions concerning your custody case violated the Medical Practice Act. You should know that for the Board to take disciplinary action against a physician in this State, the doctor must have been found guilty of gross malpractice or gross neglect in the practice of medicine or has been demonstrated professionally incompetent to practice medicine (N.J.S.A 45:9-16).
>
> Again, I apologize for the Director's unfortunate use of terms in his correspondence to you. I can identify with your plight having also been a "victim" of the legal system in similar proceedings. I trust that this will close this matter.

# 12

# FACTS ARE ONLY WHAT ARE
# REPORTED

The local newspaper, Gloucester County Times, ran an article styled *Male Victims* on the front page of their December 20, 1994 edition as part of a week-long expose about domestic violence. The story introduced a fifty-one-year-old man who had been run out of his home by his knife-wielding wife of twenty-nine years. The father of four children, he had called the police several times about domestic violence instances committed by his wife over the years including "kicking, punching, pushing, screaming, cursing, throwing various objects and hot coffee on him and slashing his clothes with the knife." Upon the arrival of the police with the wife "threatening to kill him" the police told this father to leave the home that night. There was no arrest of the wife and the husband begrudgingly filed a restraining order against the wife. At the courthouse he acknowledged "he did not want to come here" noting "he did not want to do anything that will hurt her." He believed his wife suffered from "emotional problems."

The 1993 New Jersey crime report noted that females were the victims in 83 percent of domestic violence offenses. The National Violence Survey, sponsored by the National Institute of Health reported men are as likely as women to be victims of domestic violence. According to the Department of Justice figures, men reported an average of 48,983 spousal abuse cases as compared to 572,032 cases reported by women. The large gap was assigned to battered men refusing to seek help.

There was reported to be only one place in the U.S. where men and their children can go when fleeing domestic violence. That was a seven-bed home in St. Paul, Minnesota. It was noted the most common form of abuse against men is kicking, punching, scratching, hair-pulling, and name-calling. However, statistics overwhelmingly show men are the abusers in relationships. The reason for this statistic was explained as men are usually too "macho" to call the police and ask for help; if men call police more times than not, they would be the one removed, arrested; and men think the police would laugh at them, thinking they are "wimps." Paula purchased a $6,000 car on a credit card. Is that financial abuse? Did I call the police; no, I called the credit card company and took her off the card. When she abused the checking account and stole $3,000 from family funds, I did not call the police to report this financial abuse, I took her off the joint account.

In this case, I surely felt under great duress in the waning months as Paula attacked the household financially while running amuck and shirking responsibilities at home. In counseling, hoping to resolve some of the many issues she brought into the home, it was me that was removed that evening in March 1993. I never considered a legal intervention to rein her in and I would never have left the children under any circumstance. Instead, the court forced me to leave the home and abandon my children to the ways and means of a mentally ill personality. She was the mother and the court would sanction her irrational behavior for years to come. The court did nothing to hold this mother accountable for anything she did or did not do. The system rallied to protect the mother and did nothing to protect these children much less their father.

Always looking to learn more about this system of justice, I noticed an ad in the local newspaper about an instructional session held at the community college about divorce and all its many tentacles: child support; alimony; visitations; etc... I was the lone male in a classroom of about twenty-five women. The attorney presented this class about the basics of family law and procedures, and I had seen him in court on occasions. The entire 90-minute session was this attorney fielding questions from the audience about how to get alimony; more alimony; more child support. The entire session was about money. On my way out the door after class, I questioned this attorney about a specific circumstance in my case that I took to be positive for me. His response suggested that the outcome was wrong, that the circumstance should be reopened and reversed by the court. I argued no, that what I had "won" was not an error but had been negotiated. He alleged it was a case of legal incompetence by opposing counsel. Even the few wins afforded a father are perceived errors.

The Philadelphia Inquirer, in an article dated August 19, 1994, reported the story of a father out of New Jersey Camden County Family Court who claimed the family court system denied him access to his three children and required payment of child support, alimony, and legal fees that exceeded his weekly income. Declaring himself a "broken man, they broke me," denied access to see his three children, this father filed a motion asking Camden County Superior Court for the "legal right to die by assisted suicide." He asked the four family court judges involved in his case to act as pallbearers. He argued he was financially and emotionally broken by Camden County Family Court. If granted his request, his daughters would be able to collect his life insurance benefits. Having fought the system for the last two years, the father tired of the effort. The presiding judge called him "a very complicated man." This father was briefly jailed the prior year in a state facility for the criminally insane after writing a threatening letter against a judge hearing his case. An appeals court ordered his release after five days. His filing for the right to die peacefully was routed back to the same family court for a hearing. I assume this court denied this father his right to die in peace preferring their financial and emotional torture within their justice system. The first victim in so many of these cases is justice itself.

The movie *The Ox-Bow Incident* showed the posse, the jury as it was, of about twenty-five debating how best to deal with these captured and accused killers. A few argued it was best they be taken back to town "for a proper trial;" give the sheriff time to check out the alibis as the accused demanded. The majority of this "jury" voted for justice now, that court-justice took too much time. The Major's dominant personality took hold of this jury process. He declared "there is truth in lies too if you can get enough of them." This stated paradox justified anything in the search for justice. This same logic was found in this family court as any claim by Paula supported the belief there was a crime here even if they can't prove it. They had their victim, they only needed to prosecute the accused.

# 13

# FINALLY, A WIN, BUT NOT IN FAMILY COURT

I filed a Petition with the Diocese of Camden on January 22, 1995, seeking an annulment of this fourteen-year marriage to Paula. This petition was probably the best hearing of all the facts that would ever be heard in this case. The effort required detailed writings by both parties relative to all issues, including personal and family, financial, mental health; statements from witnesses as well as from friends, counselors aware of this family's situation, perhaps the Mood Clinic and other medical professionals employed by Paula, etc.... Maybe even a response from prior Diocesan counselors Father John and the elusive Father Fred. The annulment process involved a compilation of all relevant documents and witness statements and be argued before a tribunal that was established by the Diocese to defend both parties' positions in the case. A letter dated March 13, 1996, advised: "the Diocese of Camden gave a favorable decision in your Church annulment case, of your marriage to Paula. The verdict was Affirmative, that is to say, the annulment has been granted." I was advised I was now free to marry within the Catholic church. The church agreed this was a marriage in word only. Much like New Jersey Family law touting justice for all; just in words, not deeds.

The father's support group FACE annually sponsored events the week of Father's Day. FACE had a much larger presence in Camden County that was just north of our own Gloucester County. In Camden County, they picketed judges' homes on Thanksgiving (since fathers could not be with their children on many holidays) and marched in front of the courthouse. FACE solicited members to picket other local county courthouses during this week to express displeasure with the injustice fathers routinely faced inside those courtrooms. I took my place on the protest line at the Gloucester County courthouse that stood at one of the busiest intersections in the county, Broad and Delaware streets in Woodbury. Employed only ten minutes from this intersection, I drove over from work at lunch and brought my 2'x3' sign that read "Be Fair to Dads Who Care." I was the only one to demonstrate and as conspicuous as I was, I marched back and forth along the Delaware street side of the courthouse. People could be seen looking out the courthouse windows; some cars beeped their horns as they noticed me, but I walked daily that week back and forth along a path of some fifty yards.

The Gloucester County Times, located just a block from the court-house, sent a reporter to photograph me and question why I was marching. I explained that they needed to sit inside the courtrooms and see the injustice fathers experienced every day. The photograph of my picketing was published in the June 18, 1995, Sunday edition. The picture was labeled "Fatherless Day protest" noted that FACE, the self-help group for non-custodial parents and their families, hoped to draw attention to judicial "discrimination and injustice that ignores fathers' importance to their children's well-being." In exiting the court-house for lunch one day Judge Herman acknowledged my protest with a short wave.

The courthouse had a clerk's office typically staffed by two or three women; and it was stocked with numerous pamphlets and brochures on topics such as child support; domestic violence; and other informational aids, all addressing the needs and questions of women who found themselves in a divorce or an abusive relationship. Nothing there suggested any such assistance for fathers. I would have thought a banking brochure on how best to finance an auto purchased on a credit card at 26.5 percent interest would have been useful. Or perhaps a brochure on how to protect a family's cash from a deceiving partner. In one such visit to this room; a young guy was looking around. I mentioned he would find no useful information here as this was "women's court" and there was little or no justice applicable to men in this room much less in the courtrooms. The women at the desks cringed at my comments. Within minutes a sheriff's deputy was standing behind me and told us to leave the room. I guess someone hit the buzzer.

On the July 3rd, 1995 holiday weekend there was but one-woman administrative clerk on duty in the room; I recognized her and she recognized me. I approached and said I wanted to file a complaint. For what, against whom, she asked? I said it was against the ex-wife (Paula). She asked what was the nature of my complaint and I noted that the standing TRO precluded my contacting her, harassing her. I told this clerk my complaint was that this woman continued to call me at will, ask for favors, and other considerations. These requests bothered me because her attitude and degree of trust in these usual communications were quite different from what she routinely complained about in numerous filings to date. I alleged the ex-wife was routinely harassing me. It was only logical, if I could not call her then she should not be allowed to call me. The administrative clerk advised my complaint was not valid; it would not be accepted. I insisted she take my complaint and she advised she would need to call the judge who was "on-call" for the holiday weekend, a Judge Moore, as I recall. She called the judge and came back within minutes and advised the judge refused my complaint.

I asked why, and she advised my complaint was considered an effort to harass (Paula) and the standing TRO noted I was not allowed to harass her. I asked that the complaint and denial be put in writing and she refused as my complaint having been denied there was no complaint. I asked this clerk if men, fathers were afforded any protec-tions in this family court, or was it that only women could file complaints? Were men denied "equal protection" under the law? She just stood there and said nothing. Sort of "(Moore) of the same." Had I perhaps been better versed in the law I would have sought an appeal of this denial of equal justice? What I learned that day was what I believed from my experience with family court justice, it was but a one-way street in this business. Fathers experienced this, believed it, and to fight it was useless. That lawyers and mediators told you so; that the mother gets the kids, the house, child support, alimony, and that you get nothing was New Jersey Family Court justice. In all my appearances over this ten-year plus effort it is fair to say I could not recall one instance where the plaintiff in any case I ever witnessed was anyone but a woman; men either did not file such complaints or they were just rejected upon request. This was a women's court!

While I represented myself during these divorce proceedings I sat in the family courtrooms many hours many days waiting for my case to be heard. Picture yourself in a small movie theatre with minimally cushioned seats; no drink cup holders; facing the judge's bench and his staff of two; with two tables aligned ten feet in front. The plaintiff's (the one who filed the complaint) team sits at the table to the right facing the judge and the defendant's (one who stands accused by the plaintiff) team positioned at the left table. Not unlike what one might see watching Perry Mason episodes of the old TV. These small courtrooms were generally not paneled and not adorned with pictures or statues of the likes of Thomas Jefferson or Abraham Lincoln. I suggest Lincoln might have jumped off the wall in any one of these proceedings in New Jersey Family Court. At best you might see a picture of the Governor. As a rule, all hearings are recorded for historical purposes. A sheriff's deputy was always present during any court hearing presumably for security.

The court typically "comes to order" when the judge and his staff enter the room from a door behind the bench. "All rise" and the judge welcomes all to the process of justice, New Jersey Family Court style. As noted, there is no swearing-in of the parties as we see in most public court cases. Again, I assume the thinking in family court was both parties are lying about most things. Strange but true.

The judge takes an alphabetical roll call of the cases scheduled for a hearing in that morning's session. Lateness is frowned upon as are no-shows. Lacking enough seats in this theatre for justice, the lawyers typically stood along either the left or right walls as defined by their client. In a few instances, a lawyer may advise the judge that he is also working a case next-door with another judge; that he was here now but may duck out of this courtroom to represent yet another case in an adjoining courtroom. Double-dipping is a great gig if you can get it. Lawyers typically charged $400 for any hearing they were compelled to attend in your defense whether their courtroom presence lasted fifteen or ninety minutes; that they had to be present in court for some unknown amount of time was what justified the minimum $400 fee. If a lawyer was lucky his case was called early; arguments, comments, and settlements were offered and with judicial input, a resolution was agreed to and the lawyers were back in their offices by 10 that morning. Now that is justice.

It is at this point I should introduce another of several practices of the art of lawyering. Much of the "lawyering" in these cases happens outside the courtroom; many times, noted in a lawyer's billing as a telephone call with opposing counsel to discuss issues and perhaps argue legal points of debate in a case; or such discussions that take place in the foyer of the courthouse itself. I liked to refer to these sessions, at least as they related to my case, as bartering. Here my few rights and liberties were bartered away with intimidation as opposing counsel would advise my attorney of new allegations of purported misdeeds relative to violations of the prior court orders. Or better yet, more of the she-said type stuff. My attorney then approached me with such allegations and advised we needed to resolve their claims by concession rather than face the court with new, and continuing claims of harassment, violations, etc. My impression of these bartering sessions was to make one concede, concede, concede. Lawyers hate to go in front of a judge with a list of complaints leveled against their client not knowing how the judge might react to such claims. Then too, opposing attorneys always presented their case first, usually with much hyperbole that would reportedly reflect their client's sense of fear, concern, intimidation, and insecurity relative to the court's order that typically denied any such contact in a divorce case. But this was a game, a practiced art, a con I soon enough discerned while awaiting my case to be called the day of any hearing.

Early in my pro se efforts, one complaint filed against me noted I had violated the TRO by entering the marital home which was strictly forbidden. Hearing their complaint, Judge Herman questioned why I had entered the home? I advised the court I had done so not once but on three different occasions. Opposing counsel reacted surprised by my statement as something he knew nothing about. I'm sure they wondered if one such intrusion was a violation why were three intrusions not in their complaint? I then advised the court I had entered the home upon coming to the open front door on a Saturday for the scheduled visitation. Hearing all the children crying, the mother advised the "judge" had ordered the house must be sold. I then entered the family room where all were situated and told the children "that was a lie, the judge did not order the sale of the home. The mother wanted it sold." I then left the house. The second instance was when Paula had recently asked me to help her move some furniture inside the home; no complaint was filed. The third instance was when I arrived at the home to pick up the children, now aged from four to eleven, only to find them standing in the driveway with no coats on a cold November morning. Their mother ran them out of the house as she wanted to leave before my scheduled pick-up time. I jimmied open the door and stood in the foyer as the children collected their coats and baggage for the Saturday visitation. Opposing counsel winced and the judge admonished Paula that she can't invite me into the house one week and file a complaint the next. But yet she would and did many times.

On another such hearing day, and thoroughly disgusted with lawyering as practiced against me, I took my seat in the court's gallery. I sat in the courtroom waiting for the chance to defend myself or press the issues of my case, if not both. The movie that day could easily have been "Justice on Trial." The seats were occupied by about forty people scattered among the maybe fifty available seats; plaintiffs, defendants, and a few others providing emotional support to the warring parties; mothers, sisters, etc. There were few if any witnesses in these proceedings in family court as much of any stated testimony was at best "hearsay." The lawyers took their positions along their respective walls awaiting their case to be called if not to hold up the walls of justice themselves. Called to order at the usual 8:30 AM starting time, Judge Herman initiated the roll call of cases scheduled for this morning session.

The first case of the morning was called and the day's doling of justice commenced. Case after case; argument vs argument; negotiated settlements announced, the proceedings moved along. What I noticed was that all the cases with legal representation for both sides were called first, whereas any case where a party or parties were pro se, with no legal representation, was not yet called. Nearly 10:30 that morning, Judge Herman took a breath and asked if there are any questions from the maybe fifteen people still in the room awaiting this day's chance at justice. Seeing what I had seen, I raised my hand and once acknowledged, stood to address the court. I began my statement to the court noting "we are all compelled to be here at the 8:30 start time yet here I sit for two hours. All the cases with represented lawyers are all called and heard and here I still sit. I noted, as a father, I was compelled to pay child support; that the support was predicated on my means to retain employment; and my sitting for hours waiting for my hearing put that employment at risk. The lawyers were paid to be here and I was not. Why was my case not called?" The court's immediate response was to tell me to "sit down." I guess I hit yet another raw nerve in this legal process known as family court justice.

The judge continued with some administrative issues for another ten minutes before agreeing to address my question in a more dignified effort. Judge Herman noted that the lawyers were considered "officers of the court" who provided many services in the practice of law which helped, facilitated the legal process known as justice. These lawyers filed motions; negotiated agreements; completed other legal tasks like submitting orders of the day to the court for signature. Having earned the court's consideration allowed them to collect their $400 fees and get in and out of these hearings as expeditiously as possible so that they can get back to the business of lawyering for the benefit of us all. All those free lawyer services and still I had to wait months for orders from my appearances to be presented to the court for signature confirming the court's rulings of the day. And several of them were not correct and others mailed to the wrong address. Not to mention the lawyers who, unbeknownst to me, established the sale price of my home and listed it for sale. Need we mention opposing counsel's interference in the custody evaluation that scuttled my effort for a fair custody evaluation. And let's not forget the two lawyers who erroneously reported to the court three times that I was found in contempt. Ok, now we know and could appreciate what lawyers did for me or my children. Nothing!

Those of us who did not trust lawyers, who had lost faith in lawyers, paid the additional price of acquiescing our treasured time to lawyers. But then we also got to watch them free of charge as they practiced their craft while we twiddled away our time sitting in the peanut gallery. I guess we should have been happy the Bar Association had not moved to have some fee-based system established to charge us pro se litigants as we watched and hopefully learned from this practice of law. Imagine free law classes for the pro se litigants? I can testify to what we see as law practiced on TV is not what happens in reality, and surely not in family court. What I did learn while waiting for my crapshoot at justice any day was the art of lawyering, good and not so good. I listened to both sides argue their points of law and arguments in defense of their clients, even some references to touted case law rulings. I weighed these arguments in my head and determined what did or did not make sense to me. Then the judge would weigh in with his thoughts and eventually, he ruled on the issues. Too, I learned which lawyers were good, prepared, and judged others who were not so good in these proceedings. I even considered taking my case to one or two of the good ones as I found them well prepared, knowledgeable, and argued good points for their clients. In the end, I did not approach either of these lawyers fearing I'd just hear more of the same. No, this was my fight to win or lose.

As I learned the fine art of lawyering in this case, I refused any such bartering effort by opposing counsel before any scheduled hearing. Too, I must admit to having received just one phone call some years later from the fifth opposing counsel I would face on any matter relative to this case. Paula's second lawyer did write to suggest an amicable settlement of the custody issue. When that was refused, they attacked. If and when approached in the courthouse foyer to discuss an issue before any hearing I refused by stating "I would only discuss my case in front of the court" (no bartering allowed). This approach seemed to put opposing counsel on edge as they knew little other than what was published in my formal answers filed to address their claims or issues.

Loitering in the foyer of the courthouse awaiting my chance at justice, dressed in a business suit and laden with a handful of files, I was approached a few times asking if I was a lawyer. I apologized if my appearance suggested I might be a lawyer. In yet another chance passing in the foyer of the courthouse, a woman noted "I read everything you write." That was Judge Herman's administrative assistant who was present at most hearings. I was encouraged by these few words believing someone wanted to "hear" my side of the story. I always presented all my written motions, answers, complaints, etc. in great detail to get the "facts." as I knew them, entered into the case history. In a typical hearing, these written filings were the basis for all, if any, discussion of issues. If not in the written filings' most issues were not discussed. So, the expression "to bury them in facts" and details became my mantra, in this case, to ensure the facts of any issues that I most cared about got into the court record and were not excluded. Specifics were not typically discussed in any detail, if at all, in a hearing but I could reference back to such filings in all subsequent dealings with opposing counsel and the court.

# 14

# BATTLES RAGE WHILE SINGING THE BLUES

As this case dragged on, my affection for lawyers waned. I noted their letterheads referenced law degrees and partnerships in the practice of the art of law. I decided I too needed a letterhead that defined, described who I was in this effort. The Rutgers Law library had a book of famous quotes that I perused looking for that one quote that would best represent me to all parties in this search for justice. Soon enough, there it was, and by Abraham Lincoln no less. This quote was to become my letterhead on all documents going forward; "The probability that we shall fail in the struggle ought not to deter us from the support of a cause we believe to be just." To this day I reference this quote in all my emails. Lincoln too was in a war that he lamented for the damage done, but it was a necessary battle because it was about justice. I was in this war with a family court system that denied justice to me, to my children, to all fathers. The battle continued as we looked to 1995 for the justice we sought, for the justice denied.

A quick view of my 1995 records finds us more involved in the elusive justice sought on several new fronts. Emboldened in my demand for justice, expressed in my newly minted letterhead, I forged ahead believing ever more so that what I was doing was right; legally and morally, it had to be done. I found myself frequently at Rutgers Law Library as new legal issues came to the fore. I purchased a volume of 1995 New Jersey Rules of Court – State and Federal as a source of rules on filing motions and learning how to live within this court system.

Yet another issue was soon on my plate dealing with child support payments now being collected electronically by the Probation Department, a Division of the County Sheriff's Department in the organization chart of New Jersey bureaucracy. As much as Paula enjoyed total access to family funds before having me removed from the marital home, I can only assume she presumed continued access to these funds post-divorce. In her latest effort against me, Paula walked into the local Probation Department office in September 1994 and claimed I was $1,425 in arrears on child support payments. Probation issued a directive to my employer in October advising them an additional weekly $30 assessment was to be made against my payroll check to recover this alleged debt.

Upon seeing this additional deduction in my paycheck, I immediately contacted the Probation Department and the assigned caseworker. I reported receiving no such notice of any claim of any arrearage from probation before they instituted this additional collection effort. I was told such a notice was sent and getting no response within the required thirty-day answer period, the collection effort was instituted. I asked for a copy of the said "notice" and upon receipt advised Probation, they mailed my copy of this notice of their claim to the marital home address. Paula's first attorney, in filing the initial court order establishing child support within the probation system, referenced an incorrect address for me, again. That incorrect address became probation's address of record for me. I noted I was barred from the referenced property but to pick up my children for visitations, and the address was also where Probation mailed the child support payments. A cursory review should have raised some red flags relative to my reported mailing address. Too, any such mailings were not forwarded by Paula. A review of my records also noted two prior instances where the court and Probation Department had been advised in writing that my mailing address had changed. Probation never updated its records.

I brought my payment records to the local Probation office and proved all required support payments had been made electronically from my bank account dating back many months. I questioned where was the arrearage? Seeing none, and Paula unable to substantiate her claim, I demanded Probation withdraw the claim and refund the nearly $200 they had collected in error. I also advised them that their calculation of this alleged arrearage was not correct as defined under State statute, but was excessive. They insisted I put my demand for a refund in writing and weeks later responded they would keep the collected excess funds "for the next time." I argued that there was no "this time" and there was no basis to hold my money. I never received another response from the Probation Department to my demand they refund their erroneous assessments.

I returned to Rutgers Law Library after work on nights I did not have the kids and began to better educate myself as to this institution we call the law. I made my way to the section of statutes and case law and learned the business of researching issues and cases. With a little digging there it was in plain sight, New Jersey Administrative Procedures statute that outlined, and supported by case law references, defined procedures to protect all party's rights in dealing with New Jersey bureaucrats. These procedures referenced both parties had the right to contest any administrative claim made by the likes of the Probation Department. The Probation Department poorly maintained its records and then denied this father a refund of their erroneous claims of an arrearage in child support; which was also calculated incorrectly.

I filed a suit against the State of New Jersey; naming the Governor, Attorney General, the Probation Department, case Supervisor, and agent who denied my request to refund these arrearages as proven in Paula's false claim. My case was well documented in the court filing and heard in April 1995 in the New Jersey Superior Court, now situated just across the street from the arena of our family court battles. New Jersey was represented by an Assistant Attorney General (AAG) sent in from Trenton who was accompanied into court that day by the two county Probation Department personnel involved in this action. I again represented myself pro se. I made my case and argued "Probation failed to acquiesce to (my) right to due process when advised they had used an incorrect address relative to their notice of (my) right to contest (Paula's) claim of arrearages. Likewise, subsequently advised by a family court order their arrearage claim was in error, they failed to exercise available avenues of administrative due process."

The Superior Court Judge looked at the AAG from Trenton and stated "I believe you owe (plaintiff) his money." The AAG wholeheartedly agreed and noted the state would correct the record and refund the monies due to me. In typical fashion, I merely turned and left the court followed shortly after by the state's representatives. The AAG called out to me and I merely turned and said "give me my damn money back" and continued to walk out. It took several months and two additional family court hearings to affect this refund.

The facts are the Probation Department initiates action to collect child support, all supported by family court orders. The problem was their procedures did not allow them to release or refund any child support funds collected in error unless ordered by the family court. Judge Herman heard motions on this matter in October to allow a credit due me and again in November 1994 to allow the refund of credit balance for these erroneously collected funds. But Probation still refused to refund me the monies collected in error. By Superior Court order, a check for $180 was dated June 21, 1995, to refund me these funds ten months after Paula's fictitious claim had been filed. Believe it or not, some several months later, Paula made yet another similar claim of arrearages in child support even though Probation had been electronically collecting my child support for two years. In this second instance, Probation insisted she prove her claim and allowed me to prove the claim wrong. I hoped my efforts against Probation made them more judicious in their efforts to collect claims for arrearages.

I subsequently filed a suit against the State of New Jersey and named six Departments and personnel involved in the administration of this County Probation Department alleging the State and these Departments and individuals, "by their conduct and practices in the administration of New Jersey law denied the plaintiff (me) and those in this class the right to due process as guaranteed by the Fifth and equal protection of the Fourteenth Amendments of the Constitution and New Jersey statute N.J.S.A. 2A:17-56.9." This complaint was filed on April 3, 1996. The Superior Court ruled in September my complaint had been dismissed on technical legal issues. But the effort was not for naught. I believed the Probation Department was too connected to the mother's plight to fully protect the rights of fathers. In the end, the best I could do was hope Probation would be more willing to listen to fathers who sought a hearing of the facts before they imposed their efforts to collect child support claims arbitrarily filed by mothers.

I wrote the Probation Department on July 15, 1997, to report an erroneous reference I found on my public credit report dated June 25, 1997. The credit report listed a collection action that had been filed by Gloucester County Probation for a $1,425 balance for child support that was reported $90 past due. The hearings in family court and superior court ordered Probation to refund these erroneously collected funds; there was no arrearage of child support. I received that refund in June 1995 and yet two years later Probation was reporting me delinquent on child support. This despite the state's pleadings in its motion to dismiss my complaint that they had done all they could or should have done and that their records were correct in every way. The County Probation Department referred this issue back to a state representative in Trenton. The state's response of July 25, 1997, stated that "it doesn't appear we were aware that you had been submitted to the credit bureau." The state advised a corrected record would be sent and that process took about forty-five days. I was asked to tell them if there was still an issue after having checked my credit report after the processing of this universal delete.

In a letter dated August 29, 1995, the Assistant Chief at the State's Administrative Office of the Courts, which managed the county Probation Department's efforts out of Trenton, wrote "I believe

Probation had made a good faith effort to answer each of your concerns. Therefore, I am closing our interest in this case." Two years later I can only assume the state was quite proud of its efforts for this claim of an arrearage that never had any basis in fact.

Two songs hit the charts in the early '90s whose lyrics provided me with added inspiration, as if I needed it, as I saw myself embattled, consumed in this fight for justice with the family court. Tom Petty's song *Won't Back Down* was released in 1989, and Soul Asylum's *Runaway Train* dated to a 1992 release. These songs, anthems, said in song what I believed was now my life's second cause. I adopted these songs as my themes in this fight. I played them over and over; the kids also learned the words as this was their struggle too, to a degree, as they saw me pushed from their lives; lives now guided by court orders and a mother who was not there. As I approached any court hearing I played these two songs as I drove to the courthouse. I played them loudly as I sang along. When the songs finished, I hit the replay button and started it over. I would get 2-4 renditions of either of the songs out before I arrived at the courthouse and upon arrival I was pumped up, charged, ready to face the court, opposing counsel, the day's charges, and complaints. My mantra was *"I would not back down."* I got particularly charged at the line *"you can stand me up at the gates of hell"* and sang this verse the loudest as I surely thought my time in family court was akin to standing at the gates of hell. NPR's webpage asked the public to describe how Petty's song *"Won't back down"* inspired them, carrying them through difficult times in their lives. NPR reported that over 700 people contributed to this posting. It certainly helped me through tough times.

Soul Asylum's *Runaway Train* similarly expressed my feelings that I was on a runaway train *"never going back; wrong way on a one-way track; seems like I should be getting somewhere; somehow I'm neither here nor there."* Not unlike the drum and fife corps that led the soldiers of our independence revolution into battles, so too did I utilize these songs as I approached my many battles for family court justice. I stood at the gates of hell and I surely was going the wrong way on a seemingly one-way track, but we would, must continue the fight. We could not afford to quit this battle of my life and what I saw as one for the lives of my children.

I played *Runaway Train* most times as I backed away from the home having left the children after our visits. Typically, the girls would look out the front windows of the home and wave to me while their faces expressed looks of sadness or that of being left somewhere they did not want to be. I would flash my headlights three times as I backed away from the home to let the girls know "I love you." Having turned the car around to exit the driveway, I would hit the brake lights three times as I stopped at the street to again tell them "I love you." The girls would turn the front door light on-off three times in response. As I drove down the street and back to my residence, I played Runaway Train and believed I was on a runaway train and perhaps never going back; I was going the wrong way on a one-way track. These words brought me to tears many times having left my children. I just needed to let the girls know I would never abandon them in their home situation.

Bon Jovi's song *It's My Life* was released on May 23, 2000, and would also become a belated favorite song of this cause as it too expressed the heartache of dealing with an intolerable situation. *"I did it my way;" "I ain't gonna be just a face in the crowd;" "You're gonna hear my voice"* at every issue; *"It's my life"* and that of my children; *"For the ones who stood their ground;" "Tomorrow is getting harder but you have to make your own breaks." "Don't bend; don't break."* I used the verse *"I did it my way"* in my poem eight years earlier when I decided I had to represent myself pro se if I was to salvage a future for my children and myself. This one verse in this song was mine years earlier in making my decision to take on the system known as New Jersey Family Court.

I also considered another song as I thought it too said much about how I felt in this effort to undo what Paula and the system had done, The Man of La Marche's *To Dream the Impossible Dream*. The song's lyrics say much about what I believed to be my mission in this effort but it was almost too beautiful a song to be tested in such a sordid environment as family court and its system of justice. Too, the song speaks of a dream, something I could not afford. I was dealing with reality, not a dream, but a nightmare I could only hope but awake from someday and pull my children from it. I was the father to these children; I was their protagonist who would wage this conflict for their futures as we sought justice in this court. There were unrightable wrongs that had to be challenged, and I had to fight for those rights without question or pause, even willing to march into hell. Surely, I was one man scorned and covered with scars, and strove with his last ounce of courage, but I could not afford to not reach that star. I told myself, again and again, I would never give up; I would not back down.

# 15

# ANOTHER TRY FOR CUSTODY OF MY CHILDREN

In early 1995, I filed a motion for change of custody. The motion was a long and detailed account of the situation at the home where the children were but collateral for the mother's custody that provided little benefit to them. In the meantime, Paula was on to her third lawyer, and my motion for custody introduced this attorney to the case. I told the court "I would get an attorney too but I can't find one I trust." In addition to the custody of the four children, I sought termination of the rehabilitative alimony; reduction in the child support obligation; and enforcement of a prior court order of April 1994. My motion included some 60 paragraphs of specific facts and instances that I believed supported my case for a change of child custody. Ironically, opposing counsel argued, under New Jersey case law, there was no "substantial change in circumstances" since my agreement to concede custody of the children. I noted the prior custody evaluation had been compromised by none other than the opposing counsel's interference in that process. I agreed nothing had changed in my inability to get a fair evaluation in anticipation of a custody trial; a professional evaluation was denied as was due process.

As the hearing opened, opposing counsel lifted my motion, the size of a ream of paper, and questioned the court "am I supposed to read this?" Judge Herman answered "I have" and I merely commented, "I could care less if he read it or not." Most of my allegations were typically denied as situations taken out of context or me just being an angry and bitter person.

I argued I found the children's care at the home under the mother's management was deteriorating on several fronts. My concerns for the children's well-being were detailed to the court in my filing for a change of custody as a record of the current situation, and not in the best interest of these children now aged eleven, nine, eight, and four years of age.

I questioned the orthodontist care proposed two years ago for the two oldest children that had fallen prey to this divorce action. The children had not received regular dental care in three years. A prior reported head lice infestation had now plagued the girls for the fourth month; the pediatrician refusing to renew the fifth prescription of head lice medication on the concern the children could be poisoned at such dosages. Bees had again swarmed in the master bedroom similar to that which occurred last year. The two-car garage had become a trash dump that threatened the safety of the children and the home itself. The home had run out of oil service for the fourth time affecting heat and hot water service. I had counted fifteen different babysitters aged thirteen to eighteen years of age to care for the children in the mother's absence. The children had become wards of the community. One frequent sitter was seen in public wearing clothes I had purchased for Michelle which were thought to have been lost in the piles of laundry in the home. Paula went to the sitter's home to demand the return of the stolen clothing.

Because of the general lack of care and maintenance of the marital home that I owned a half interest in, I sought the right to visit the property to maintain the landscape, take the trash from the garage and to the curb. Allowing this father to take custody of the children when the mother left the marital home for church services or other events.

I refused Paula's request to take the children to an acknowledged sixth counselor. I complained Paula continued to shop the children to various counseling services. I participated in a couple of these sessions and questioned the counselors if they knew of certain instances or were aware of other facts. I found these counselors to be sympathetic to the mother and I challenged them on the need to have these children burdened with such psychological hogwash. Ironically, it was the mother who sought such "expertise" for the children when she refused such "expert" prescribed medication and care herself. Too, when I insisted these counselors address issues known to me, Paula would seek new counseling services without my consideration. One counselor, in a private session with me, acknowledged he had heard nothing of the one-child being wrestled to the floor several times by the mother; the child was being isolated within the home. My complaint stated these children were brought into such sessions and advised to discuss their issues and concerns. Little, I alleged, was said in the presence of the mother. I would not allow her to continue this counseling charade disguised as parenting.

The April 21, 1995 hearing produced changes that I took as positive; the court eliminated the rehabilitative alimony as Paula acknowledged she had elected not to continue pursuit of her education; the court wanted a progress report from the current counselor working with the children; Paula could not arbitrarily change counselors without my consideration; the court ordered its in-house court mediator interview the four children to get a better assessment of the custody issue and the children's input. Paula's request for the release of the children's passports for travel to Colombia was again denied. I drafted the order that detailed the court's rulings of this hearing. It was signed by Judge Herman on May 3, 1995. No longer would we allow lawyers to drag out the resolution of these orders for months.

The court's May 25, 1995 letter instructed all four children to meet with the court's mediator. In a letter dated May 23, addressed to the court's mediator, I advised a neighbor had informed me my oldest daughter, Michelle, their daughter's best friend, was at their home crying and distraught. Reportedly, the children were told by their mother that should Adriana, not quite ten, be allowed to leave the home and live with her father, the house would need to be sold and they would need to move. I always wanted to maintain this home for all the children but I would not allow one child to be subjected to continued abuse at the hands of the mother. I had no intention to let one circumstance change the living situation for the other children. I made this issue known as well as providing the neighbor's name and contact information. I believed the children were being coerced by the mother, and the court's mediator needed to be made aware of such efforts.

In a subsequent letter to this mediator, I exposed the head lice infestation the girls had endured for four months, even though the court was told in March that the problem, first identified in February, had been addressed. I informed the court in June the pediatrician had refused any additional prescriptions after the preceding four had failed to resolve the problem. The HMO refused a referral to a dermatologist and subsequently canceled a visit from a visiting nurse to review the home environment that would allow for such a condition to persist for months. The HMO suggested the local Board of Health be called. Nothing was done by anyone. Over the July 4th holiday, my sister and I had the children at my apartment and we spent two days combing through the girls' hair and pulled out an incredible number of head lice and nits. One child had 19 nits alone. The kids were allowed to stay over the long weekend outside the visitation schedule as Paula announced she was not feeling well and went home to bed.

Then there was the situation of a hive of bees that had taken up residence in the attic over the master bedroom. Last year the room was closed off as bees swarmed inside and the kids noted a hundred dead bees in the room. A beekeeper was called and he merely killed the hive and left it there with a hole in the ceiling sheetrock dripping honey onto the rug below. A year later yellow jackets had taken possession of the abandoned hive and room. The hole in the ceiling would not be repaired for several years.

Opposing counsel answered this latest litany of complaints by requesting the court deny any change of custody for these children; denying the father's right to inspect the marital property as to care and condition, and requesting the children be allowed to continue with additional counseling, and allowing Paula the right to the children's passports so they can travel with her to Colombia. Their answer noted Paula found new employment, her fourth job this year; the head lice condition was again under control; the bees had returned but fortunately, no one had been stung; the referenced condition in the garage was addressed, noting "I have slowly been cleaning out the garage as I have time ... having a spotless garage is not on the top of my list of important life issues;" and continued counseling to help the children cope, and as for the requested travel to Colombia with the children we were offered an affidavit "promising to return timely with the children and acknowledging that Paula would be held in contempt of court if she did not return the children." My response to the court noted this answer was not timely filed under the rules while noting my previous letters to counsel addressing all such issues went unanswered implying an "air of unaccountability and arrogance."

The hearing of August 25 had several positives for me but this court would not allow any circumstance to unseat this custodial parent. Paula could not take more than two of the children on any visit to Colombia. Should such a trip occur the father would have custody of the other children; Paula must ensure the children get regular dental care; I was allowed to arrange for the long-sought orthodontist care for the two oldest children; I was given the right to inspect the marital home upon two weeks' notice to address my concerns for the bee infestation and allowed to access the marital property once a month to provide maintenance to the property; mow the lawn and trim trees and shrubs; Paula was ordered to give the father first option to take custody of his children when her plans called for her to leave them overnight. I always took custody of my children in all such instances. Too, the children's daily phone call with their father was to be maintained; and the opposing counsel's request for me to pay his legal fees was denied.

The general disrepair of the home was obvious from the street. Molly, the youngest child, heard another on the school bus pointing to their home, ask if it was abandoned, and wondered if anyone still lived there. Katie was so embarrassed by the look of the home that she got off at a different stop and walked to her home.

I addressed a letter on September 8, to the K-6 School Administrator to acknowledge my wish for the school to keep me informed as to all matters relative to my children. I asked that copies of routine tests and normal school correspondence be forwarded to me. Also, I wanted to be advised when the children missed school. The school answered noting I was not on record as the school's emergency contact, but two neighbors. Having joint-custody of the children, I insisted I be the emergency contact.

I addressed opposing counsel on September 29 and copied Judge Herman and the court's mediator. The letter was yet another effort to make all aware of what I described as a deteriorating situation at the home as to the welfare of Adriana, not quite ten years old, and who on several occasions had expressed a desire to live with me. The letter referenced a situation where this child and mother were in an environment of increasing conflict. I noted having spoken with Paula on the phone one evening at the end of my call with the children. I discussed the arguing between these two and told Paula I thought this child was being isolated within the home and she had to do more to prevent this emotional abuse of this child. Paula agreed with my interpretation of the situation but stated the isolation was self-inflicted. I asked her to consider giving me custody of this child to reduce the tension between them and be able to help with her school work. Paula was again agreeable to a change of custody of Adriana to my care.

My letter to Paula dated October 20 and copied to her counsel and the court, noted my "concerns" for Adriana's school progress based on the recent mid-term report. I scheduled an October 23 meeting with a school administrator, teacher, and counselor about her struggles with school work. I also noted that Paula needed to advise the school when she left the home to travel and that I had the right to custody of the children in such absences. In a recent experience, during Paula's most recent trip to Colombia, I was accosted by a school administrator who questioned why I was at the school to pick up the children? I had to explain the mother was in Colombia and that I had custody of all the children in her three-week absence. After we met with the school staff, I addressed a letter to the Chief School Administrator, and copied counsel and the court, thanking the staff for the time to discuss Adriana's progress at school. I noted I did not think the standard remedial effort offered to any number of struggling students would be sufficient to pull my daughter up to standards. The school advised it would institute its Pupil Assistance Team concept to assist this child. Likewise, I noted both of the parents being present had competing agendas but that I reserved my right to bring this immediate issue to family court to get it the attention I thought it deserved.

My letter to opposing counsel dated October 23, and copied to the court and school staff, was an attempt to shed truth on this meeting with the school staff. I noted Paula's espoused efforts to help this struggling child were but lip-service to her responsibilities and the realities at the home. I told them the mother had not asked to see this child's mid-term report although she had seen those of the other two children; that she left the home two nights a week for a bible class and personal counseling; and that I had counted at least fifteen babysitters in the home over the past two years. My children were "wards of the community" as they were so often left in the care of neighbors or sitters. Paula's contribution to this meeting was to express her concern for this neglected child while defending her lack of participation to help her. She then reneged on her agreement to allow a custody change of this child to live with me claiming she "would retain custody of all the children for as long as God wills it." Or as long as the family court tolerated the abuse of these custodial children.

Yet another letter to opposing counsel was sent on December 4, 1995, to again lodge my complaint relative to the mother's conduct at the marital home. The court and the school counselor were also copied. My letter referenced events of the past week involving your client and my children. I am inclined to describe them as "crazy" but then I am not really a part of "the system" and surely not a lawyer so our perspectives are different. I am fighting the system, as the record will reflect because it is a flawed system and one that has put my children at risk. I advised I would seek a plenary hearing to address the care and well-being of my children, but especially relative to the mother's treatment of Adriana.

I reported an increased level of conflict between the mother and this child at the home. I referenced several times my nightly calls to the children were punctuated with episodes of the mother having wrestled this child to the floor while pinching and scratching her. The other children witnessed these brawls but did nothing to interfere with them. I advised if such treatment continued, I would file a complaint against his client with the Division of Youth and Family Services (DYFS). Also, Paula had recently invited me into the home to help move a large box from her car and into the home; I turned off the outside spigots from the basement for the winter; fixed the computer printer, and declined an invitation to stay for dinner.

This Saturday I returned the children to the home and returned to the car to look for some misplaced item. Finding it, I returned to the front door and was asked by Paula to come into the home to get this distressed child (Adriana) to stop kicking the walls. I stood in the foyer and consoled the child and advised her she could not kick the walls. I told Paula the child "was probably frustrated" and with that, Paula made a gesture towards the open door. I moved away but inadvertently in the same direction as she did. Paula then erupted into a demand to call the police. The children screamed in anxiety asking the mother to not call the police on daddy. I calmed the children assuring them I was in no jeopardy and left the home and property.

Upon return to my apartment, I received a call from a state trooper who said he was at the home and was advised an arrest warrant would be issued against me for violating the restraining order and entering the home. I told the trooper he knew nothing of this case and that I had been invited into the home that evening and just days before by Paula. Conveniently, Paula could not find a copy of the TRO so there was no basis upon which to issue a warrant for my arrest. The children were quite distressed at every instance the mother threatened my arrest. I was the stable force in their lives while they were forced to live under the care of this erratic custodial mother.

There was much "chatter" written in 1995 addressing the role of fathers in divorces where it was still assumed, if not ruled, the mother was the preferred custodial parent. One article noted New Jersey lawmakers took the first steps that could result in a wholesale revision of the state's divorce laws. A commission was established in 1993 to recommend changes to divorce laws. Hearings were held with testimony from all sides of the issue. Some suggestions were deemed easier than others to address, including a parenting plan to be agreed to; giving both parents access to their children's records; and providing sanctions when the custodial parent violates a visitation order. Another proposal that was deemed more controversial was one that would prohibit judges from ordering divorcing parents to pay for their children's college education. The argument here was that in many intact families, parents simply tell their children they will or will not pay for some or all college expenses. No court demands married parents to contribute to college education expenses. In many divorce cases, judges ordered fathers to contribute to such expenses when fathers complained the same court denied them reasonable access to these same children. Another proposed change suggested child "emancipation" at age eighteen and relinquish their "right" to continued child support. Yet another issue that surely caused much disdain was the custodial parent be required to account for how child support was being spent.

In this case, child support was established from the state's income tables that determined the level of financial support based on the incomes of both parents and the number of children in the marriage. This table included expenses for housing; food and clothing; education; and all other types of miscellaneous expenses a family might incur raising children. I suggested my court-mandated support payments and other out-of-pocket expenses accounted for ninety-five percent of the care and support of my children. In addition to the basic monthly financial support payment that totaled over $1,500 a month, I paid for all the back-to-school clothes and supplies; gifts for birthday parties; various school expenses like book sales or day trips; I paid for all outside expenses for sports teams or equipment. On Wednesday night visitations I sent the kids home with lunches as Paula had them on the school's free lunch program based on her income. They hated showing their meal tickets for a free lunch in a community of solid middle-class families. There was never a second accounting of this support obligation that included any consideration of the mother's current income. In their high school years, it was me that took all the girls shopping for their homecoming and prom dresses yet could not see them off to these social events.

A New York Times article dated April 26, 1995, headlined *Divorced Fathers Make Gains in Battles to Increase Rights.* This article referenced the New Jersey's Assembly passing a Bill that limited child support payments up to the age of eighteen, but it was never passed into law. The article noted "increasingly, courts and legislatures around the nation are rethinking some tenets of divorce law, with father's rights in mind. By and large, the changes aim to give fathers more access to their children and, under certain circumstances, to reduce their child support payments."

A Philadelphia Inquirer article dated December 5, 1995, headlined *Fingers Point at No-Fault Divorce* as a fairly recent phenomenon of no-fault divorce law first signed into law by then California Governor Ronald Reagan in 1970. The article "acknowledges that many factors have combined to trigger the upward zoom of divorce rates, including the brave new ethos of individualism and self-expression" but those no-fault laws further accelerated the pace of divorce. The author noted divorce weakened ties between fathers and their children, reducing the number of adults in a society committed to children's issues.

The Inquirer article headlined *Save the Fathers* on June 18, 1995, stressed the need for father's involvement when so many family courts did little but to delegate fathers to a paycheck. Statistics quoted in this article from the National Fatherhood Initiative (NFI), a nonprofit group founded in 1984 as a catalyst for social change, noted:

America has never seen so many children in families without fathers.

The United States was now the world leader in fatherless families.

40% of America's children go to sleep where their biological father does not live.

40% of these fatherless children had not seen their father in the past year.

The NFI's message is that fathers play a unique and irreplaceable role in the lives of their children; that they are the natural agents for socializing young males and guiding them on the pathway to manhood... and that being a good father is the essence of masculinity and requires giving children your time, keeping your commitments to your children, and accepting responsibility for ensuring that your children are healthy, well-fed, safely housed and well-educated.

The Wall Street Journal, in an article *Courts let Custodial Parents Move* dated February 10, 1997, highlighted a father's effort in New York state to stop his seven-year-old son from being allowed to follow his custodial mother and new step-father to an assignment in Saudi Arabia, 8,000 miles away. The trial judge ruled it was in the child's "best interest" to move with his mother even if that meant the child's contact with his biological father was limited to faxes and emails. The article noted recent research "that children of divorce do best if they are not shuttled frequently between bickering parents and if the parent, they spend the most time with is happy." The article noted companies also welcomed the change. At AT&T Corp., a spokesman says court approval "will free up more employees to face the notion of transferring across state lines." Fathers and children be damned!

Fathers seldom being given custody of their children were distraught as they saw their children being moved to distances that denied them a right to participate in their children's lives. Several cases referenced in this article confirmed the courts acquiesced to the custodial mother's right to move children in their pursuit of a new relationship; a new job. One California court noted it was "unrealistic to assume that divorced parents will permanently remain in the same location." Divorce dissolved a marriage but the custody rulings tore children from their fathers.

My December 12, 1995 letter to the School Administrator, and copied to counsel and the court, acknowledged other instances where the mother had again brought Adriana to the floor and punched her. I advised I would be filing a motion with family court to bring the issue of this hostile environment to attention and would file a complaint with DYFS requesting they investigate these allegations of physical and emotional abuse being inflicted on a ten-year-old child. Specifically, in this letter "I address this situation with you because you are the educators and counselors that have direct contact with Adriana and the other children in this family. I ask that each of you accept your moral, legal, and professional responsibilities to protect the interest of this child and these children in this situation, in this year of the campaign to 'Put Children First.'"

# 16

# WHAT DO WE WANT FOR CHRISTMAS? JUSTICE!

The year-end was fast approaching and we looked for a reprieve in the action so to speak, a holiday time-out perhaps. No, that would be too easy and Paula never missed an opportunity to put me in jeopardy. The original April 2, 1993 court order defined for both parents a routine and holiday visitation schedule. Paula enjoyed custody of the children every Christmas Eve from noon until noon Christmas day. I was to never have the children any Christmas Eve and Paula claimed that right for the next twenty years. That said, her lawyers had twice asked the court to incarcerate me for sundry violations of the same court order. I faced their claims but never gave them much credence but agreed they wanted me arrested, jailed, as perhaps a more effective weapon since they could not win most of their arguments on merit or facts.

Christmas 1995 was on a Monday, and Paula demanded I have the children back at the house by noon Sunday as her Christmas Eve visitation would begin at that time. The kids and I went off on our scheduled visit and we returned to the home at 12:05 PM and sat at the bottom of the driveway, as I was not allowed any closer to the home. It was a cold December day and there we sat. I turned the car on every-so-often to heat the van interior. The girls had no access to a bathroom as they could not get into the house and I had no means to contact Paula.

We sat in the van until 12:30, then 1:00, and now 1:30. Finally, a neighbor approached the car. I rolled down the window and the neighbor said Paula had called her and claimed "there must have been some mistake; Paula was up at my apartment looking to pick up the girls." The neighbor then asked me to give her custody of the children and Paula would pick them up from her house. I told the neighbor there was no misunderstanding, it was obvious Paula was somewhere else and was not yet in a position to take custody of her children. I advised, "I don't leave my children with anyone." Nothing personal, but I asked her to advise Paula I would take the children up to my apartment, some twenty minutes away. She could claim them there. We left the property and returned to my apartment.

Paula was not waiting at the apartment upon our arrival. Finally, at 2:30 PM, Paula pulled up to the curb and beeped the horn. I went to the door and told the kids to wait as I went out to Paula's car. I engaged her from the passenger side door asking why she was so late, now two and a half hours late while demanding just the prior day I return the kids by the noon deadline? Her notion of some misunderstanding of the drop-off point was a lie. She rolled down the passenger side window a couple of inches so she could perhaps hear me better. I again questioned why she was so late relative to the visitation schedule; that we sat in the driveway for ninety minutes on a cold winter day waiting for her? She then exposed a small tape recorder and I told her to take that "and shove it...." The girls came out to the car and they all left the apartment complex.

I picked up the girls at noon on Christmas Day, and we went to my apartment where we opened gifts. We then headed to my sister's in Poughkeepsie, NY to meet with other family members and enjoyed our version of a Christmas holiday. We returned home the following evening and I never gave a thought to what was just another incidence of Paula's late arrival; it was to be expected, Christmas Eve or not.

My apartment was just ten minutes from the office, and I was at the top of the emergency call list should the alarm go off at the office building. Having been called a few times, I would go to the office to be met by the local police who would check out the building and grounds. I arrived at my place of work this Wednesday, December 27, 1995 at 7:00 AM. Two Deptford police cars were in the front lot and two officers were standing near the door. I thought the office alarm must have gone off. I got out of the car and as I approached the door one officer called to me by name. Yes; surely, they knew my name from the call list. They announced they had a warrant for my arrest. Stunned and caught off guard, I stopped in my tracks some fifteen feet from the officers. What was the charge? Violating the TRO. One officer asked, "are you going to run?" I looked down at the dress shoes I was wearing and advised "if I had known, I would have worn my sneakers." I proceeded to unlock the office door and was informed bail was set at $2,500 cash and I was to be taken to the local police station a mile down the road. My hearing was scheduled for about 11:00 AM. Fortunately, I had my checkbook not to mention the $2,500. I reached out to another employee who had just arrived and explained the circumstances and I expected to be back by noon. We arrived at the Deptford police station within minutes. Escorted down a hallway, my right arm wrist was handcuffed to a bench seat. What, no padded cells? Did I miss breakfast?

There I sat contemplating my situation. Sometime later that morning an officer was talking to two other gentlemen, visitors, giving them some verbal layout of the building while standing in the front lobby. A door to the right was referenced as going somewhere. At that point, I stood up, cuffed to the bench as I was, I called down the twenty-foot hallway and asked "what was behind that door?" One questioned, "what did you care, you're not going anywhere? "I just wanted to know what was behind that door." I was told to sit down and so I did.

I was ushered into the Municipal courtroom and fairly well dressed that some might have taken me for a banker suspected of fraud. This hearing was very brief as the Municipal Court Judge read the charge against me, as filed by Paula. Charged as "defendant has violated restraining order signed by Judge Herman," the case was referred back to family court. Nothing more; no evidence; just Paula's statement. Paula was two and a half hours late and I was charged with violating the TRO. They took my check for $2,500 and I was back at the office near noon. What I would have given for the same opportunity to protect myself some months ago. My request to file a complaint was denied as but a ploy to harass the ex-wife.

But for immediate access to my checkbook and $2,500 cash to post bail, I would have been remanded to jail. Why? Because I dared to question, complain that the custodial parent was two-plus hours late for the court-mandated visitation schedule, she insisted I comply with it just days earlier. That the four children and I had to sit in a cold car on Christmas Eve awaiting her late arrival did not matter. This was the same mother who on several occasions physically assaulted her child with punches and wrestled her to the floor. The same family court system of justice chose to ignore all such complaints against this mother. This system provided a sanctuary to the mother at every instance. This is the justice we knew in New Jersey Family Court. The system only protected one, the mother. To hell with the children and get this father.

My letter dated January 2, 1996, copied below, was addressed to Judge Herman and copied to opposing counsel, school staff, and current counselor, pleading for an immediate intercession in this case for the welfare of Adriana being abused by her custodial mother.

I request an extraordinary hearing, to be held as soon as possible, hopefully within twenty-four to forty-eight hours. My daughter (Adriana) is under extreme duress at home. I have noted incidents in prior correspondence, dated December 4 and 12, 1995. The degree of abuse, both physical and emotional, has continued to be inflicted on Adriana by the mother. Just tonight, during the nightly telephone call, it was again reported by Adriana and confirmed with the other children in the home, that the abuse has continued to escalate against this child.

Adriana noted that she was again brought to the floor in the home as the mother "restrained" her. This effort at restraining a ten-year-old has become an almost daily routine. Never in twelve years have I ever had to resort to this in managing my four girls. On the scheduled overnight visitation on Friday, December 29, 1995, Adriana arrived at my apartment, again distraught and in tears. I questioned what had happened? She noted she and the mother had another confrontation and again she was restrained on the floor in the house. Adriana related that the mother had punched her in the chest while holding a pencil in her hand. Also, the mother had pushed and held her face against a wall. Both of the child's arms had fingernail scratches the length of the forearms that were inflicted by the mother that evening. The oldest child said she implored her mother to "please stop."

Tonight's telephone call noted more alleged conduct by the mother that I can only describe as outrageous. Again, all directed at Adriana. During the restraining effort, the mother threatened to call the police on the child. This threat to call the police on one's ten-year-old is nothing more than psychological abuse meant to intimidate a child. Most adults would be intimidated by this. The children are aware that the mother had me arrested last week. They were in the home when the state trooper was called to the home earlier in the month. This is nothing more than an effort to exert one's influence using fear and intimidation, now even with the children.

Adriana also advised that she is ignored by the mother upon her return to the home after a visitation. The two younger sisters were instructed by the mother to "stay away" from her, she is nasty, she will hurt you. Adriana is increasingly isolated in her own home by the mother and sisters. I believe the sisters have learned not to challenge the mother or they too will be forced to endure what Adriana does on almost a daily basis. Adriana has historically shared one of the bedrooms with a younger sister, Katie. Reportedly, the last few nights the mother has allowed this sister to sleep in her bed with her and the youngest child. Adriana, who is very timid, afraid of her own shadow, has never liked to sleep alone. Previously, to avoid confrontations with the mother, I have advised her to go to her room and do homework or play. Her response has been, and I know it to be a fact, she doesn't like to be upstairs alone. Isolated in her room at bedtime she now sleeps on the floor in her oldest sister's room rather than sleep alone.

Paula allowed Adriana to spend New Year's Eve with me. I picked her up at the house at 7 PM on December 31 and returned her on January 1 at 7 PM. Paula told me "yes, she could go because she wanted a happy new year." I answered, "Adriana deserved one too." Adriana and I had a normal time together. I cooked meals, she watched TV, I helped her with her homework. There was not an effort to restrain her. She cried when it was time to return her to the house, her "home."

Much of what I report here was related to the daily phone call this evening. While speaking with Adriana for approximately twenty minutes it was confirmed the mother was within arm's reach of her while on the phone with me. I told Adriana to advise the mother she was allowed to tape the call, which was being taped, but you specifically instructed she could not monitor the calls directly. Most of the daily calls have been taped by the plaintiff. I request you subpoena the tape from the call last night, January 2, 1996, as evidence of what I have related in this letter.

I called DYFS, New Jersey's child welfare bureaucracy, on December 13, 1995, and spoke with a representative. I reported that Adriana had been punched by the mother, etc. I was advised it was one person's word against another and that I should file for custody of the child. The conversation lasted all of three minutes and they did not even ask for the address where the child lived:

Judge Herman, I implore you to intercede on behalf of Adriana, and the other children. I did not waste the time to file a Motion to address this tragic situation. The law and our sense of responsibility require we do all we can to protect the child. I am at my wit's end as to what to do next. Adriana has asked if she could stay with me on Wednesday night, January 3 rather than return to her home. I'm sure the mother would call the police and I would be charged with some criminal offense, but I have to do something. The system has to do something. Please do not let this be one of those circumstances where all the obvious signs were ignored as the problem becomes just another case study. I have advised school personnel and the school counselor of previous episodes at the home but this has produced nothing to date. You are the only person who can hopefully stabilize this situation for Adriana and the sisters who must live it daily.

I will do whatever you require and would be available at any time to address this matter, but I beg of you that it be addressed immediately. What do I tell Adriana? I cannot let it go on. Please help this child. She is a dear little girl caught in a very bad crisis at age ten. I, her father, am helpless to protect her. I await your response.

In answer to this letter, on January 3, the court signed its own order to show cause and scheduled a hearing for Friday, January 8, and subsequently deferred until January 17, 1996, at 11:30 AM. Paula answered the court's motion to show cause in a certification dated January 11, 1996. In it, she denied much of the day-to-day abuse I alleged she inflicted against this child. She quoted various books on parenting and marriage conflicts and how they impact children. She asked the court to compel me to attend counseling sessions and to limit the daily phone calls with the children to five minutes each.

I wrote a letter to the School Administrator, dated January 12 noting my expedited hearing relative to Adriana had now been deferred until January 17. In this letter I reiterated the alleged abuse being suffered by the child at the marital home. I requested the four teachers who have taught Adriana, write their observations of the personality they have known Adriana to exhibit during the year each taught her. I asked the school counselor, who I knew to have met many times with Adriana to help her cope with this home situation, also submit such a statement. I would request the same of the counselor who has seen all the children on several occasions. I would expect the teachers/counselors would or would not be able to identify Adriana as a "problem" student, one who was hostile and threatening to other students, unrulily in class, etc. Was she a child better defined as timid, shy, quiet, friendly, reserved? Or hostile, domineering, loud, unruly, aggressive? Also, please note in a separate statement whether or not school records reflect Adriana having been given any school detentions over this time to address such behavior or for other misconduct. I must admit, I have no recollection of any such incidents but perhaps my memory has failed me. The mother claims she is forced to deal with the "real" Adriana.

I requested the school's statement(s) be directed by fax to Judge Herman and to opposing counsel in time for the hearing on January 17. I realize the school does not relish having to participate in such an exercise but I, as a father, am compelled to protect Adriana and the other children, even if it is from the mother. Our moral code and the law require we do "what is in the best interest of the child." Should the requested statement not be provided for some reason I would appreciate a response as to why they were denied, likewise by fax to Judge Herman and opposing counsel. Of course, to produce evidence contrary to the mother's comments to me, I would request of the court the right to compel such testimony from third parties such as school personnel, who I suggest have had an opportunity to identify a child's behavior and would be considered as disinterested third parties in matters such as this.

In a filing dated January 15, 1996, we were advised opposing counsel had withdrawn as Paula's legal representative in this case. Again, thanks for nothing! Paula would represent herself pro se at this pending hearing.

Upon opening this hearing of January 17, Judge Herman said he found my letter of January 12 to the school "outrageous!" Not that the mother's alleged treatment of this child was "outrageous" but that my letter to the school was outrageous. The mother admitted to the court she had punched this child and tackled her. She testified it was her only means to control the child. The judge ordered Adriana was to speak with the court mediator; neither party was to discuss the hearing with Adriana; the court mediator was to contact the school and counselor for a report; Paula was ordered to not physically punish Adriana or face a contempt of court citation; both parties were to return February 21 to review the matter. Finally, an admitted incident of domestic violence in this case and the court did nothing to hold this mother responsible for her actions. This court is not about justice for all.

I received a copy of a letter the school's attorney had faxed to Judge Herman the morning of the hearing to address my asking the school to provide a record of what the teacher's observations were relative to this child in distress. The letter from the School's Solicitor on the subject follows.

I represent the Board of Education. I received a telephone call today from the district superintendent. She told me that on Friday, January 12, 1996, a letter is ostensibly written and signed by (father), was faxed to the board office. The fax was discovered after the board office was closed for the teacher in-service and the Martin Luther King holiday.

The letter advised the district that:

The father is scheduled to appear in court before Your Honor tomorrow, Wednesday, January 17. He requested the child's teachers prepare written statements regarding their observations about the child's behavior and personality and fax them to all parties. He also indicated he might want all four teachers to appear in court to testify."

As a matter of practicality, the time frame is impossible to meet. Also, to lose four teaching staff members, potentially all at the same time, to a court hearing would be crippling to the educational process in the district. Our teaching staff members are educators, not child psychologists. However, if the Court issues an order or subpoena compelling the production of documents or reports the district will comply.

Seeing this letter from the school district's attorney I was compelled to respond to this lawyer in my letter below dated January 19, 1996, and copied to the court.

I received a copy of your letter to Judge Herman relative to my concerns about the welfare of my ten-year-old daughter. I asked the teachers for a definition as to whether this child was known to them to be timid, shy, quiet, loud, unruly, aggressive, etc. The same behavior traits or conduct that a teacher might make in observations in the routine report card or in committing a child to detention for an hour after school. I know the teachers are not child psychologists but I suspect most parents trust the teacher's observations as to conduct, and other habits without regard to professional credentials.

I hardly believe the school system would be brought to a crash, as you allege, due to any required appearance by any one or all of the teachers. Surely, if the system can be shut down by snow for four days, an in-service day (whatever that is), any number of legal holidays much less the usual vacation schedule, I would argue most parents would not be bothered by just a one-or two-hour absence in the name of any child's welfare. But lawyers being what they are, you have the right, if not the obligation, to argue the absurd in the name of your client.

For the record, I have waited three months for the school to meet with me to discuss an enhanced program for the benefit of Adriana. It must be all that snow that slows the wheels of the education system. It took the legal system ten minutes to remove me from the lives of my children and the home on the word of one woman.

Should the system fail to provide for all, it is the immortal words of Mr. Lincoln, "the probability that we shall fail in the struggle ought not to deter us from the support of a cause we believe to be just" that should drive the rest of us. I would guess there were even lawyers in his day who argued for slavery. As their argument was wrong, I suggest so is yours.

Paula subsequently found new legal counsel, a Catholic priest who worked for a local non-profit providing legal services for clients deemed unable to afford an attorney. Here was someone I found I could trust and work with on this case, a rare bird for sure, someone who I believed cared as much about the welfare of my children and what was best for them in getting issues resolved. The February 21, 1996 hearing resolved some issues relative to this child in great distress at home and being brutalized by the mother. The court's order that day was drafted and filed by opposing counsel the next day and signed by the court in short order.

This order, signed March 6, 1996, gave me extended custody of Adriana from Wednesday night through Sunday; I was in charge of her school work and getting the school to address efforts to bring this child's progress to maximum effort, and the court's mediator was to interview this child. This family court did not find the mother guilty of any offense against this child. There was no mention of her physical assaults against this child. No warnings; no dismissal without prejudice; nothing! The court left the other three children in the mother's custody to deal with this threatening personality on their own. Family Court justice as we knew it. I was charged but not convicted of any offense three years ago but I was removed from my children and my home.

A neighborly grandmother would at times stop by the home after the kids were in bed to visit with Paula. I assume she felt Paula needed some comfort time. On one such visit, she entered the home in the midst of one of these brawls where Paula was sitting on Adriana on the floor and there was reported much yelling, distress, etc... Paula asked this neighbor for the phone as she was going to call the police on this child. The neighbor interceded and stopped this abuse that night. Her husband crossed paths with me a few weeks later and noted "we never knew what was happening" and I merely answered "nobody knows what goes on behind those closed doors."

Never willing to concede anything to this system of justice, I was most bothered by the $2,500 cash bail demanded of me on the most recent post-Christmas arrest at the office doorstep. These were personal funds I used to support my children's immediate needs, many of those same needs Paula refused to meet or just begged off saying "I have no money." So again, I found myself searching for justice at the Rutgers Law Library. I would defend myself in court when these charges were to be heard, but I wanted my money back and not sitting in some state coffer. Sure enough, there it was, New Jersey law allowed for a hearing to reduce, if not negate, the imposed bail if the person charged could meet certain criteria as to being trusted to show up for the hearing. I met all the stated criteria for a release from this egregious cash bond. I filed a motion contesting this cash bond against me.

A hearing was scheduled for February 2, 1996, to address my motion to reduce the $2,500 bail if not eliminate it. The Assistant County Prosecutor was to prosecute this case. The County Prosecutor, in a July 13, 1995 headline story in the local press, noted that this Lead Prosecutor headed the Prosecutor's Office efforts to address domestic violence. That same article noted the county had experienced a fifteen percent increase in such cases. The Prosecutor noted, "Gloucester County has a better awareness of domestic violence than other counties statewide and credits (this Prosecutor) for her dedication." Maybe this prosecutor should look into a father's rights as denied at the local courthouse. That might garner them yet another headline in the pursuit of justice for all, not just mothers.

I walked into this bail hearing pretty confident I would win this argument, as the actual hearing of the charge of harassment and violating the TRO was not scheduled until June 3, four months down the road. This prosecutor began by pounding her fist into her hand demanding "we want this defendant, your honor." I wondered seeing her punching fist if I had done so would it have been perceived as a violent moment, subject to arrest and bail? Remember, in 1994 I was admonished by the court just for distributing an article that discussed the difference between anger and violence. The prosecution gave no weight to my motion and the supporting legal argument that I was no risk to flee this charge, the basis of any bail, is it not? Judge Herman made quick work of this zealot's diatribe announcing "give him back his money, I see this guy more than I see most people in my family." I walked out of court and the bail money was returned to me in an order dated February 16, 1996. Bail was reduced from $2,500 to ROR (released on own recognizance). The prosecutor subsequently modified its motion to correct the date of the incident from December 27 to the 24th. Just get their facts straight is all I ever asked, as if that was important. This prosecutor was subsequently appointed a family court Judge in Gloucester County. I'm sure she demonstrated the unbiased mindset and disposition that would suit her well when adjudicating justice for all from a New Jersey Family Court bench.

At the June 3rd trial, I faced the charge of having violated the TRO by questioning why Paula was so late for the Christmas Eve visitation exchange. My defense was that Paula's actions continued to be contradictory at best and themselves a violation of the same TRO I stood accused of violating in this incident. I was subjected to Paula's whims and schedule, no complaints allowed. That the children and I sat in the driveway for ninety minutes on a cold December day, awaiting her return prompted my question to her of why she was so late? And I got arrested. I then laid out a long history of five pages that detailed numerous violations of this same TRO, all initiated by Paula to fit her schedule and lack of concern to take care of the children in her custody. I alone did what needed to be done to take care of these children. If not me, who?

I grew weary, frustrated with the reality of Paula's lack of concern and care for the children versus what was espoused in any court hearing. I began to log day-to-day events of what happened. I always suggested the children provided more to the mother in the level of child support she garnered with their custody than they ever received from the mother in day-to-day care. My daily record log noted incident after incident where Paula was late to claim the children; when I had gone to the marital home at Paula's request to assist with things; I took the children out on all Halloweens as Paula was not feeling well or would not do it; I took the children on thanksgiving weekend as Paula was tired; I took custody of the children last July 4th weekend as Paula went home; I bought the gifts for birthday parties as Paula had no money; I fed the children when Paula failed to do so as required; I was making them lunches for school; etc., etc., etc.

Perhaps this long history of near-total neglect of the children had begun to wear on me; that I was to never have the children any Christmas Eve; perhaps I tired of the fraud perpetrated against me and the children daily; weekly; year-after-year by this person who called herself mother, the court's chosen one; that prompted my disgruntled response to yet another late arrival. We all were victims of her neglect of any responsibility to these children she only claimed in court.

I was found not guilty at this June trial prosecuted by the county. The judge found my comments to "shove it (tape recorder)" to be "boorish." Again, a question of Paula's late arrival gets me prosecuted in this case. What also came out of this trial, the court's order as to visitation was to be honored by both parties; the orders were not subject to interpretation by the parties or changed at will to suit one's schedule. Of course, I was always willing to do whatever to accommodate Paula's wishes, as it afforded me more opportunities to be with the girls, provide for them. But it also angered me to see the status quo at the house as compared to what the court chose to believe. Paula had custody of the children and I was being used by her to facilitate her continued misuse of the restraining order. I was damned if I allowed her to continue to use me and damned if I did not do all to accommodate her and gain access to the children and provide for their needs.

Available New Jersey statistics for the period 1992 through 1994 noted complaints of domestic violence totaled 39,300; 41,100 and 41,800, respectively for the three years. These complaints were filed by women against men eighty-three percent, eighty percent, and eighty-one percent respectively for the referenced three-year period. As previously noted, I was denied the ability to file a complaint against Paula. In my thirteen years in family court hearings, I never once saw a case where the male was the accuser in a DV case. But the DV complaint filed against me, as contrived as it was, was sufficient to have me removed from my home and my children. The court never found me guilty or innocent of that complaint. The charge remains open against me to this day, twenty-six years later.

# 17

# THE FRAUD CONTINUES: INSIDE
# COURT AND OUT

As the court-ordered in the August 25, 1995 hearing, I was authorized to initiate orthodontic treatment for the two oldest children as was contemplated in October 1992. I reached out to the local orthodontist and arranged for him to see the two oldest children and begin the treatment anew. I counted four letters written to Paula in May and June 1995 asking for input on the subject that went unanswered. Having finally begun this treatment we heard from opposing counsel suggesting the process be delayed while Paula sought out other sources, hopefully, less expensive. I advised I did not want to delay it any longer and I would go with the orthodontist we had selected some three years ago. I requested the billing be separated into two coupon books of twenty-four monthly payments, split seventy-five percent, and twenty-five percent, representing the court's assignment of the shared payment of medical expenses. The split billing of these expenses would eliminate any co-mingling of my balance with Paula's balance due.

The first visit appointment was on April 29, 1996. I took Michelle and Adriana with me and it was agreed that weekly follow-up visits would be necessary to ensure the braces held in place and any necessary adjustments could be made. Braces in place for both of the girls, I scheduled weekly 7:00 AM visits on Wednesday for Adriana, now in my custody five days a week. After three weekly visits, I asked the medical office how Michelle was doing with her weekly visits? I was advised they had not seen the child since I had brought her for the initial visit. I asked Michelle why she was not getting to the weekly visits to check up and make any needed adjustments to the braces? She said the mother could not take her. I reached out to Paula and told her these weekly check-ups were necessary. Could I take Michelle with me for the scheduled visits with Adriana on Wednesday mornings? Paula agreed and allowed Michelle to spend Tuesday nights with Adriana and me. The girls enjoyed the opportunity to spend the night together, without all the drama at home. I cooked them meals and made lunches for the next day, and both got to the weekly orthodontist visits. Some weeks we had two visits if there was some additional slippage in a brace, but these visits continued for the next two years until the braces were due to come off. Finally, something was working and there were no hassles.

At the end of this two-year program in 1998, we arrived at the orthodontist's office and the girls were anxious to get those wire braces off. I was approached by the doctor who advised there was an issue with an unpaid balance. Now I assumed Paula would be in arrears on payments but I was unprepared to learn she had paid nothing towards her $2,000 balance for this court-sanctioned treatment for these children. The doctor said he could not take the braces off with this unpaid balance; the braces were his collateral. The girls wanted them off; they were due to come off but how does this balance due get paid? The girls were disappointed and I must admit I was shocked to a degree. We rescheduled for another appointment. I wish they had advised me earlier of this issue, but it not being my bill I can only assume they were not at liberty to discuss another client's account. I paid the $2,000 balance owed by Paula and the braces were removed the next week. This situation was to create yet another court hearing to resolve yet another dispute in this case. This dispute took this case deeper into the bowels of the New Jersey Family Court of injustice in 1999. The final resolution of this issue was not to be had until 2003.

In a June 5, 1996 letter to opposing counsel, I advised I had learned a lesson at trial for asking his client why she was so late returning home the prior Christmas Eve. All my efforts to appease, acquiesce to his client's arbitrary and random changes to the court established visitation schedule was at my peril. Yes, I did everything that would allow me to take care of the children's needs, scheduled or not, but that I alone was the one to be charged, arrested, held on bail; and forced to defend myself at trial. I advised I would not, could not continue to put myself in jeopardy answering to his client's every whim, in violation of the TRO. Even the court acknowledged the TRO was not subject to arbitrary change by either party. I asked him to impress upon his client there could be no more violations of the TRO. I'm sure the children would suffer. I then noted the scheduled, court-ordered inspection of the marital home was refused by Paula upon my arrival. Too, the children advised me the mother had lost her job, her third this year. Finally, I noted the mother refused to take Adriana, now enjoying extended visitation with me, with her and her three sisters for the Memorial Day weekend. The child was left crying in the driveway as Paula drove away with the other three children.

Yet another letter dated June 20, 1996, noted I took custody of the children for Father's Day, which I styled as nothing but a "Hallmark" event. I took the time to cut the lawn which had grown to a foot high. I then referenced a late call to the children at the house at 8:30 on Tuesday night. Again, Adriana was in great distress as the other children had confronted her to address their concerns should a permanent custody change be ordered and she leaves the home to live with her father. They told this sister that if she leaves the house would need to be sold and they would all have to leave the house, their school, their friends. All problems at the home were attributed to this one child. I spoke with Adriana for some twenty minutes to try to calm her down. She noted her mother had spit on her and pushed and pulled her out the front door and left her locked outside the home for several minutes. "How is that for motherly instincts, counselor?" This was the second time that week where this child was forced out of the house by the mother. The other time she was locked in the garage for thirty minutes. I reminded counsel this was a ten-year-old child. Twice this child was forced from the car at night close to home and made to walk several hundred yards down the county road in the headlights of the car.

Yet in another letter to opposing counsel, I referenced that his client had suggested she would consider leaving the home and custody of the children to allow her to pursue further education, and new employment while relieving some of the pressure on her to maintain the marital home. Counsel's letter dated June 22 advised the mother's employment with a school district would be renewed as of September and that she was willing to consider my buyout of her equity in the marital home.

A hearing was held on June 26, 1996, to address the custody of Adriana, among other matters. Judge Herman entered the court and while sitting, in what I would describe as a somewhat agitated voice, announced: "there is going to be a change here today." He ordered physical custody of ten-year-old Adriana was to change to the father. God, I almost cried in court; finally, this child was free of that terrible situation at the house. She was to continue counseling and the designated counselor was at my discretion. The child's visitation with the mother was at best whatever could be agreed to. The court also ordered the four children to be brought to the court on July 8, 1996, so they could meet the Court's Mediator and the Judge.

I thanked the Judge, and I told him I wanted him to meet these children so he could see for himself why they were so important to me. The adjustment in child support relative to this child's change of custody was to be negotiated between myself and the opposing counsel. If no agreement could be reached, we would return to court to determine the level of the defendant's child support obligation. What was noted, no complaints or charges were ever filed against the mother for her months of abusive treatment of this child. The court merely took the child from her custody after many months of abuse. And the other three children? They were left in the custody of this acknowledged abusive mother. I must question if Judge Herman deemed this custodial parent unfit relative to her treatment of this child? Perhaps a paradox of family court justice, could a custodial parent be unfit parenting one child and yet deemed fit in parenting for the other three custodial children in the same home? Or would the court argue it was the child who was unfit? Only in New Jersey Family Court.

Opposing counsel and I exchanged letters addressing Paula's child support obligation under the changed circumstances where the one-child was now in my physical custody full time. It was suggested Paula's child support be netted against what was my established level of support. I argued that netting Paula's child support against what I paid failed to establish a record of her obligation to pay support for this child now in my custody. If she lost her job the Probation Department would not even know his client was obligated to pay any child support. I asked for a meeting to discuss several issues including Paula's level of child support; negotiations for my purchase of Paula's interest in the marital home; the visitation schedule; new counseling services Paula advocated for the children; Adriana's possessions in the marital home; and the youngest child's formal schooling that was to begin in September.

Lacking any agreement on the child support issue, I filed a motion to enforce litigant's rights on August 9, 1996, and to also address the fact that the mother had enrolled Molly, now five-years-old, in the Camden school district and not in the local district where the family resided. I also asked the court to have Paula reimburse me for a portion of my child support for the foreign exchange student allowed to live in the marital home for two months during the summer, at the expense of care afforded to my children using my child support. An amended motion dated August 19 included the incident where Paula forced two of the children, Adriana and 8-year-old sister Katie, from the car on a county road to walk some 300 yards home in the head-lights of her car at night. Katie was allowed back into the car after having walked half this distance, Adriana was forced to remain on the road. Michelle told the mother that it was not fair. I'd be curious to know what the police might have said seeing children forced to walk in the headlights of a car. But this issue failed to garner a comment in this Family Court.

Since the change of custody, Adriana attempted about ten visits with her siblings at the marital home. Some forty percent of these failed with Adriana asking me to come and take her home. I noted Molly was now subject to being restrained by the mother, the same physical control used against Adriana. I asked the court to order the mother to never again evict any of the children from her car to walk in front of it; and that the court order the mother undergo a psychological evaluation as to her mental fitness to retain custody of any of these children. The court neither said nor did anything to rein in this mother's abusive treatment of these children.

Paula's effort to take Molly from the local school and enroll her in the Camden school district where she was a teacher's aid was of great concern to me. The local school, just a mile from the home, was well rated. Paula wanted companionship as she traveled the thirty plus miles one-way into Camden. Molly, just entering first grade, would make good company for her on this drive. I suggested she get a mannequin but not take this child into a failed school system; one that had such a completely different culture and language environment. The move afforded this child no advantages.

I also made a counter-offer to Paula to consider no child support payments be required of her in exchange for letting me make the monthly mortgage and property tax payments in place of my child support obligation. One: I feared Paula's financial issues put these required timely payments in jeopardy. I had gotten into the habit of confirming the mortgage and tax payments were made as my name was on the property deed. Two: New Jersey Family Court refused to mandate any accounting for child support payments. Those payments were directed to the custodial parent and the court would not hold the custodial parent accountable as to how those funds were disbursed. Also, Paula's limited income wasted these tax deductions while my child support payments were not a tax deduction. In a financially distressed family situation, these tax benefits should not be wasted. This agreement would eliminate Paula's monthly child support obligation. It would provide me fiscal peace of mind relative to securing the mortgage and tax payments. A win any way I looked at it.

Opposing counsel filed a cross-motion on August 21, 1996, suggesting among other things that Adriana's right to her bedroom furniture be limited; yet a new counseling session at the Family Institute of Philadelphia, the eighth such request for counseling for these children; and modifying my visitation to every other weekend.

With a break in the hearing, I approached opposing counsel, this Catholic priest. Judge Herman had just ruled the custodial parent could place Molly in the school of her choice. I was shocked and devastated by this ruling. How was that decision in the best interest of this child? Desperate, I asked opposing counsel to find out what it would take, anything, that would keep Molly in the local school district and out of Camden's schools? The opposing counsel addressed the issue with Paula and returned within ten minutes. It was agreed, Molly could remain in the local school if I would forgive the $400 arrearage in child support Paula had incurred for the few months Adriana was living with me four days a week. Done! Opposing counsel seemed perturbed by Paula's decision. He had just argued to the count minutes ago the merits of Molly being allowed to attend the school the custodial parent wanted her to attend. Was the best interest of this child really about a $400 debt and nothing else? The child was nothing but a bargaining chip in Paula's world of custodial parenting. I would later tell Molly I bought back her lifetime future for all of $400.

The hearing of August 30, 1996, to address all of the above issues produced the following order, and signed by the court on September 18, 1996: I agreed to pay the mortgage and property taxes as of September 1996 in place of child support payments and shall be considered in satisfaction of his child support obligation; Molly would remain in the local school district; Adriana's bedroom furniture would follow her to her new residence. The court did not address or order Paula could not evict the children from the car. The court denied my reimbursement for the child support used to fund the exchange student living at the home.

I had witnessed a hearing in court some months prior that was to shock me. A young family was in court dealing with the issue of a marital home that had gone into foreclosure. The father, the defendant, was in tears as he explained he had made all the required support payments to maintain the home for the young child. The mother, the court-sanctioned preferred custodial parent, elected not to pay the mortgage but to hoard the support payments for personal benefit. The court stated it could not compel the custodial parent how child support should be spent; the mother controlled the funds and, in this case, elected to not pay the mortgage. The home would proceed into foreclosure. The father's credit record was likewise ruined with such a foreclosure but the court would do nothing. The mother merely asked the court to confirm she could remain in the home until evicted by the bank. Judge Herman answered disgustingly, "I don't care what you do." A custodial parent could take the child support payments and go to Atlantic City every week in the hopes of winning big; there was no accounting in New Jersey for how any custodial parent spent child support funds.

Witnessing that hearing scared the hell out of me. The custodial parent in my case was a known abuser of fiscal responsibility; a manic spender and very self-serving. As mentioned, Paula routinely told the custodial children she had no funds to pay for almost anything and I, the non-custodial father, provided for all such needs. This became an immediate issue that had to be addressed as I wanted the children to remain in the marital home that Paula found to be a "prison" in her mind and words. The agreement to allow me to pay the mortgage and property taxes in place of child support was a game-changer for me. It provided all I wanted, secured the home; and garnered tax deductions for me. I did not understand a system that ignored such financial considerations in these situations.

Opposing counsel and I ironed out our differences from the August 30 court hearing. An order was drafted by counsel and presented to the court for signature on September 5, 1996. In my letter to counsel dated September 5, I thanked him for his efforts in this case. You were the best of the six lawyers to date on this one. I will take care of my children, do not doubt that. I have a moral right and a legal right to protect their interest.

School starting for the girls; Adriana's custody situation settled; hopefully, this case would settle into some degree of calm. I had been in court ten times since January. Ridiculous! Counsel announced he was leaving this case. Paula advised he had to continue to represent her. He advised he did not. We hated to see him go. Paula's various legal representatives appeared quick to leave this case at the first opportunity. Unfortunately, the children and I were stuck with her.

I had to write opposing counsel yet again on September 9, 1996, to address yet another issue. Paula had subsequently received two weekly child support payments after the court agreed I would be responsible for the property mortgage and taxes in place of child support. The Probation Department confirmed weekly checks had been mailed to Paula on August 30 and September 6. I asked Paula to refund these two payments to me, as they were needed to make the mortgage payment by the fifteenth of the month. Paula merely answered "I don't care about the mortgage or the house and could care less if the house went into foreclosure." I knew this to be the case and the decision to allow me to make these payments was a monumental win for me and the children who cared to preserve this home. Paula never refunded me these two child support payments totaling $800 although the court had ordered such payments to stop on August 21, 1996.

The school year started early September and Adriana and I were living in an apartment in Deptford, some fifteen miles away from the marital home and local school. I drove Adriana to school in the morning, left work in time to pick her up when school ended at 3:00 PM, and took her back to the apartment. I then returned to work, just two miles away. A neighbor, a member of the local school board, called me soon after the start of the school year to advise I violated the law. Adriana did not live in the local school district but in the Deptford district, where my apartment was located. I advised this friend I was paying property taxes on a house just two doors away from his and within the district. He advised the law only allowed those who physically lived within the boundaries of the district could send their children to that district's school. I asked how could I afford a second home within this district, the wealthiest in the county? I told him I would look into options and he advised I had until the end of the month to resolve the issue.

I began a frantic search for options as I wanted to keep Adriana in the same school her sisters attended. That weekend, as I drove through the neighborhood after I picked up the other children, I noticed a mobile home park, just a mile away from the school, and situated on a side road almost equidistant between the school and the marital home. I drove through the park and sure enough, there was a home for sale at the park's main entrance with a sign in the window. I approached the home, never having ever been inside one, and an older woman answered. I asked about the selling price and when it might be available for possession? ASAP, as she had lived there some thirty years and was looking to move to a retirement community eight miles away. This was perfect as it would allow me to be within a mile of the other three children at the marital home and it put Adriana physically back within the local school district. We agreed on the $7,500 sales price. I never really noticed this mobile home park as it was located on a road I hardly used and was partly hidden behind trees. By the end of September, we were living in the mobile home within the community, a mile from the school, and a mile from the other children. If I was ever the recipient of good luck, a break in life, this was a God-send.

New Jersey would pass a law some years later to account for divorce situations where parents shared custody of children but lived-in different school districts. The law now allows the family to choose which district they want the children to attend even if they both did not physically live within the same district. That law resolved a difficult issue but did not help me then.

The mobile home was dark inside, with the original rug and dark wall paneling. It had two full baths, and a bedroom at each end of its seventy-foot length; had a large AC window unit that cooled the entire living area; a small kitchen, and a living room. Maybe all of 750 square feet but it was to be our new "home" for the next six years. My sister and a friend helped me pull up the old rugs and we replaced them with a new carpet. We painted the interior walls a bright white to get some light into the place; added new white curtains, put in new tile in the kitchen, and added a washer and dryer. We were living a dream that just a few weeks ago I would have not thought possible. I paid cash so I only needed to pay the monthly ground rent which allowed me to also carry the marital home expenses in my budget. The other girls were also excited to know Adriana would remain in their school and they would see her every day. Acquisition of these new living quarters also alleviated their fears the marital home would need to be sold now that Adriana was living with their father. Too, I was that much closer to the kids should issues arise.

We did not want to call our new home a trailer, or even a mobile home. I came up with the moniker "the house-on-wheels" and we all forever referred to this new home by that name. Things were sure looking up for us. After three years of almost constant conflict, it did not take much to lift our spirits, but this house-on-wheels did all of that and we loved it. Nothing fancy but it was our new home for Adriana and me.

# 18

# A NEW JUDGE AND WE START
# ALL OVER

Sometime in the last quarter of 1996, in a general reassignment of judges within the various county courts, Judge Herman was reassigned out of family court to the criminal division. I hated to see him go as I believed he had begun to see the situation this family lived under. I wrote to thank him for what he had done for the welfare of my children. Specifically, I thanked him for getting Adriana out of the mother's custody and into my care; I thanked him for agreeing the marital home need not be sold; that I could exchange the payment of the mortgage and property taxes for the child support obligation. I would see Judge Herman several times on back-to-school nights as his son was in class with Molly at the regional middle and high schools. Although many fathers had issues with Judge Herman's handling of their cases, I can say at this time he did what he did to save a bad situation for me and my children. He received tenure on the judicial bench once he was reassigned out of the family court and into the more "civilized" environment of criminal court.

A new judge was assigned to our case, Judge Tomasello, and how best for Paula to introduce him to this case than to file another DV complaint against me. Paula walked into the courthouse office on May 7, 1997, and swore out a complaint against me. The complaint stated, "defendant(me) knowingly and recklessly caused bodily injury to the plaintiff (Paula) specifically by hitting the plaintiff with a kitchen metal pot which was thrown by the defendant striking her lower left leg." The complaint was served upon me by a knock on the door at the house-on-wheels that same evening. A local police officer handed me the complaint and told me to report to the family court to answer this charge on July 10, 1997. So here we go again. Just when we hoped things might have settled down Paula needed to stir the pot, excuse the pun.

The reality of the new circumstance was, having taken up residence in the house-on-wheels just a mile from the marital residence, I saw the children more and more. The two younger children, Katie and Molly, went to a sitter's home in the mornings just five houses away from the marital home as did several other children from local families. The school bus stopped at this neighbor's house to pick up as many as ten children from the neighborhood. My two youngest children had noted their preference for the lunches I made for them on Wednesday night visits for Thursday's school lunch, as it included a favorite sandwich on Italian rolls; a desert snack of their choice, and a drink box. Too, I would draw stick figures on the brown lunch bags in some stage of action. I made a habit of dropping off daily lunches for the girls at the sitter's in the mornings and would visit with them until the school bus arrived some fifteen minutes later. Soon enough, the girls noted they had not had breakfast so I began to bring a breakfast snack of grapes, orange slices, something that would carry them until lunch.

On May 23, 1997, Paula wrote me a note outlining her unilateral modification of the visitation schedule that would have her attending night classes for the summer months and the new school year beginning in September. So much for those court-sanctioned visitation schedules. Her new schedule outlined classes until 7:50 PM and to 10:00 PM on two different nights. Too, the after-school sitter asked the children to be picked up by 5:30 PM so she could enjoy time alone with her family. Could I agree to pick up the children? Of course, I took every opportunity to be with the children; even suggesting she leave them with me instead of the many babysitters she had utilized over the years. Judge Herman had ruled I was to be given the first option for the care of these children. Not knowing much of what Paula was doing or when all I cared most about was that the children got home promptly and safely after school.

Relative to this flying pot incident, I had called the home this May evening for my daily phone call. At 5:30 PM, Michelle, all of 13 years, said she was the only one home; she had not heard from the mother and the youngest sister was at the sitter's and the other at a friend's home waiting for the mother to pick them up. I called again at 6 PM and again at 6:30 PM and still no word from the mother as to when she would be home. I told Michelle I would go get the two younger sisters who were located at homes about five miles apart and then come and get her and bring them all to my place. I would feed them dinner and we would wait for the mother to show up. We arrived back at the house-on-wheels and I, pressed for time, decided the quickest meal was spaghetti and meatballs.

All four kids sitting at the dining table at about 7:15 PM and having just been served the meal, Paula charged into my home. In a very agitated voice, she yelled that the kids did not belong there, and instructed the three to get into her car, now! I asked Paula to let them eat the meal served on their plates and I would return them to the house soon thereafter. I also reminded her the children could not be left at the neighbors' hours after school waiting for her unannounced return. No, get out, she demanded. Standing just three feet away from me in the small kitchen, I asked again if she would allow the kids to eat the meal. I would bring them back to the house. No, was her response. As the incident raised the level of anxiety amongst the four children, I dropped the empty pot to the floor of the kitchen in disgust. They left and Adriana and I were left in total dismay at what we had just experienced.

We showed up in family court on May 29, 1997, with newly assigned Judge Tomasello to decide justice. Paula, never under oath, to tell the truth, was asked to describe what had happened and she said I threw a pot and hit her on her lower leg causing a bruise. I told the court this was more of the same we had endured over the prior four-plus years; false claims that looked to put me in jeopardy. Judge Tomasello then stated, "as far as he was concerned, this case starts today." I was then told to give my version of this incident and I noted: "if I had wanted to hit her, I would have, she was just three feet away."

The court took a breath to announce its decision; based upon the "preponderance of the evidence," I was "guilty" of domestic violence. My only comment to the judge was "this is not like TV" to which he responded, "no, it is not." But if it was on TV it would be considered a comedy at best or black-humor at worst. The verdict in this "trial" reminded me again of justice, Ox-Bow style; her word against mine, and I had no right to justice, surely not in family court. No witnesses, no additional facts needed. What evidence? A woman's word against that of the man. I was to be advised that a second conviction of domestic violence against a TRO was, under New Jersey justice, a mandatory thirty days in jail. Now that caught my attention knowing Paula's propensity to abuse justice at every chance. The court then took it upon itself to modify the TRO into a Final Restraining Order (FRO) negating any chance of ever getting the restraining order lifted. This would be the only initiative this judge ever offered in this case.

In reality, this family court system would not have agreed to lift this restraining order anyway and surely not with Paula's desire to see me in jail. The restraining order was the weapon of choice in family court. The court then agreed to my request that I have the children when there were a few instances of a fifth weekend in a month. On such dates, this adjudged violent father would have additional time with his children, and the mother is relieved of that much more responsibility. Now that made perfect sense in the realm of family court justice. Guilty of domestic violence but at least the court did not think me violent. This mother was not charged with assault after having previously admitting to punching and tackling a child in her custody. Those incidents, like so much of what this mother did or didn't do, were just ignored by this court.

I wrote a letter to Paula and Judge Tomasello dated May 29, 1997, announcing I was voluntarily relinquishing my "right" to visitation with my three non-custodial children. This most recent trial that found me guilty of domestic violence found me defenseless against any complaints this woman could file. I would continue to bring Adriana to the home so she could visit with her sisters; I would look to maintain my daily phone calls with the other three children, but I would not continue with my scheduled visitations with the non-custodial children. I would not adopt my schedule to facilitate Paula's schedule; I would no longer feed the children or look to provide for them because the mother does not. I accused the court of bias against fathers. I would refer the home situation to DYFS, New Jersey's failed child care bureaucracy but expected nothing from them as they had previously refused to intercede when Adriana was being routinely physically assaulted by the mother.

Nothing changed but for the fact, I had relinquished my visits with the three other children. I felt I could not protect myself from whatever situation might present itself on such visits to the marital home. Adriana and I suffered through these missed visits. I'm sure the three children wanted the time to get out of the home their mother managed and go with me for what could best be described as a "normal" time of relaxation; being fed meals; and just out from under the whims of the mentally ill mother. Michelle soon remarked to Adriana "daddy doesn't love us anymore." Enough, I could not take the missed visits with the girls and they surely wanted to go with me. On Saturday, June 21, 1997, I returned to the marital home at 9:00 AM to again take part in my scheduled visitation. I remained in the car, parked some 100 feet down the driveway of the residence. The three children ran from the home to greet me and I asked them to get ready to come with me for our day of visitation. Within minutes, the children, still about in the driveway, advised a police car had pulled in behind my car. The police officer approached and stated Paula had called in a complaint that I was at the home in violation of the visitation order; the same schedule in place since March 1993 and just modified in an order signed by the court on June 19, 1997. I advised there was an order that spelled out my visitation rights, even as of the last hearing, and signed two days ago. The officer advised he would go into the home and if Paula presented evidence contrary to what I had stated I would be arrested and taken to the county jail.

The officer exited the home with a copy of the FRO, received just yesterday in the mail. Paula's interpretation of this order was that it took most of my visitation rights away as this FRO noted: "visitation, as ordered, is modified to permit visitation when there was a fifth Friday in a month." This order granted me these fifth weekends in a month as additional visitation with my children not my only visitation with my children. I explained to the officer the mother had deliberately distorted the facts of this referenced change, as it only applied to those few months that had the fifth weekend. Unfortunately, but to no surprise, Paula could not produce the original court order that clearly defined the complete visitation schedule.

The officer then produced a copy of my May 29 letter wherein I relinquished my visitation with these children because I could not protect myself from Paula's many erroneous claims against me. I advised the officer the letter had no legal standing as it was not a part of any court order. If anything, ironically, my letter proved my point, I was defenseless against Paula's charges. To further highlight the absurdity of Paula's reference to this new ruling on the visitation schedule, I noted the FRO referenced "the defendant was barred from the residence." I questioned the paradox of their interpretation of this FRO relative to the claim I only had visitation with these children on the fifth weekend of any month. If barred from the residence yet entitled to the referenced visitation, how was I to exercise that visitation if I could not accept the children at this residence? The FRO made no mention of any alternate pick-up location. Threatened again by the officer, I left the home without the children in tow. The officer did not want to debate the merits of either party's claim but ordered me off the property and not to return without a court defined visitation order.

Addressing this very threatening situation, and yet another example of Paula's lies and the abuse of facts to expose me to extreme jeopardy, I filed a motion to enforce litigant's rights on June 25 for a hearing on July 18, 1997. The court's order of that day noted: "visitation reinstituted for the defendant." The fact was my visitation had never been discontinued or abated. Paula lied to the police about what was the visitation schedule. My request to allow two of the children to visit an aunt in Utah for two weeks was granted. My application asked that Paula be held in contempt of court and was denied. No surprise.

Sitting in family court awaiting your case to be called, you had the opportunity to experience justice dispensed. All watched, listened as any judge had their irrational moments on various issues of the day, and I would surely agree I was the recipient of a fair share of such irrationality. One case in front of Judge Tomasello was that of an ex-wife who reported she was in line at an intersection near her residence waiting for traffic to clear. While waiting, this woman complained the ex in her relationship drove through the intersection, never acknowledging seeing her. The woman claimed she felt threatened just seeing the ex-randomly pass through this intersection. The ex, not previously charged in any domestic violence incident, explained he was on his way home to his new residence and had not noticed the ex-wife. This judge ordered him to find a new way home that did not take him through this intersection. I found this ruling to border on the ridiculous. Did this man not have the right to use public roads near his new home? The court did not rule he was not allowed to live within miles of this woman, and their passing at this intersection was random. He was not parked at the intersection to stalk, accost her. Perhaps the woman should move her residence if she felt so threatened.

Another incident of note was heard by Judge Herman. An ex-wife had filed a complaint alleging the ex-husband had failed to make scheduled child support payments. The man explained he mailed all such support payments weekly by certified mail so there would be no issue of non-payment. All payments had been returned as "unclaimed." The judge ordered the man to open the evidenced envelopes and the required support check fell out of each. Judge Herman admonished the woman for her conduct. This was a perfect example of why child support payments were pushed onto the electronic payment system. The level of games was matched only by one's imagination. I too experienced such a claim in the early stage of this marital separation. I left the weekly support payment in the baby's car seat. I was accused of non-payment.

A comment in the *Notable and Quotable of the Wall Street Journal* dated June 9, 1997, extracted from an issue of Women's Quarterly, referenced:

> Pennsylvania's Protection from Abuse Act (is) a well-intentioned and useful weapon in the fight against domestic violence, but all too often a 'weapon of opportunity' in the hands of vengeful spouses and opportunistic lawyers seeking to gain the upper hand in divorce and custody cases. Indeed, indiscriminate use of the act, which allows a wife to obtain a 'protective order' against her potentially violent mate, maybe fueling the domestic violence it was designed to quell. As a result, many women are unwittingly discovering that taking out a protection order against their husbands or lovers may incite violence- sometimes with tragic consequences...
>
> The problem may not be that the law doesn't work, but that it works too well. Protection orders are intentionally convenient, cheap, and easy to obtain; but convenient, cheap, easy justice comes at a price.

It sounds like some old cowboy lynching.

> The act contains civil remedies for criminal behavior (bodily injury, rape, spousal assault) but lacks the due process guarantees, the moral authority, and the persuasive force of the criminal law. A protection order is a legal hybrid, neither fish nor fowl. Thus, a plaintiff who alleges immediate and present danger of abuse may, without a court hearing, be granted 'such temporary order as the court deems necessary to protect the plaintiff or minor children'. In layman's terms, a spouse or partner can find themselves out on the street on nothing more than the word of an angry partner. By the time the hearing is held, reputations, careers, and families may be in ruin. Insult is added

to injury when the charges are later dropped or dismissed (as is often the case).

Paula's initial complaint against me was heard and dismissed but I was left out on the street. A crime perpetrated by another crime. No truer words are spoken to define the abuse of the filing of a restraining order on the word of a woman who seeks to gain the upper hand in a custody and divorce case. This was family court justice at its worst.

The flying-pot experience behind me, I was in the house-on-wheels, and about a week later there was a knock on the door at 8:00 PM. A local police officer served me with yet another complaint. I assumed Paula felt emboldened with the guilty verdict issued in family court that she now sought to up the ante and pressed for a criminal charge of assault by flying pot in the local municipal court. The hearing date was two weeks away. I arrived for the hearing and the 4:00 PM roll call of the scheduled cases. Typical cases heard in these municipal courts are traffic violations; disputes between neighbors; and might I suggest flying pots in the neighborhood. Our case was called for the hearing a little after 5:00 PM and Paula was late as usual. A no-show, the case was dismissed by the court. As I pulled out of the municipal building's driveway at 5:30 PM, Paula was seen driving in. I said nothing and continued my exit. At about 8:00 PM that evening there was again a knock on the door and the local police served me with yet another complaint of the alleged assault by the flying pot. I noted to the officer the court had dismissed the charge just hours before. I was told the charge was reinstated upon Paula's late arrival.

I again made my way to the municipal court for the rescheduled hearing two weeks later. I told Adriana she should come and watch "a civics lesson" in action; see cases being heard and what people say and do at such efforts seeking justice. Paula was there on time for this hearing. Finally, our case was called near 6:00 PM; the parties identified for the record; I was representing myself pro se, and the Municipal Prosecutor would prosecute Paula's case. The prosecutor was my barber's son from the town where I grew up. This prosecutor did not know me. Bringing nothing more than my wits, the case opened with Paula stating the child, Adriana, was in the court, and children were not allowed in court hearings. Well, that was the rule in family court but this was the municipal court. I advised the court "she was my witness" to the alleged assault. Now, I had no notion to call Adriana for anything but I could not give Paula an easy win out of the gate. The judge agreed I was entitled to my witness and Adriana was asked to please exit the courtroom and sit in the adjoining room where the local police officer who took Paula's complaint was seated. The officer knew Adriana from school.

Administrative issues resolved, the prosecutor placed Paula under oath (strange but interesting) and she proceeded to tell the story she conjured up of this alleged assault that won the day in family court. No questions needed to be asked or desired in that exercise of injustice. Paula reported she entered my home at 7:15 PM, no knock, and demanded the children leave the premises immediately. She had custody of the three children. Angry at the situation, I threw the pot at her striking her lower leg. The next day she filed a complaint of assault against me at the local police station. The prosecutor then called the police officer who had taken Paula's complaint and asked him a few basic questions. He then presented pictures taken of the bruise that reportedly evidenced the alleged assault. The officer was then excused to the waiting room.

Ok, I admit her story made me look guilty, but then I was allowed to mount my defense; not like in family court. I had nothing but my instincts and facts as I knew them and told the court I had but one question of the plaintiff. "Had the plaintiff advised the police officer that she had fallen the prior day at the schoolyard and had bruised her leg?" Paula answered "yes." I had not seen any pictures and didn't know much of anything about the bruise on her lower leg. The children had mentioned the mother had fallen and bruised her leg at the school just the day before the alleged incident at the house-on-wheels. I had no more questions for the plaintiff. I advised the court I wished to call the police officer back into the courtroom and upon his taking up the position I noted I had but one question for him. "Had the plaintiff advised him that she had fallen in a schoolyard the previous day and had bruised her leg?" He answered "no." I glanced at the judge and saw him roll his eyes and I then dismissed the officer; "I had no more questions, Your Honor." The seasoned prosecutor looked a little stunned.

Paula's allegation being a lower-level criminal charge, a misdemeanor, Municipal Court weighs guilt based on evidence and facts, and not gender bias. To my surprise and dismay, the judge then announced he would call the witness to the alleged crime, Adriana, and only he would ask her questions. Adriana was brought in and seated at the table and the judge was very careful to lower her level of anxiety as her appearance was surely not something I had ever imagined or anticipated. My claim that "she is my witness" was just an afterthought to Paula's effort to have Adriana removed from the courtroom. The judge went through some basic introductory questions and then asked this child to give "an eyewitness" account of the flying pot incident. Had the pot hit the plaintiff? No, the pot was dropped to the floor by her father in disgust and it slid a short distance but surely did not hit her mother. The judge then pronounced me "not guilty." I gathered Adriana and we were out of there before Paula and the prosecutor could absorb the hit in the case of the flying pot. This local prosecutor was subsequently appointed as a family court Judge in Gloucester County.

Paula soon requested my agreement to allow the children to go to yet another counseling service she had found, the ninth I had counted to date. I denied her request but did suggest she consider reentering the medical therapy she walked away from at the Mood Clinic some years ago. Maybe even get a prescription for a truth serum.

Paula wrote letters to me on August 11 and the 15th asking for yet another change in the weekly visitation schedule to suit her scheduling conflicts. The latter communication referenced the broken lawn tractor and questioned if I was coming to the home to fix it? These requests from a woman who calls the police on me at will and then filed yet another complaint just weeks ago. I did not respond to these requests. Similar letters dated in September advised she had an invitation to a dinner party and Paula would allow the three children to spend that Friday overnight with me. She then advised a neighbor would be watching the children every Friday and I could pick them up there for my scheduled visitation. The girls asked if they could spend all Friday nights with me rather than waiting at a neighbor's house for her return. Again, Paula asked me to fix the tractor, and take care of the lawn as allowed by prior court order.

A Wall Street Journal article dated October 3, 1997, headlined *More Dads Raise Families Without Mom*, noting "deadbeat dads may dominate the headlines, but another type of father is emerging: the fastest-growing type of family today is headed by a single father. The number of single dads with custody of their children has exploded to 1.86 million in 1996 from 393,000 in 1970, according to the census bureau surveys. Altogether, five percent of families with children under eighteen are headed by single fathers today, up from one percent a generation ago."

The article commented that "the law has become friendlier to parental custody." There has been a "substantial change" in state laws and judicial opinions away from a presumption in favor of the mother. "The overwhelming majority of states now simply have a best-interest-in-the-child standard. Still, fathers rarely won custody without the mother's consent." New Jersey's interests were surely aligned with the mother and the tender years' doctrine was still the prevailing law of this family court.

These statistics and trends fell on deaf ears and were victims of the entrenched bias in the New Jersey Family Court. This court catered to all of this mother's whims, actions, and misdeeds. Yet when I filed motions alleging the mother failed in many areas of custodial care, Judge Tomasello stated "I am not a fact finder." No heat in the home; limited meals provided; a record of physical abuse of these children; this judge demanded I present my claims to DYFS, New Jersey's equivalent of a failed child welfare agency. If DYFS saw an issue then they would be the impetus for a complaint, not me, the non-custodial father. We noted we called DYFS and they advised: "If things are that bad take your claim to family court." The hypocrisy of this court and this judge for "what is in the best interest of (my) children" was only matched by my contempt for his unwillingness to do what he had a moral obligation to do. This judge would fail me, the children, justice on many occasions.

Was this judge not a "fact-finder" when he found me guilty of domestic violence in the case of the flying pot? There is no jury in these proceedings but this judge. Who else to weigh in on the truthfulness, validity of all the statements made to this court in oral and written presentations if not this judge? Yet Paula made one false, unsupported allegation against me, no questions asked, and this same judge, the "I'm not a fact-finder" judge, weighed in and found me guilty. I agreed there were no facts in that hearing other than a statement of truth versus a false statement and I was found guilty. Four years earlier, Paula filed a DV complaint against me and I was removed from my home and children before a question was asked. The court required no third party to confirm her complaint.

In December 1997, the children complained the house was very cold; that they were walking around the home wrapped in blankets and used sleeping bags at night to try to keep warm. Hearing this, I called the fuel oil supplier and ordered fuel oil to be delivered to the house. I assumed Paula did not have the funds to pay for oil. On delivery, I was advised the 275-gallon tank only took fifty gallons. Not an oil supply issue, I then called the local Chief of Police, who had asked me to reach out to him in any dispute to reduce the level of conflict at this home. The same chief who escorted me out of this home in March 1993.

I advised the chief the children complained of the home being cold and he asked the name of the oil service. He called the service and requested they visit the home under some pretense to check on the heater. The repairman showed up, no heat in the home, he repaired the furnace. I paid the $210 billing. A few days later the kids again reported no heat in the home. Again, I called the chief who again called the repair service and asked them to follow up at this home as to any service issues. Again, this service visit confirmed a new issue and a $284 bill was generated. I paid that bill too but at least the home now had heat in late December weather. The chief advised me repairs had been made but questioned "what is wrong with that woman?" The chief asked, "who does not look to fix a heater in a cold December in New Jersey?" I told him the children and I have had to live with her for these many years while she ignored reality. The chief asked me to continue to use him to facilitate the resolution of issues and I appreciated his concern for my children. The chief advised, "stay away from her." I merely answered, "but she has my children."

# 19

# YET ANOTHER CUSTODY TRIAL. WHY NOT?

O n November 19, 1997, I filed yet another motion seeking a change of custody of the three children who lived at the marital home. This motion would be considered by Judge Tomasello, so I thought it necessary to spell out the case history in support of my argument why I should be considered the parent most capable to care for these children. I needed to convince this court of a standard of the law that there had been "a change in circumstances" relative to the original custody agreement.

I noted the custody of Adriana had been changed to my care due to Paula's physical abuse of this child and her continued mistreatment by denying her access to her sisters; Paula's financial condition had continued to deteriorate such that I, the father, now provided most of their needs not afforded by the mother; I referenced the prior custody effort had to be abandoned due to the evaluator's misdeeds, which were precipitated, if not coordinated, by Paula's prior counsel; Paula had recently left her employment with a state agency at $18,000 a year to take another job that paid $12,000 with fewer benefits; Paula acknowledged she had credit card debts totaling $10,000 and referenced being "harassed" for payment, and her new job did not provide for three months of summer employment; she bought new bedding in an effort to eradicate a head lice infestation that lasted six months; Paula admitted to keeping the home at sixty degrees during the prior winter as she could not afford oil to heat the home and the children used sleeping bags to keep warm.

I was now purchasing all the new clothing for the children totaling some $3,400 over the last two years and Paula admitted her take-home pay was consumed by paying off debt and new car purchase. Paula acknowledged she only bought bread and milk with other food staples provided by church food banks and neighbors; that it was me who was taking the oldest, non-custodial child to the two-year orthodontist treatment Paula could not fit into her schedule; I now meet my two youngest children in the morning and give them fruits for breakfast snacks as they get no breakfast at the home; I was providing daily homemade lunches as Paula qualified for free lunches under a federal program, Paula does not make lunches for the children; I was providing all financial resources for all other school expenses for supplies, day trips, projects; Paula's efforts over several years to complete her education has resulted with a "new" unsanctioned visitation schedule that has the children spending even greater time with me as Paula is away for school or other social calls (fifteen specific dates were listed identifying Paula having relinquished custody of the children to me for the period August 15, 1997 thru November 10, 1997); Paula failed to maintain the marital property such that it has fallen into general disrepair. I asked that the two youngest tax-dependent children be assigned to me as tax dependents as I provided for their substantial support and care.

Paula sought the services of a fifth lawyer. The first I heard from this new attorney was his call to me suggesting an agreement might be worked out between the parties. He wrote the court on December 11, 1997, asking for an adjournment of my motion to be heard on January 9, 1998. I wrote a letter to opposing counsel on December 15, 1997 spelling out my concerns and requested a serious effort to bring this five-year saga to an end. I acknowledged Paula's obvious financial issues and her longstanding effort to complete her education and my concern for the welfare of my four children. I would not demand any immediate child support payment but allow her to accrue such payments against any home equity she would earn while I took possession of the marital home. I admitted to being suspicious of their efforts but hoped this to be a legitimate effort to resolve this case. It was not.

I received a letter from the court's law clerk on January 6, 1998, advising the judge had decided to send this matter to the court's mediator for mediation. A January 20 date was set for that mediation review. I filed an amended motion dated January 8 contesting the court's order that this case is referred to the mediator. Specifically, I noted I was seeking a trial not more mediation in this case; that such delays in the past produced little benefit for my children but more delays of a hearing of the facts of this case. This same court had recently suggested this father take his complaints of child neglect to DYFS as the court would only act upon specific recommendations by DYFS. DYFS's response was "if the situation was as dire as you presented it to be, you should seek justice in family court." DYFS refused to get involved in this case.

My motion argued opposing counsel had failed to answer the recent motion within the required date, noting they did not contest my allegations but merely looked to defer action at the expense of the children. Having been deferred 28 days to date, they had yet to answer the motion dated November 19, 1997, or initiate any communication on the channel they had suggested on the phone call of December 11, 1997. Mediation, in this case, had been fraught with Paula's efforts to contaminate such efforts. Finally, I advised I would file an appeal of the court's effort at yet another mediation, as such mediation would not provide heat for the custodial children; mediation would not feed the children; mediation will not bring the sisters together in one home; mediation would not cloth the children; mediation will not address the mother's dire financial condition; mediation will not resolve most of the issues of this case.

On January 9, 1998, the court ordered the parties to submit within ten days the names of three custody evaluators; parenting plans, and that a plenary hearing would be set on the issue of custody. Likewise, the judge made a particular point to note the custody trial required the Case Information Statement (CIS) needed to be completed in detail, by court rule. The CIS was a state-developed financial information record of about ten pages in length requiring a complete detail of each parties' assets, debts, and a detailed accounting of monthly expenses and all sources of income. The CIS required all income and expenses to be detailed by a weekly calculation as compared to monthly reporting. For example, an annual expense for auto insurance would be calculated by dividing it by fifty-two weeks and not twelve-monthly premiums. Since child support was calculated based on a level of weekly income, the CIS required all family expenses to be converted to a weekly dollar value.

On January 19, 1998, I submitted the names of three prospective evaluators. Opposing counsel produced their candidates' list on January 23. The court's clerk advised me by a phone call that the hearing had been postponed to March 18, 1998. This change of date was prompted by opposing counsel having called the court clerk, ex parte (without notice to me), and asked the hearing date be changed. I timely filed a parenting plan and completed the CIS as required.

A February 17, 1998 letter from opposing counsel to the court confirmed that the hearing of March 18 had again been rescheduled to May 20, 1998. Again, I was not a party to any such effort and was not agreeable to the date changes for the custody hearing. I wrote Judge Tomasello on February 17 to address these ex parte efforts by opposing counsel to defer scheduled hearings. I got no response from the court. Likewise, my letter to the court dated February 18 noted all three of the evaluators I had submitted for consideration required the court to clarify, in writing, what was expected of them for this evaluation. Who was to be or could be evaluated in this effort; what test or tests were to be given and to whom; access to all medical records of the principals in this custody evaluation allowed? The court never issued a response that defined the parameters of this evaluation process.

I wrote a letter dated March 3, 1998, to Judge DeSimone, Chief Judge of the Vicinage that covered three South Jersey counties. I expressed my frustrations at getting due process in my dealings with this family court. I noted being pro se and had filed a motion for a change of custody for my three children, but that court dates were being arbitrarily changed by the ex parte efforts of opposing counsel. I was merely advised after-the-fact that a scheduled court date had been changed. Too, opposing counsel had yet to submit a notice of substitution of attorney four months into having made an appearance in written responses in this case. I worried that having never officially entered this case he might now leave the case. I noted I would be in court for the immediate hearing date of April 3 and would ignore the most recent noted change of the hearing date to May 20, 1998. Judge DeSimone responded that my correspondence had been forwarded to Judge Tomasello and the local Family Division Manager.

Judge Tomasello wrote to opposing counsel and me on March 17 to advise "a case management conference would be held March 24 at 9:30 A.M., mark your calendars accordingly." I arrived for the hearing on March 24 and there sat Judge Tomasello but no opposing counsel. I believe the judge was embarrassed, as well he should have been. His law clerk participated in these arbitrary changes of hearing dates without any consideration with me. My letter to Judge DeSimone got the issue addressed; there were to be no more postponements. The judge called the opposing counsel's law office from the bench and asked why he was not in court for this scheduled hearing? Opposing counsel replied his secretary was on vacation and he never got the notice. I guess we know why they never ask attorneys to take an oath, to tell the truth. The hearing was held with opposing counsel hanging on the phone. The custody trial was scheduled for May 20, 1998. No more unauthorized, ex parte orchestrated delays.

As arbitrary as picking a winning lottery ticket is the selection process for choosing those who present themselves as professional evaluators in child custody cases. There is no screening process by the courts; these charlatans merely get on the list or, as with the first custody trial, I found him in the phone book. Both sides suggested the names of candidates. Why or how this evaluator was chosen is lost to my memory. Perhaps chosen because of his quoted rate; availability;

some reference to professional qualifications, who knows. Court Rule 5:3-3 notes "the court shall establish the scope of the expert's assignment in the order of appointment." Two of the three evaluators I had proposed required certain psychological testing of the parents. This third evaluator's plan noted significant time dedicated to interviewing the parents and children and also noted: "parents may also be required to be evaluated with psychological testing." Judge Tomasello set no such parameters for this custody evaluation although court rules required the court to define what specific efforts were to be done in any such evaluation. One of the evaluators I had nominated was chosen to perform this custody evaluation.

In a seminal custody case of New Jersey family law, Lepis v. Lepis, the Appellate Court stated custody evaluations are serious endeavors, which require a forensic custody evaluator "to assess the personality and cognitive functioning of the person being examined to assist the court in a best interest determination." The evaluator chosen for this custody trial, with no formal direction from the court, was left to do or not do anything in his evaluation process to justify his expert opinion. This professional's effort could at best be described as littered with fraud. I alleged so in my subsequent complaint filed August 14, 1998, with the New Jersey Division of Consumer Affairs, Board of Psychological Examiners. My complaint highlighted my concerns with the work product and the testimony of this evaluator. The professional work consisted of nothing more than a total of four interviews with the parents and the children for a total of four hours. One such session included all of the family members. No psychological testing was done; no, he did not secure Paula's medical records from Mood Clinic or from the psychiatrist who had been working with Paula for the past three years or more. The evaluation consisted of nothing more than a general discussion of family issues. One could have garnered as much sitting at a table in a beer hall.

At the opening of this trial, I told the judge that Paula had not completed the CIS in any detail as he required was a court rule in the pre-trial hearing weeks ago. Her CIS was all but blank sheets except for a few lines about her income with almost no accounting for any of her expenses, assets, or debts. My CIS was completed in detail. The judge then held up a CIS and questioned me "who would complete such a report but an accountant type?" So much for his demand, the CIS be completed in detail as required by court rules. But this was the family court.

So, let the trial begin. The evaluator made several false statements at the start of the trial. Working from a copy of his evaluation report, I called him as a witness. He reported having testified previously in this court. Judge Tomasello said "no, he had never seen him before." The evaluator then noted his office had received a call from the judge, who has read this report, required him to be present for this custody trial. Again, the Judge noted he had not seen or read the evaluation report and surely would not have called him to court. That was the prerogative of either of the parties. It was subsequently disclosed opposing counsel made the call to this evaluator advising him to be in court for this trial. Then there was a reference on his Curriculum Vitae listing himself as a Fellow, Professional Academy of Custody Evaluators, and a Registered Custody Evaluator. I called both New Jersey and Pennsylvania licensing boards and the New Jersey Psychological Association for information about this referenced "Academy." No one knew or had ever heard of any such academy much less its professional standards to achieve the acclaimed title of Fellow. No one knew of any registry of custody evaluators.

As my witness, I then started to pick apart his evaluation report which made several dubious claims. No psychological exams had been administered by him as part of his evaluation, although Judge Herman noted they were standard practice in custody trials. His evaluation report made mention that I had no auto accidents in the last twenty-five years and that Paula had no accidents in five years. No, he was not aware that Paula had totaled two cars and had four other auto accidents in the last ten years. He only asked for the last five years and I happened to note my record dating back twenty-five years. What auto accidents had to do with a custody evaluation was best answered in the evaluator's Curriculum Vitae? His professional work referenced counseling accident victims. Are we headed for a train wreck?

Now to get into some of the more serious stuff. He admitted he did not get Paula's medical records from the Mood Clinic. Although a resident of a Philadelphia suburb, and a psychologist with a Ph.D., he admitted to never having heard of the Mood Clinic. Might I suggest the equivalent of an auto mechanic never having heard of Craftsman tools? His report noted as "background information" the mother "reports that when she was in marital counseling in 1988 her counselor believed her to be depressed; she was seen at the Mood Clinic at the University of Pennsylvania for an evaluation. She states that she was diagnosed as having bipolar disorder and was prescribed Lithium. She reports she never followed through with taking the medication." Concerning her depression, the mother stated, "I always have depression, but it's more being overwhelmed with the situation." For the past four years, the mother has been seeing a psychologist twice a month. No, this evaluator made no effort to seek the records relative to that professional counseling. Further comments included she acknowledged "I am struggling financially. I am considering bankruptcy." It is then reported "they (children) have hand-me-downs from me, new clothes from him (father)." "The home is not dirty or infested." She works full time "there are nights I nearly collapse and no cleaning gets done." One might have asked who cooks meals on such nights?

Sitting through many hearings in family court awaiting my case to be called, drug and alcohol abuse were acknowledged social ills that contributed to much family discourse. Most agree that these are obvious issues that affect a family. Here, in this custody trial, a professional evaluator ignores a major mental illness and the mother admits its effects on her life while also admitting she elected to ignore the treatment of the illness. His recommendation, keep the children under the mother's care that is acknowledged by herself to be somewhat limited. The evaluator's report also made comments relative to his interviews with the children including the oldest child, in eighth grade. Michelle is quoted "I like seeing (dad) on weekends. There are times I want to see him more, but overall, I like how it is now." Asked about living with her mother this child stated "I pretty much like being there because I'm with my mom. My mom is a close friend of mine, not just a mom." One thing she did not like was the mother has "lessened up" on keeping the house neat. As for remarks about her father's home, this child noted "my dad is the security. He is always there for us. He's dependable. He helps us with our homework. He's on a schedule. He's reliable." "I just love him. He is always there." One of the things she did not like at her father's house was that it "lacked spontaneity." Her father was a perfectionist who pushes us hard to get those "As."

The evaluator's report commented on his interview with Adriana, the child who Judge Herman removed from the mother's custody last year. Adriana is quoted as "my mom and I don't get along." As for her father, she noted "I get along with my dad better...we don't fight and it's calmer. It's more fun living with him." She mentioned numerous things she did not like at the mother's house including "we were always at babysitters; but when she was home, she'd just lie on the couch and sleeps. Some nights we would not have dinner." Adriana was asked to rate each parent on a scale of zero to one hundred. "She felt that her father would get a score of one hundred and that her mother would get a score of zero." The evaluation report made no comments or even acknowledged the physical and emotional abuse the mother inflicted on this child that prompted the court to remove her from the mother's custody. There was no discussion of why she did not live with the mother or why she rated her mother a zero as to parenting skills.

The evaluation report's comments relative to interviews with the two youngest children, aged eleven and seven, were all but non-descript, useless babble that included nothing about the children's emotional contact with the mother, or physical well-being but noted that they were both reportedly good students.

In my continued cross-examination, I asked this evaluator "is bipolar disorder a mental illness caused by a chemical imbalance in the brain?" He answered, "that is one theory." I questioned what might be another theory? He answered, "bipolar disorder was stress-induced." He then testified "(mother) was asymptomatic relative to the bipolar disorder illness." I can only presume my line of questioning struck a nerve as opposing counsel began to question the "form" of all the questions I asked. Three, four times I tried to rephrase three or four questions, and each time opposing counsel objected, and each time the court sustained his objection.

His recommendations stated he thought it best to allow the second child to remain in the custody of the father. He then recommended the other three children remain in the mother's custody. He did recommend the father be allowed all the additional time with his children in the mother's absence. He then explained his rationale for his recommendations. "The oldest child found the mother to be not only a good parent but also a good friend to her." "Both parents are doing a good job of parenting, albeit in different and complementary ways." "It is the father who would more likely jeopardize the other parent's relationship with the children and discourage it rather than encourage it. I feel it would be better for the children to be with the father, rather than at home alone, on those evenings that the mother is at school." The father "expressed concerns that the mother was treated for bipolar disorder in 1988, and that she was arrested for shoplifting. I find no indication of any problems similar to those since that time and no indication that her parenting has been affected in any way by such a disorder since that time as well." He might have thought to ask what was the purpose of the mother's referenced four-year-long effort at psychological counseling. He never sought those records either. So, we are to continue the status-quo, the mother is to remain protected by the system, and the dad is to just keep taking care of things when mom fails to do her share. The fix was in. Frustrated that the court allowed opposing counsel's numerous objections to my posed questions. I asked for a break in the proceedings so I could collect my thoughts. It was near noon, the court agreed and we adjourned for a lunch break.

I met with my two sisters who were sitting in the courtroom watching the proceedings. I was upset and disgusted that the "expert" so blatantly dismissed this mental illness issue as something akin to the common cold; stress-induced, he testified. Paula's conduct weighed little against her and I only needed to be there to take up more of her responsibilities in her absence. The status quo was sufficient. Distressed beyond belief, I returned to the court in tears advising the court I wanted to stop the trial as I saw no way to change anything of these circumstances. I had again failed to win the freedom of my daughters. The court agreed and ordered me to pay fees of $1,500 to opposing counsel and $1,500 to the evaluator. The court's order of the day noted the defendant's motion to dismiss is granted; the mother, bankrupt as she reports, was allowed to travel abroad with her youngest child.

I subsequently filed a complaint with New Jersey that this expert's testimony refuted established scientific knowledge on a subject for which he claimed no professional or educational experience. His suggestion that the mental illness of bipolar disorder was a byproduct of stress was nonsensical. He never sought the medical records from the Mood Clinic; never sought input from the psychiatrist who treated this person for at least two prior years; or from the psychologist treating this person for the last four years. No psychological exams were given although they were considered standard in such custody evaluations. The evaluator stated he saw no evidence that the custodial parent showed any signs of bipolar disorder during the hour interview he had with her. Or that the shoplifting habit was an ongoing issue. He did not consider why the mother had already lost custody of one child.

My complaint to the State Board noted:

To make or agree to such a statement a testifying expert would have to know the symptoms of the illness and then know the facts of the preceding ten-year period. This statement could also be construed to imply this evaluator believes an unmedicated bipolar personality just lapses into an inactive phase of years duration. This is also questioned to some degree in that Paula is quoted as being chronically depressed.

Various public medical journals stated the facts about mental illness, bipolar disorder. The Attorneys Medical Advisor reported the following in Section 49:4 Mania, the expectancy of developing the bipolar illness is approximately one percent and is equal in both sexes. The presentation of mania is often quite dramatic and almost invariably brings the patient to the attention of mental health professionals. The average age of onset of bipolar illness is approximately thirty years of age. The typical patient profile for bipolar mood disorder...a strong religious background.

The fundamental feature of a manic episode is an elevated, expansive, or irritable mood. The elevated mood is euphoric, often infectious in nature, and can be quite entertaining to witness. If untreated, the elevated mood frequently progresses to potentially dangerous and unpredictable irritability which can be very difficult to manage, especially if it is combined with psychotic features. Although sudden onset is possible, most episodes develop gradually over a few days or even weeks.

Drug therapy was the preferred treatment for a bipolar mood disorder, but its application was considerably more complicated. While lithium was a breakthrough for the treatment of bipolar disorder, it had a narrow therapeutic window, and toxicity is common without strict compliance and frequent blood level checks.

Recent studies suggest that bipolar illness is not always a benign, remitting illness; it has a variable prognosis ranging from complete recovery to functional incapacitation. Likewise, The Columbia University College of Physicians and Surgeons produced a "Complete Home Guide to Mental Health. Once thought to be the work of the devil, depression and bipolar disorder are now known to be accompanied by disturbances in the brain's chemistry. Depressed mothers and fathers have difficulty being parents and often cannot attend to their children's emotional needs.

But then what do I know, I don't have a Ph.D. in psychology; I don't claim to have achieved the status of Fellow of an unknown Academy. Yet he is qualified as an expert in a family court custody trial of young children forced by this court to live with a mentally ill parent who refused treatment. The State Board of Psychological Examiners acknowledged receipt of my complaint against this evaluator in a letter dated September 23, 1998. The complaint "would be reviewed at a regularly scheduled meeting after it has received the information it needs to conduct its investigation. This process could take three months or longer.

In a letter dated July 19, 1998, the state Board of Psychological Examiners advised the board had reviewed materials submitted by yourself and the psychologist. "Pursuant to the Uniform Enforcement Act, the Board can only take action where the licensee's conduct rises to the level of repeated or gross acts of malpractice or professional misconduct. After a careful and thorough review, the Board has determined that there is no cause for disciplinary action in this matter. The Board now considers this matter closed." This Board never reported if it found this licensed professional's work, in this case, a "gross act of malpractice or misconduct." It just advised it could only take action if there had been some unknown number of such reports against a professional. It sounded vague to me for a board charged with protecting the public interests.

I wrote a letter to Christine Todd Whitman, Governor of New Jersey, dated September 20, 1999, and copied the Board of Psychological Examiners, addressing the Board's response to my complaint filed against this custody evaluator. Excerpts below.

The Board's response suggests they see no problem with the evaluation report because the evaluator's file does not reflect an undefined number of complaints. The cause for concern in this family tragedy is the custodial mother's announcement that "I always have depression" and for the first time in six years an acknowledgment of a diagnosis of bipolar disorder by the Mood Clinic at the University of Pennsylvania. She readily admits she elected not to treat either of these mental illnesses. How is this in the best interest of the children? It is not.

The impact of these two unmedicated diseases on the family has been significant. The welfare of four children is not given any consideration by either the evaluator or the Board despite the fact the custodial parent admits to a serious mental illness. The argument, in this case, is about this evaluation and the welfare of the children. Is this a reasonable standard for the welfare of children in New Jersey? The courts, unfortunately, make much of this professional product for the basis for too many custodial decisions.

My letter to the Governor prompted a response from the Board's Deputy Director dated January 31, 2000. I was advised the Board will again review this matter at its February 7 meeting. A July 26, 2000 letter from the Board's Executive Director noted: "the Board is not persuaded by your additional information to change their original decision and therefore, voted to sustain its original decision."

The November/December 1997 issue of the New Jersey Reporter ran an article, styled *All in the Family*, noting angry fathers were swaying the debate over a divorce. The article referenced father's groups had pressured the State Legislature to address what they saw as "trampled rights and biased courts." The former chairman of the Bar Association's Family Law Section answered "we have seen father's rights groups become a kind of a new Gestapo." Gestapo? Like when court orders are blindly issued to remove fathers from their homes and children, without a trial, never to return. I can appreciate the Bar's concern for such efforts that might expose these Gestapo-like efforts to the light of day. The chairman of the New Jersey Council for Children's Rights noted "we wanted to put the bench on notice that we are not going to take this sitting down." Almost sounds like a threat that could get a father removed from his home. No, let their reign of terror on fathers continue unabated.

Testimony at State hearings noted another relevant fact that nearly thirty-five percent of the litigants stated there had been allegations of violence in their marriages. In most cases, men claimed they were wrongly accused of violent acts. Father's argued lawyers favored litigation and not meaningful mediation. Another hot button issue was whether judges should be allowed to order divorcing parents to pay for college costs as parents who are not divorced had no obligation to pay any college costs for their children. Then too, there was an issue that all the child support paid to the custodial parent goes with no accounting of how those funds are spent. So much for the touted case law Guglielmo, supra, 253 N.J. Super that referenced "child support runs from parent to child, not parent to parent, both parents were obligated to provide for their children." Not in real life family court proceedings in New Jersey. More of that legal pollution.

In June 1998, the Philadelphia Inquirer Magazine ran a lead story on borderline personality, specifically addressing the mental illnesses of bipolar disorder and schizophrenia. The article noted, "bipolar disorder has come to be associated with flawed brain chemistry." What might have been had this evaluator been qualified to do responsible, professional work? Instead, we got just another fraudulent effort to deny this father and his children a fair hearing of the facts.

The Philadelphia Inquirer quoted an article from the Los Angeles Times on March 28, 1999, titled *High Court Tells Judges to Screen the Experts*:

> The Supreme Court told federal trial judges last week that they must screen out testimony from all experts whose opinions are not based on solid science. Plaintiffs often use hired experts in their efforts to prove that products are defective, a necessity for victory – and winning damages. But the U.S. Supreme Court has displayed much skepticism about such experts. "Six years ago, it said judges should act as 'gatekeepers' and scrutinize testimony from scientific experts." The ruling issued extends that review to all kinds of experts, whether they are engineers, psychologists, accountants, or handwriting analysts.

So much in this evaluator's opinion that bipolar-disorder was not necessarily due to a chemical imbalance in the brain but perhaps stress. Are we all bipolar? I had three kidney stone attacks attributed to stress. Am I bipolar?

I wrote a letter to Paula on August 4, 1998, and advised her I would not be making any contribution towards her purchase of a new refrigerator. I noted she was again not working these summer months; not taking any classes in the hopes of completing her education, but had taken yet another trip to South America to visit her parents in June. How does this contribute to the welfare of the children she claims custody of in court but neglects day-to-day? I asked why she could not work; not afford to finish her education but she could afford to take annual trips to South America? Guess who took custody of the three children while Paula spent 19 days in South America?

# 20

# ANOTHER MOTION. WHAT ELSE?

So, what next in a case that seemingly has no resolution and no justice? We file yet another motion, what else? This latest, dated November 19, 1998, asked for reduced child support; changes in the tax deductions for these dependent children; change in the visitation schedule, remedy Paula's default of medical care expenses, and to consider the change of custody for the third child. Katie, now almost twelve, wanted to live with her father.

The judge's law clerk advised that the December 18 hearing had again been postponed for an unknown reason, but that the court wanted me to draft a proposed visitation schedule for consideration. I wrote a letter to the court dated December 18, 1998, noting my continued frustration with Paula's abuse of the visitation schedule using me as her de facto babysitter. I confirmed the children and I routinely sat at my residence waiting for the mother to show up. Most times an hour or more past the scheduled visitation time.

My motion argued my level of child support was subject to review because as a non-custodial parent I had significant unscheduled visitation with the children. I now had unscheduled full custody of all the children every weekend; Paula's late arrivals and early departures continued; she had recently filed for personal bankruptcy which further supported my claim I was the sole financial support of these children; Paula acknowledged the daughter, Katie, wanted to live with her father; the mother had failed to pay any of her $2,000 share of the orthodontist's bill from the two-year orthodontist treatment provided to the two oldest children.

The court ordered its mediator to interview Katie, relative to my claim that she wanted to live with me. I questioned why the children were subjected to mandated interviews when they wanted to live with me but there was no such mandate when these same children were the subject of "state-sanctioned hijacking" by the mother six years ago? Katie met with the court's mediator on January 21, 1999. I filed yet another order to show cause alleging yet another physical assault by Paula against the non-custodial child, Adriana, who was at the home one evening waiting for me to pick up the children for our Wednesday visitation. Paula punched this child in the stomach and took her to the floor with a vice-like pinch that bruised the child's arm in four spots. I asked the court to charge the mother with domestic violence against this child.

At this March 5, 1999 hearing opposing counsel went into a full defense of Paula's position claiming there had been no change of circumstances relative to the care of the third daughter, so no custody change should be considered. Opposing counsel then argued, but did not deny, all my additional visitation time and custody of all these children were but non-recurring and incidental expenses which are not subject to child support considerations; in fact, they asked my child support to be increased by $58 weekly. My child support obligation was the payment of the mortgage and property taxes that already exceeded the support guidelines. As for Paula's unpaid $2,000 bill for the orthodontist treatment, opposing counsel argued "since this obligation is presumably either satisfied or discharged (Paula listed this debt in her recent bankruptcy filing) there was no basis for judicial intervention. If this court were to consider ordering reimbursement from the mother, the court must look first to the mother's ability to pay such a cost, as compared to the father's financial position." This lawyer must have known child support debt could not be relieved in a bankruptcy filing. I sure knew it. But in this court, any gambit in defense of the mother was a fair legal argument. In another exchange, opposing counsel made an obvious effort to disparage my living accommodations, referring to the court that I lived in a trailer. Judge Tomasello turned to me to question this situation at the trailer. I told the court I lived in a mobile home, not a trailer. The judge restated his question to reference the mobile home. Opposing counsel also asked the court to award $2,640 in legal fees to himself.

The court ordered that my application for change of residential custody of Katie was denied but did order she could now officially spend three Sundays a month with her father; all other issues of my application were denied. The judge stated he would only entertain the complaint of an alleged assault of the child if it were substantiated by DYFS. Judge Tomasello stated this court is "not a fact-finder;" that is the job of DYFS. Paula's application for increased child support was denied. The good of this court effort was that I officially got more time with Katie and vice versa. Too, it was ordered if Paula failed to show up by 7:00 PM, two hours past the 5:00 PM visitation time, the non-custodial children could stay with their father if they so desired. Opposing counsel was denied any fees as the judge noted the father had made a case on several issues.

But what became of the $2,000 debt I had paid for Paula's share of the orthodontist billing? Opposing counsel argued I was not obligated to have made that payment; that it was a gift by the father to the mother. My response was "it was a gift to the children, to the mother it was child support." The court stated "I'm satisfied that the debt is an aspect of child support. I'm satisfied that it's part and parcel of the child support order so I'm going to indicate that it is a judgment that's due and owing to the father. I'm not going to order its liquidation (payment) at this point ... and at some point, we'll find a way for actual payments to be made, although I don't see a way to pay for that right now." Wait, did I hear that right, this court just took a position of sympathy for this custodial parent who did not meet her child support obligations?

I waited for the court's written order of the hearing. Having been written up, signed by the judge, and distributed by the court's law clerk, I read through the order in the foyer of the courthouse. This order made no mention of the $2,000 judgment for child support owed to me by Paula for her share of the orthodontist bill I had paid six months ago. I went back to the law clerk's office and I asked the clerk to come out to discuss the issue. The clerk stated the judge said there were no current means to collect the judgment. I argued he ordered a judgment for this debt; we need the judgment referenced in the order so it could be recorded and filed against the mother. Not convinced, the clerk left and returned within minutes with a second law clerk and they both then argued with me what good is a judgment if it can't be collected. I said it is judgment and it will be collected, but it must be recorded. After some ten minutes of debate, the law clerks asked me to put my concerns on the matter in writing and it would presumably be addressed. I did as they requested and never heard another thing from the clerks or the court on the issue. Having endured the court's concern for Paula's means to pay this debt, which is clearly defined as a child support obligation, it then argued with itself if it could ever be collected.

Opposing counsel's letter dated June 18, 1999, advised he no longer represented Paula and not to forward any documents. Bye, we won't miss you!

Believing the law clerks hoped I would just go away and ignore their silence if not their ignorance on the subject, what other avenue was available to address court issues if the court itself chooses to ignore the law? I researched information as to how to file an appeal of this order. Lots more paperwork and a new routine but it had to be done. I could not let them give me some semblance of justice and then take it back because of some law clerks' ignorance of judgments and justice. I suggest the court has access to an entire bureaucracy in the Probation Department that is charged by law to collect child support ordered by all family courts. Why not utilize their talents and resources? Probation collected from me, legitimate or not some years prior, and then some. But then I am the father in this case and the court does not protect me or the children; this court only protects the mother.

To address the mounting issue and debt of unpaid child support, most states, prodded by the federal government, established procedures that required child support to be collected by wage garnishment and allowed tax refunds to be seized at the federal and state level. Then there were the more public efforts to identify deadbeat dads, as society liked to call us. Our local county, as did all in New Jersey, routinely staged early morning raids, roundups as they called them, at any scofflaws last known address, and places of employment looking to catch these deadbeats and haul them off to court and jail if need be for non-payment of child support. One newspaper pictured Governor Whitman positioned behind one captured "deadbeat" from one of these roundups with his hands up high against a wall. The picture suggested that even the Governor was an active participant in the effort to collect child support. I agreed with these measures as children had to be cared for financially as well as emotionally.

But in this case, against this mother, in this family court, the judgment for child support was ordered; but the court, sympathetic to the mother, refused to put its ruling in writing much less enforce collection. No, instead the court worried how this deadbeat mother would pay this two-year-old $2,000 debt. The court pocketed the judgment and did not send it through channels for collection. Perhaps it could order Paula not to make her annual trip to Colombia until this debt was paid. Perhaps a courthouse bake sale or take up a collection within the courtrooms from divorce lawyers who plied their trade in defense of mothers. Maybe a fee charge for those pro se litigants who looked to learn some law while sitting in courtrooms waiting for their crapshoot at justice. Such is this family court; I could get no consideration for all the additional support I provided to my children. Meanwhile, Paula was given sanctuary by this court so that she need not pay the support even the court had acknowledged was due for the children she only claimed in court.

I can only guess these law clerks had yet to progress to a level of education that would have made them aware of this basic tenet of law. But these law clerks seemed well-groomed to represent mothers in future family court proceedings. Again, justice denied in this family court that only concerns itself with the welfare of but one, the mother.

# 21

# WHAT NOW? WE APPEAL!

I launched my research effort at Rutgers Law in support of my appeal of the court's ruling on several issues including the $2,000 judgment having not been recorded as part of the court's summary of the day's decisions. Case law in State v. Pohlabel, 40 N.J. Super. 416, 423 (App Div. 1956) notes "we stated that where there is a conflict between the oral and the written commitment, the former will control since it is the true source of the sentence. We conclude that the same principle should generally apply to a conflict in a written opinion of the trial judge and the form of the judgment prepared by counsel which is intended to embody the written opinion." This standard of New Jersey law of almost 60 years was ignored by this court in this case. Did they think this father lacked the standing to secure equal justice?

I purchased a transcript of this March 5, 1999 hearing as it was my evidence of the court's spoken intention as to this $2,000 judgment. My motion of notice to accelerate the appeal of the order of said hearing relative to the custody of the three children noted: I questioned the validity of the court's decision that Paula's physical assault of the non-custodial child would not be considered until and unless DYFS first investigated a report to substantiate this claim; that the mother failed to provide basic needs and necessities for the custodial children in her care at the expense of the defendant (father); that the court awarded a $2,000 judgment for child support but then failed to record it or order its payment. Too, the court denied the third child's request for a change of custody to her father; but did extend visitation

I referenced Rules of Court 1:2-5(1) and an unwritten but touted moral code that justice demands a timely hearing of all matters relative to the custody, welfare, and protection of all children. I requested an accelerated appeal for a hearing for justice due to these children, a constitutional remedy of the timeless legal cliché "justice for all." The appellate court denied this effort for an accelerated appeal on November 18, 1999. All we could do was try and hope, but having been denied we pushed ahead. The appellate court did note Paula had failed to respond to this filing and any such response would be deemed late and not admitted. Paula need not respond in this case, as the court itself took up her defense. And Paula's complaint of alleged domestic violence some seven years ago had me removed from my children within two days and that before any hearing of the facts on the matter. An expedited hearing as to the welfare of these children was worthless commentary in New Jersey Family Court.

The appellate court issued its opinion on April 3, 2000. The court sustained the trial court's ruling that Katie's custody should remain with Paula but that the additional third-weekend visitation is allowed. Too, it agreed that my documented additional support of his children over and above that already ordered did not constitute a change of circumstances to warrant consideration by the court. Likewise, my request to claim all the children as tax dependents was also denied. Paula's physical assault on the non-custodial child was correctly deferred by the court pending an outside review by DYFS or criminal charges against the mother." No third party had to investigate Paula's 1993 claim of a perceived threat against her. The court itself ordered my removal from the home before a word in my defense was spoken.

The appellate division's response stated, "defendant's argument that he was somehow subjected to a higher standard of the law is clearly without merit and does not warrant discussion in this opinion." Lastly, relative to the judgment against Paula for non-payment of the orthodontist bill, the appellate court ruled this was child support, and "recognition of the obligation should, indeed, be memorialized in the order." The judgment for $2,000 was ordered on April 3, 2000, and likewise noted the "court does not determine liquidation (payment) of this claim." And all this from the appellate court spouting it too was all about equal justice. But this is the New Jersey Family Court. Perhaps the appellate court also had not heard of the Probation Department's mandate to collect child support ordered by the family court or were such enforcement efforts only for orders issued against fathers.

I assumed the appellate court made no effort to discuss its opinion or defense of my claim I was held to a "higher standard" as there was no defense to be made. The double standard of this New Jersey court was as obvious as it was indefensible. So, no double standard as to the father being held to a higher standard relative to this mother. Justice is fair in New Jersey Family Court, so says the court. A $2,000 judgment for child support gets recorded but the court makes no effort to enforce collection. The mother's neglect of her care and support of the custodial children is accepted, as seemingly "no change in circumstances;" and the court turns a blind eye to the physical assault on a child. Just months ago, Paula's claim of being hit with a pot had me convicted in this same court after all of five minutes. No third-party testimony, no questions, no facts were required to document her charge against me other than the court's preponderance of Paula's words. My questioning of Paula why she was two-plus hours late had me arrested and held on $2,500 bail. One would suggest the bias is so entrenched in this family court's processes and practice of justice it can't see its discrimination against this father. This was not justice but judicial contempt for justice itself.

On July 20, 2000, I filed a petition with the New Jersey Supreme Court appealing the appellate division's opinion of the court's order dated March 5, 1999. My certification in support of this appeal to the New Jersey Supreme Court presented all the facts and figures of the trial court and appeal efforts. But facts were no defense against the

State's bias against fathers. The text below was part of my argument for this appeal to the state supreme court.

The aforementioned facts of this case are not denied by neither the mother nor the courts but rather just ignored relative to consideration of changed circumstances. The legal and moral merits of this appeal brief are an effort to expose the inequities and double standards of family court justice relative to the court's judgment, summarily sanctioned by the appellate opinion. Of all the aforementioned changed circumstances, both the trial and appellate courts expressed concern for the mother's low income imposed by none other than herself and her neglect. Not one syllable of either the trial transcript or the appellate court's decision concerns itself with the care and welfare of the custodial children. The courts suggest it is surely the children and the father who must bear the burdens of the mother's failings. The statutes, case law, and local rules and procedures justly dictate the court's judgment and opinions are wrong. Chivalry is alive and well in family court; the 'best interest of the child' is all but a legal cliché and defendant fathers are but second-class citizens in this parody of American justice.

I challenged the courts' lack of interest in who provided the necessities of life for these children but was rebuffed by the court's opinion that the mother was exempt from a review of these matters because her money was her money. Case law supports (my) argument. Specifically, Lynn v. Lynn; Martinette v. Hickman; Connell v. Connell; Orr v. Orr; Hallberg v. Hallberg. The legal issue was whether the mother was obligated by New Jersey law, rules of court, and case law to provide a proportionate level of support for the custodial children and had the circumstances of that level of support for the custodial children changed substantially? The court suggests the mother is not required to complete the Case Information Statement (CIS), and she did not. Only the father's income and expenses were part of the analysis. How can there be an analysis of changed circumstances when one set of circumstances can only be compared to itself? The court's decision doomed this exercise of justice, and the father and his children are doomed to inequity of justice. The law is clear, child support is an obligation of both parents for the benefit of the children.

The trial court's only compelling response to my complaint relative to his assumption of total support of his children was to suggest "you ought to stick to the order. And if there's a deficiency concerning the children's needs clothing-wise or nutrition-wise, then the appropriate state agency will make the investigation." What state agency does the court suggest? DYFS, a failed bureaucracy, itself answering a complaint about its institutional failures to protect the children of this state and three times failed to respond to this case. When the father told the court, he could not sit idle while the children were neglected, Judge Tomasello responded "you're caught between a rock and a hard place." My issue of the equal application of justice in these family court proceedings also fell on deaf ears, dismissed with summary prejudice as were so many of the issues at hand.

In September 1999, the Supreme Court of New Jersey advised my appeal had been denied with no comments offered, signed by Deborah T. Poritz, Chief Justice. I have serious doubts she ever read this appeal. Judge Poritz was the former Attorney General of New Jersey previously served by me on two prior suits lodged against the New Jersey Probation Department and my complaint filed with the New Jersey Board of Medical Examiners relative to the corrupted custody evaluation of 1994. Her promotion to the New Jersey Supreme Court suggests the "Peter Principle" is alive in New Jersey's legal aristocracy.

Perhaps now is the time to define DYFS, that failed New Jersey institution of child neglect, that these courts valued, trusted to do its job. DYFS came under serious scrutiny in late 1997. A new federal law required states to release certain information about a child's death when "abuse or neglect is suspected or proven." Previously that information was conveniently considered confidential. From the period January 1997 into 1999, DYFS reported, as required by this new federal law, about 300 children had died whose families were, at the time, being investigated by DYFS. Of eighty-five cases under direct

DYFS management, forty-four children had died as a result of abuse or neglect from January 1997 to October 15, 1999. The DYFS Director refused public access to the case records to protect the privacy of others mentioned in those reports and was reluctant to answer questions about the investigation of these cases. New Jersey lagged behind the rest of the country when it came to proving child abuse claims according to federal statistics. New Jersey substantiated just fifteen percent of these cases whereas the national average was thirty-three percent.

The New York Times reported on August 5, 1999, a New York City non-profit, Children's Rights Inc., filed suit against New Jersey and DYFS alleging DYFS was doing a very poor job monitoring children in crisis. The suit aimed to reform child welfare in New Jersey and claimed DYFS was underfunded, mismanaged, and overburdened. Dr. Richard Gelles, author of the report and Dean of the School of Social Work at the University of Pennsylvania noted "the DYFS picture is not just bleak, it is one of chaos and tragedy." The litany of specific examples where children had died while the case was under DYFS management was telling. One such referenced case was that of a seven-year-old having been found dead and stuffed in a plastic bin, and his two brothers having been found locked in the basement of a house belonging to their mother's cousin. DYFS believed the children were still with their mother and closed their case file, unaware the mother was in jail on an unrelated child abuse charge. A federal judge allowed this lawsuit to continue in a ruling dated February 2000. The issues and woes of DYFS were well-publicized and widely reported once this lawsuit was initiated. The local and regional newspapers were littered with articles about the failings of DYFS and all the issues confronting New Jersey as it tried to manage this human crisis of children under the failed protective custody and management of this state bureaucracy. Unfortunately, the New Jersey family and appellate courts thought well of DYFS. One state bureaucracy protecting another.

As noted in the transcript of testimony I presented in Judge Tomasello's court on March 5, 1999, relative to my Order to Show

Cause, I alleged Paula had again physically assaulted the non-custodial child visiting at the marital home. The motion noted we had contacted DYFS, as this court required, to complain about the assault. The response from DYFS was to take the case to family court, they would not intervene. Likewise, I testified I had reached out to two different sources at the county government, one being the Prosecutor's Office, and both advised the matter should be addressed in this family court. This judge again refused to be a "fact-finder" and told me the court needed DYFS to substantiate this case, and then they would bring the issue to court. I advised I had addressed the issue with DYFS and even the Prosecutor's office advised me to skip DYFS and bring the issue directly to family court. Judge Tomasello responded, "if the Prosecutor's Office doesn't believe in what DYFS does then I guess we all ought to go home." I should have asked this Judge why he trusted DYFS when no one else did?

In yet another early scene in *The Ox-Bow Incident*, citizens of the town gathered to hear of the murder of the local rancher. Men piled out of the saloon; agitated and demanding justice as others gathered from the town's main street. Another sent for the local judge to take control of this brooding mob. The judge arrived and espoused justice would be served as demanded, but pleaded for this posse to wait for the sheriff's return so he could lead this mob's search for justice. Chided that "court-justice" took too long; the judge declared it was the sheriff's job, not his job, to manage this mob. Sounds a lot like Judge Tomasello. What's another lynching in the search for justice for all?

This matter, among other issues of that hearing, was appealed to the appellate court and subsequently to the New Jersey Supreme Court and both agreed with Judge Tomasello's handling of this issue of a child having been assaulted by the mother. Please, don't ever tell me that New Jersey Family Court gives a damn about "what is in the best interest of the child." They proved time and again in this case and why I always referred to the state's laws and case law refers to the axiom "the best interest of the child" was but a cliché of New Jersey law. The family court only protected the mother, the father and the children had no legitimate standing in this court.

Judge Tomasello and the state's appellate and supreme courts confirmed family court had no obligation, no need to intercede for the benefit of this abused child. They are not "fact-finders" as to the mistreatment of this child and confirmed, "justice is blind" when it comes to the family court cliché "what is in the best interest of the children" in New Jersey. I counted fifteen articles in regional newsprint from the New York Times, the Philadelphia Inquirer, the Courier-Post, and the local Gloucester Country Times that headlined New Jersey's attempt to grappled with the extent of the budding DYFS scandal as our case made its way to trial. These articles covered stories of cases of child neglect, child abuse, children who had died, and the resulting lawsuits that attacked DYFS from all fronts. For these courts to think that they need not intercede for the protection of this child under physical assault by her mother was unconscionable. But it does speak to the level of contempt these courts had for these children in the application of the law in its efforts to protect this mother. Upon calling the county DYFS office the father was advised DYFS would not intercede in the case; "take it to family court;" the County Prosecutor's office advised the defendant to address the situation to the family court. This court and higher courts denied such efforts declaring this child's welfare was best determined by DYFS; the child is damned!

Surely expecting more of the same from New Jersey's courts and its entrenched bias for the mother in such family court cases, I prepared a filing of the facts of this case as handled in New Jersey courts. I filed a petition in the Federal District Court located in Camden, New Jersey. My notice of removal was filed with New Jersey announcing my intention to seek a review of my arguments for justice in Federal Court as I alleged New Jersey denied the defendant and his children equal protection under the law as espoused in the Fourteenth Amendment of the Federal Constitution and the constitutional right to due process under the Fifth Amendment of the Federal Constitution. The arguments and case history were the same; just a different venue for a hearing outside the New Jersey Courts' bias against this father and these children. Again, I argued that equal parties in a divorce were treated very differently under the laws of New Jersey relative to family court practices and opinions. I alleged New Jersey practiced "genderism" by favoring the plaintiff-mother over the defendant-father while applying justice as best defined in *The Ox-Bow Incident*: hang the guilty father. My pleading included a Writ of Habeas Corpus in that the child Katie, aged thirteen, was being forcibly held against her will by the court's mandate she remains in the custody of the mother.

The New Jersey Family and Appellate court's decisions to ignore the welfare of these children bordered on criminal neglect. I suggested their willingness to ignore the facts; turning their eyes on the situation they imposed on these children would today be the equivalent of the abject handling of the Sandusky scandal at Penn State; the Nassar scandal with the US Women's Gymnastics Team and the pending Strauss scandal at Ohio State. Such entrenched abuse is not limited to sports teams but I suggest it is also embedded in New Jersey Family Court.

In its best efforts to fix, if not resolve, the crisis and scandal that was DYFS, New Jersey reconstituted this bureaucracy under a new name, New Jersey Division of Child Protection and Permanency (DCP&P). There that should fix the DYFS problem and save the neglected children of New Jersey. Now if they can only get New Jersey Family Court to give a damn.

A letter from the Federal Court noted my effort to remove this case from New Jersey courts was improper in that my appeal to the State Supreme Court had yet to be finalized. The State Supreme Court decision was not finalized until September 2000, I found myself too emotionally and physically exhausted to refile this case in Federal Court. A decision I regret to this day as I believed this was a case to be won. That said, with the girls growing up, I became more and more involved with them in many things in and out of school. I just did not have the energy to continue to wage my campaign on so many fronts.

# 22

# A NEW JUDGE, THE SAME OLD INJUSTICE

Family court judicial assignments were again shuffled in July 2000 and the dice were rolled again. We were introduced to yet another Judge, Robert E. Francis. As much as I never felt very welcomed in Judge Tomasello's court my sensibilities of fairness would be tested by Judge Francis. I think it is fair to say I didn't like him and he didn't like me.

With the start of a new school year, I reminded the high school I wanted to be copied on the performance of all the children as allowed by the federal Family Education Rights and Privacy Act. Likewise, seeing the girls more and more on weekends and school nights we were very busy doing homework, projects, studying for tests. Too, the two youngest girls were very involved in softball. I bought all the girls' gloves and taught them how to throw and catch a softball, catch fly balls, and field grounders. We all went to the open field just across the driveway from the house-on-wheels and had fun every weekend the weather allowed. Molly joined a softball travel team at age ten while Katie took up travel ball two years later. All four girls played little league softball in the community. Paula took no interest in any of these events. As the two youngest children developed and got more involved, we raced across New Jersey, to Delaware, to Maryland, a weekend tournament at West Point, NY, and into Philadelphia for tournament games on spring and summer weekends. Some of the best times were had during those crazy softball seasons. Parents, grandparents, and siblings were the typical fans of all these softball games. A teammate questioned Molly that after so many games, months, and years of playing ball together they had never seen her mother. Molly answered, "and you never will."

Unfortunately, the only way to get anything resolved in this case, and that was a very long shot at best, was to present issues to family court and hope for the best and expect nothing. We finished the year 2000 again in court addressing custody issues. What else? I met with Paula, at her request, at the marital home (yes, in violation of the FRO). All the children were present as she wanted to discuss yet another promised transition of the children to my custody. Again, Katie and Molly made it clear they wanted to live with their father. Michelle, who all but raised Molly, would never leave the home without Molly. Michelle brought Molly with her for years whenever she went with her friends. I expressed to Paula my desire to get all the children back under the roof of the marital home; to provide for them and negotiate a settlement of her equity in the marital home. The only concern expressed by any of the children was when Michelle asked the mother if she could make it on her own? Strange but true, this child worried more about the mother than this mother ever worried about her children. During this gathering, Paula was clear and repeatedly expressed that she only wished to take into account the children's desire to live with me. Paula expressed her willingness to consider a change of residential custody for the children had come "only after months of soul searching about the children's wishes and best interest." Yet again more words than deeds.

Judge Francis called our case from the day's docket of scheduled cases of February 9, 2001, to mark our appearances and begin yet another exercise of justice denied. Judge Francis, in introducing the case to the court gallery, noted that after numerous prior hearings in this court "defendant is of the impression he does not get justice in family court. He contests everything, appeals many issues, and then appeals the appeal. He even quotes Abraham Lincoln." My response to the court was "you got that right." Am I to assume this judge read some of the years' prior court filings in this case? Judge Tomasello acknowledged no such concern for case history noting "as far as I'm concerned this case starts today" choosing to ignore the prior three and a half years of the case history with Judge Herman. But this was now year eight in our search for justice. Maybe things will change. Maybe not. The children and I waited for Paula's next move and again she wavered, reneged on her prior offer to leave the marital home, and make for a peaceful change of custody of the children over to me.

I filed yet another motion for a change of custody of the three non-custodial children still in Paula's legal sphere of control; not to be confused with emotional and financial support. Paula's answer to this motion was replete with time-worn family court innuendo employed by mothers in defense of their privileged position as the preferred custodial parent. One this court bought hook, line, and sinker for years, and surely in this case.

Paula's answer to this most recent motion stated "she has known for about two years of Katie's desire to live with her father." Of course, she then noted, "(her) psychologist's recommendation of not having any custody change without a proper psychological evaluation of all parties involved." Paula's response then launched into the regurgitated verbiage employed by most in her class to promote their position of preference within this court. Paula stated "both the (mother) and (father) are contributing to the best of their abilities. The disparity of assets and income is of extraordinary size but the father will continue to claim and accuse me of being uncommitted and a failure." Further along in this response, Paula claimed "(she) maintains and will maintain her position, that she doesn't intend to negate or diminish her responsibilities but will continue to provide as much as she can do within her limited financial possibilities. The father claims the (mother) is a freeloader and irresponsible. The (mother) states that she has not lived free of rent but has been made a 'prisoner' of a $180,000 home she struggles to keep to be with her children."

Paula then referenced her psychologist's considerations and observations of this case stating "the (father's) total irrationalities have unfortunately become the children's reality. No wonder they think they want out!" This psychologist appeared to be an absentee witness in this case. Never identified; never qualified; just quoted. Paula's commentary asked the court to "order an evaluation to establish the presence of parental alienation and thereby move towards putting an end to the (father's) irrational and obsessive allegations, accusations, and motives." At this point, the filing also urged the court "to order a psychiatric evaluation of the (father) to help him move beyond his obsession for revenge that is harming all parties involved." Well, Paula does like her psychologist and counselors who promote her claim to motherhood, even if she did not provide for the children physically, financially, or emotionally. Now if they could only have convinced her to continue to work with the professionals at the Mood Clinic that she elected to abandon some ten years ago.

My response asked this response be denied as it was filed late under court rules. That said, I stated:

> The fact Judge Tomasello refused to interview any of these affected children did not negate their desire for justice predicated on their free will and expressed wishes. It merely delayed and postponed the inevitable, the exercise of justice for these children... We are here again seeking justice for these children because they request it, desire it, and by constitutional right, demand it. They are the custodial children not the chattel of the mother. The mother's inability to contribute a fair and legally mandated level of support for these children she claims only in family court is hostage to her inability to take control of her problems and assume the level of responsibility mandated by New Jersey law and that of a higher moral law. The financial and emotional neglect of these children she only claims in court is complete.
>
> New Jersey case law as referenced in Sheehan v. Sheehan, 51 N.J. Super. 276 (App. Div. 1958) is ignored in this case. There is little to suggest family court applied case law to question this mother despite all the changed circumstances she acknowledged. This system only protects the mother. Sheehan noted, "while a judgment involving the

custody of minor children was subject to modification at any time upon a ground of changed circumstances, the primary consideration of the court remained the welfare of the children, and the basic issue was whether there existed a change in circumstances which would affect the welfare of the children.

More espoused legal lingo, maybe even morally inspirational. But, again New Jersey case law was full of eloquent language that typically bore little fruit in this family court. When Judge Tomasello declared "the case starts today," there was no history of circumstances this judge would consider even after three years. And now Judge Francis acknowledged that the father complained a lot about the lack of justice in New Jersey Family Court. The extent of Judge Francis' bias was yet to see the light of day but he was a typical standard-bearer of this family court's contempt of this father and these children.

The two youngest children, now aged thirteen and nine, who sought shelter from the storm with their father, as to that of their life with the mother, are quite capable of making their own decisions on this matter. Katie, in seventh-grade, having been tested at her father's request, skipped seventh-grade math and was placed with the eighth-grade high honors math class. Her eighth-grade English teacher suggested she take the high school level PSAT test as her vocabulary was so strong. The first of many colleges, Yale University, wrote to acknowledge her academic potential, and that was just as a freshman. Molly also did well academically.

The court ordered on February 9, 2001, yet another evaluator would be selected from the court's compiled list. I demanded that neither of the two prior evaluators is considered due to their exposed fraud, and the judge would make the final selection of the evaluator. I filed a motion on February 20, 2001, asking the court to reconsider its order stating that the only dispute with the mother was the value of her equity in the marital home and when would it be paid. The mother had agreed the two youngest children could live with their father and Michelle, now seventeen was well capable of making her decision relative to custody. Adriana had been in my custody for five years. I knew, Michelle, the oldest sibling, would never leave the homestead and leave her two younger sisters behind to fend for themselves in that home. Paula's now late-filed answer dated January 31, 2001, asked, among other things, the court denies any change of custody; order a review of child support; a report from a court-appointed psychologist; and that the court reviews the report her counselor had prepared. And then yet again requested a complete psychiatric evaluation of the father.

The court never produced its list of suggested psychologists and psychiatrists for yet another custody evaluation until March 26; some two months after this hearing. Justice does run slow at times. What about a five-day rule? Can't we get something like that when the best interests of the children are the concern? Not sure what became of the court's demand for yet another custody evaluator in this case. Knowing and having experienced two prior such scams, I had no interest to test yet a third. Fool me once; fool me twice; fool me a third time, shame on me. No such third evaluation was ever done and no more money was wasted on that mumbo-jumbo from court-sanctioned charlatans who prostituted themselves as family court child custody evaluators.

But before we go any further, we should take a look at this new judge to the case, Judge Robert E. Francis. Judge Francis had made a name for himself in 1996 as a jurist on the Superior Court-Law Division and only recently transferred to the family court bench. A New York Times article noted, "a New Jersey Judge (Judge Francis) ruled that New Jersey State Troopers patrolling reaches of the New Jersey Turnpike on the lookout for drug suspects singled out and pulled over black motorists in widely inordinate numbers over three years because of race." Judge Francis "based his decision largely on defense surveys and statistics showing wide disparities between the number of black motorists on the road and the number of blacks pulled over by the troopers. Judge Francis concluded that the evidence in nineteen narcotics cases had been seized in violation of their Fourteenth Amendment rights afforded all by the Constitution, which guarantees equal treatment to all under the law." Judge Francis noted, "the statistical disparities are indeed dark." He added "the defendants have proven at least a de facto policy on the part of the State Police out of the Moorestown station of targeting blacks for investigation and arrest..." The Gloucester County Public Defender, who represented these defendants, stated "it confirms what attorneys throughout the state have known for a long time, that the State Police have been targeting minority motorists on the turnpike and other highways in the state." He hailed Judge Francis's decision noting "it took a courageous decision on the part of the judge to acknowledge in legal form what's been going on."

This case garnered national attention and prompted the federal government to take a look into the national issue of racial profiling by police. Judge Francis was lauded for having the "courage" to address this controversial issue. Wow, having read this about Judge Francis I would have thought this judge cherished the Constitution and believed all people, maybe even fathers should be treated equally, maybe even fairly. But that was when he sat on the bench in the New Jersey Superior Court-Law Division. He then moved to family court and the blinders go on, and the cherished tenet of "justice for all" gets chucked out the Family Court courthouse window, and the obvious bias against fathers is palpable.

The local lawyers who practiced law in New Jersey Family Court knew well eight years ago that fathers could not get equal justice in custody proceedings any more so than black citizens could in their efforts to run the gauntlet of State Police who preyed upon them on the New Jersey Turnpike. Those facts were found in the family court's statistics as were those presented against the State Police trolling that portion of the turnpike that passed through Gloucester County. But what goes on in family court, as documented as it was, was not as exposed as are traffic stops on the turnpike, although the bias was equally acknowledged by the legal profession. As noted, a father would have to look long and hard to find an attorney in Gloucester County who gave him more than a nominal chance at obtaining custody of his young children, even if the mother had a major mental illness and elected to stop treatment. New Jersey Family Court had its gauntlet for fathers to run as they were processed through this system of injustice.

What is it about family courts that so corrupts judges' sense of the law; equality and fairness? The tender-years doctrine blatantly gave mothers a superior position carte blanche. One would think the more recent doctrine of the best interest of the child would be subject to review under some circumstances. No, it never happened in this court. Mothers were afforded protections that fathers never acquired. Mothers seemingly get their preferred legal status by birth rite. Fathers rarely got it and were forced to forever prove any legal status despite the cherished Fourteenth Amendment of the Constitution. This bias, discrimination against fathers was such that divorce lawyers advised fathers they had little chance for custody of their children in New Jersey Family Court. The statistics supported those claims and exposed the court's judicial bias against fathers. Marty told me I should go to California and cut ties to my children; don't fight the obvious, you won't get custody of your children. The other attorneys I interviewed also stated the obvious. The attorney from the MESP effort advised I had no chance for custody, that the thought of me getting custody of my children was "DOA" upon mention of the topic no matter what the circumstances were in my case.

Judge Francis inflicted his sense of justice on these children, this father, in his handling of the issues of this case brought before him. Perhaps these children and the father would have fared better had the hearing been held in the toll booth at the number two entrance of the New Jersey Turnpike, just three miles from where they lived with their mother. Any place would suffice that might afford a father and his children justice not available to them in the county courthouse. There was just something about such judicial hearings held within the walls of this New Jersey Family Court that inevitably perverted justice for this father, for his children.

Paula's acknowledgment of being diagnosed with bipolar disorder and electing to not take the medication had a profound impact on her ability to live a functional life. The serious effects of bipolar disorder on an individual's life were published, common knowledge among medical professionals. Her inability to manage her own life was then imposed upon the children in her custody. For some unknown reason, she expressed a psychotic degree of hostility against the one child in particular. After three years of hostile behavior, the court did not remove the mother, it removed this child and left the other children behind to fend for themselves.

Unfortunately, none of this known medical knowledge ever made it into the two custody evaluations or the many family court hearings for consideration of the best interest of my children. No, there was an acceptable level of fraud practiced in family court under the guise of justice for all. One can only imagine what our infamous custody evaluators would say about such acknowledged medical information. The first such "expert" declared the Mood Clinic's diagnosis was wrong after an hour's interview with this mother. The second "expert" suggested bipolar-disorder condition was stress-induced, even in benign remission. But the New Jersey professional review boards, the Board of Medical Examiners and the Board of Psychological Examiners, made no mention of these flawed theories, seemingly giving them some credence by not questioning the ridiculous testimony bantered about by professional charlatans in New Jersey Family Court proceedings addressing the welfare of my children.

# 23

# THE CHILDREN OVERRULE THE
# COURT

Michelle, graduating third in her high school class, was accepted early into the University of Chicago and Washington University-St Louis (WashU), while having applied to other top-tier universities. I took the four girls on a road-trip to visit various universities in the Midwest where Michelle had an interest in attending, including the University of Notre Dame, Northwestern, and Boston College. Arriving on campus in St Louis she immediately fell in love with WashU, and the deal was done. All other college applications were withdrawn.

A scare almost disrupted all these plans as the day before graduation the high school principal called me and reported Michelle had missed a total of fifteen days of school of which all were unexcused absences. Under state law, she was not eligible to graduate as she had not attended the minimum number of school days. How does this happen under the mother's watch? On a back-to-school evening in sixth grade, this child's teacher noted to me "Michelle was like the mother of the class; all the girls brought their problems and issues to her to resolve." I merely answered, "she is also the mother at home." Michelle ran the home in the mother's absence, mentally and physically, so I presume Paula was not inclined to push her to attend school. Somehow, upon notice of this issue, an effort was made by Paula to secure excuses that satisfied the school and she was allowed to graduate. Michelle was a Merit Scholar as well as a participant in New Jersey's Governor's School; she was the school's representative to Girl's State; and also a New Jersey Bloustein Scholar, all state programs to identify the upper echelon of its top students.

Yet another hearing was held on August 9, 2002, to address my continued custody claims and the pending college costs for Michelle who would be attending college in September. The court also ordered if a custody change was to be entertained it would require another custody evaluation to be performed and that DYFS would need to conduct a home study. Even as DYFS was under full legal assault for its institutional neglect of New Jersey's abused children and advised several times it would not get involved in this case. Perhaps this judge, while having read the case history to a degree, did not read the local newspapers.

The hypocrisy of this court's demand for yet another custody evaluation was obvious if I were to contest the mother's standing as the custodial parent. There was no such evaluation that established the mother as the better parent. The mother merely needed to file a DV complaint; I was removed from the home and this court leaves her in place to be the custodial parent. The DV charge was never adjudicated but dismissed without prejudice. The equivalent of a forfeit in sports; fathers lose every time.

Having gone away to college in Arizona, I wanted my children to experience that too. I preached it and the girls accepted the unwritten rule that if a college was within a day's drive it was too close. At this latest hearing, Paula told Judge Francis she could not afford the fancy, private schools this child had considered. She argued the child could go to the local community college or a four-year state college. The judge asked me my thoughts on the subject and I answered that these children were not your average students, but exceptional, and considered so on a national level relative to test scores. Private and public universities across the country recruited this student. I stated, "the children should be able to go where they can and not just where it was cheapest." With that, the judge stated "I agree" and pointing his finger in my direction said, "and you can pay for it." He then ordered the emancipation of the three oldest children, then aged eighteen, sixteen, and fifteen such that the mother was relieved of any obligation to contribute to any college costs for any of these children she claimed in this court for the past ten years. This court's justice of a thousand cuts continued when it came to justice for these children. Paula refused to complete any of the college financial aid packages for any of the children, and all we could do was advise schools the mother refused to participate in that process. Some schools refused to consider financial aid if financial information was not available from both parents. Paula contributed nothing to the college education of any of these children, and this court sanctioned it.

The judgment of Divorce, dated August 8, 1994, under the subject "College Education Costs" stated "the parties agree both parents should be responsible to contribute to their children's college educations. If the parties cannot agree as to their respective contributions, either one of them may make the appropriate application to the court."

In his rush to injustice, one could only assume Judge Francis denied or forgot state statute N.J.S.A 9:2-4 that states "both parents have equal rights to the custody of children. Both parents are equally charged with the care, education, and maintenance of the children." The court never participated in any review of the ability of both parents to contribute to the education of these children. It issued its blatant denial of justice for this father and the children as prosecuted against them for the duration of this case. The duty of parents to support their minor children was described by Blackstone, Commentaries, 447 as "a principle of natural law." But this was New Jersey Family Court. Judge Francis believed equal protection, justice under New Jersey law, only applied to those who transit the New Jersey Turnpike. It was not a consideration of this family court.

The hearing then moved on to address my request for child support for Katie and Molly, now aged fifteen and eleven, respectively, as both had "moved in" and were living full time with Adriana and me at the house-on-wheels. Knowing Michelle would soon leave the marital home for college in St. Louis, the two youngest children must have wondered what was to become of them at that house. Unbeknownst to me, on the last day of school in mid-June 2002, Katie and Molly stayed on the school bus as it passed the marital residence and got off the bus at the house-on-wheels a mile away. I can only assume they too tired of the legal process, the court's denial of their wishes to get out of that house and live with their father. Paula promised several times she would allow them to live with their father, only to deny it days or weeks later. Michelle moved freely between both homes as she planned her late August exit to St. Louis. Judge Francis ruled this two-month-long living arrangement for the two younger children was but "an extended summer visitation" and we left the court that day. I now supported three of the four children full-time at the house-on-wheels while paying child support to Paula who now lived alone at the marital home. The divorce judgment deemed the marital home was to be the residence for the children who had now fled that residence.

Despite it all, the girls and I loved the new living arrangement as they were out of the mother's domain; the three younger sisters were back again living together full-time. I could do all I wanted to provide for the girls. Paula would stop by infrequently on weekends and offer to take the girls out for ice cream but she always brought them back to me. The girls and I piled into the car in late August 2002 to drive Michelle to St. Louis for her first semester at college. The case issues calmed down as the four of us settled into the house-on-wheels. We were again a family.

Having dropped Michelle off at college, the children and I again met with the mother, at her request, in late August to "negotiate" yet another change of custody agreement. Paula agreed to vacate the marital home and receive a determined payoff of her equity in the home. The girls and I spent a weekend at the marital home, in the mother's absence, and a violation of the FRO, doing nothing but cleaning the home and working in the yard to create a better curb appeal for the pending appraisal needed to refinance the property for the buyout of Paula's equity. A few weeks into September, Paula, perhaps seeing the home cleaned up, now demanded the negotiated payoff value of $35,000 plus another $20,000. I refused her extortion demand and the deal was dead. She continued to live in the home, paid for with the child support for the children who abandoned the home more than three months ago.

On October 21, 2002, Paula, aided by her psychologist (everybody needs one), filed an order to show cause to enforce litigant's rights demanding the return of the two youngest children who had fled her residence in June. A hearing was held on November 9, 2002, and Paula alleged these children were being held "hostage" by their father and acknowledged the children had not come home since June. She asked the court for a "crisis intervention" to "evaluate and assess parental alienation and the emotional and psychological well-being of the girls," and last but not to be denied "on-going therapy for all the parties." Paula's filing claimed a formal police action was not filed against me for fear of upsetting the children now living with me full-time. She had me arrested three times in the presence of these children; called the police several other times to the home to threaten me and threatened to call the police on Adriana several times. I did not believe her expressed level of concern on this issue relative to this case history.

My nine-page response to this motion reminded the court that four months ago these circumstances were reported to the court. The court then defined the children's living status as but an "extended summer visitation," contrary to my having told the court the children had moved in with me at the house-on-wheels. If a kidnapping of these children was to be believed, I told the court these serious charges must be addressed in criminal court and I would demand a jury trial. The judge was somewhat confused as to all the circumstances and asked Paula why the children had left her home? Paula responded with the most honest words she had spoken in the ten-years of this case. She told the judge "they want to live with their father." Judge Francis then ordered Katie and Molly would stay with their father and he would retain residential custody of them. There was not to be another phony professional evaluation; no more custody trials; no more fraud perpetrated upon these children, this father, justice itself.

The children finally had their freedom from their mother and this court system that had denied them for ten years. No professionals; no therapy; no lawyers; no psychological tests; they just plotted their escape in the summer of 2002. They exercised their rights; the same rights this system had denied them for years. Yes, these children were hostages but to a corrupt system of brutal denial, bias, and contempt imposed by this family court. The children had no value, no rights; they were the property of a mentally ill parent. As the father, I fought this corrupt system of justice and the brutality it imposed on my children. From family court to the appellant division to the supreme court of New Jersey; DYFS; lawyers and the fraudulent professionals who denied my children their rights. Every system failed to protect these children and all failed miserably. These children survived despite family court, New Jersey's abysmal venue for justice for these children. The children had finally escaped family court justice.

I asked the court to assign Paula a level of child support for the additional children now in my custody. Typical of this court, Judge Francis ruled I had to continue to pay full child support to Paula for the children the court had just acknowledged had left her custody six months ago. The judge also ruled Paula could also claim the two youngest non-custodial children for the 2002 tax filings. As crazy as that exchange was, I was most gratified the children would remain in my custody and care. I would deal with the child support issue in due time but for now, I had these children out of the control of the mother. When Michelle returned home from college for Christmas break, she too took up residence at the house-on-wheels.

The court then ordered the three children in my custody to be interviewed by the court's mediator, to establish a visitation schedule with their mother. Having done little but visit these children sporadically on weekends since June there would be no scheduled visitation with the mother but for her casual visits. These children were but pawns in this family court's systemic efforts to protect, maintain, defend this mother at all costs. To hell with any other considerations or facts. There was but one consideration in this court, what is in the best interest of the mother; the interest or concerns for the children, and surely the father be damned.

As for the court awarding Paula the right to claim the two youngest children as tax dependents, the IRS did not think too highly of that. Tax law, not family court orders, governs tax issues. An IRS opinion filed with the United States Tax Court dated February 24, 2005, involved a case with similar concerns. The tax code states it is the parent who has physical custody of the dependent(s) who claims them unless relinquished by the custodial parent by signing Form 8332.

Paula filed her 2002 tax returns early and claimed the two children who had fled her custody months ago. I never signed a release of these tax-dependents to Paula. Federal and state tax filings earned her substantial refunds including an earned income credit for these dependents no longer in her custody. My 2002 returns were rejected as there was a duplicate claim for these two dependents. A tax audit in October 2003 brought this matter to a head and someone had to prove custody of these children. Paula, lacking any standing on the issue, was hit with demands by both the federal and state tax authorities for repayment of the substantial tax credits and ill-gained refunds plus interest and penalties. The IRS and New Jersey Revenue vigorously enforced their judgments, collecting them back from Paula over the next three years. Unlike the $2,000 judgment for child support awarded to me on March 5, 1999, and put into writing on appeal in 2000. New Jersey courts made no effort to enforce collection against this mother and this judgment debt that was still unpaid three years later.

In year-ten of this saga, the court finally ruled these children, having escaped their home, had served enough time of the verdict it imposed upon them. One might ask, what was their crime? They wanted to live with their father. But we did learn yet another truth of New Jersey Family Court: if the mother's complaint alleges the father is abusive, this court will have the father forcefully removed from the home before any hearing of the facts; if the mother is deemed abusive to a child in her home, this court will have the child removed from that home; if the mother's abuse continues the remaining children must flee their home. In the New Jersey Family Court, it is this abusive mother who is protected.

# 24

# THE END OF THE BEGINNING

I had been exposed to Judge Francis' ways on several occasions and thought him right up near the top of the list as a hard-nosed personality type in the way he treated many who sought justice in his court. I will relate here a hearing Judge Francis presided over while I was sitting in the peanut gallery waiting for my case to be called.

The case of a young couple, an ex-wife vs. the ex-husband who was representing himself. The young man hobbled into court in a full-length cast on his right leg. Barely able to sit, he hung to the edge of the seat so he could extend his injured leg. This ex-wife's lawyer complained that this ex-husband's scheduled child support payment was not collected by Probation, and he subsequently stopped-payment on the replacement check he had written. This ex-wife wanted the defendant jailed for not paying the obligated support. Jail for not paying child support; in this court? Is the accused male or female? The judge then turned to the ex-husband for his side of the story. He explained that having broken his leg, he was now on disability and in the interim was being paid by his employer's disability insurance carrier. The child support obligation could not be collected electronically by Probation from his employer's payroll, as he was temporarily off that payroll and on that of the disability carriers' payment system. To make the scheduled support payment he issued a personal check to the ex-wife.

The judge interrupted and called the resident sheriff's deputy to the bench and spoke to him briefly. The deputy left the courtroom and within minutes returned with three more deputies who took up positions to the right, left, and behind this hobbled ex-husband. Dare we suggest a Gestapo-like gesture by this court? The ex-husband continued with his explanation of the missed support payment. He told the court he was advised by the Probation Department that all support payments were to be paid through them and Probation told him to stop-payment on the check he had written to the ex-wife. He was to write a replacement check to Probation who would then issue the support payment to the ex-wife. That was the proper procedure as dictated by the Probation Department. This reasonably explained the stopped payment of the check but reason was not a valued commodity in this court.

The judge referred back to the ex-wife and her counsel who stated she still wanted the judge to put the ex-husband in jail. The judge advised if he did that then there would be no support payments with him jailed. This judge ignored the reasonable explanation for the stop-payment; giving it no consideration. The judge told the ex-wife and her attorney to take a ten-minute break and decide what they wanted the court to do in this case. A recess was called, the ex-wife and her attorney left the courtroom. I made my way down to this young guy, still surrounded by three sheriff's deputies as if the court anticipated this crippled man would flee the premises. Pure intimidation of the worst kind. I approached him and told him his explanation made complete sense and not to worry as they would not send him to jail, all they wanted was to intimidate him, but most of all they wanted his money. After a brief break, the ex-wife returned to court. Had they decided? Yes, they wanted the court to put the ex-husband in jail.

Judge Francis, having conceded the penalty consideration to the ex-wife rather than maintain control of the case, was shocked she elected to jail this ex-husband. Judge Francis immediately questioned the decision as the support payments were now in jeopardy if he ordered the ex-husband, with a broken leg in a full-length cast, to jail. The judge then began to argue the merits of their decision which was his to make but one that he had abdicated. How a judge allowed an ex-wife to decide justice was beyond my imagination but again this was the family court. I can only imagine what the appellate division would have said in that they typically rubber-stamped trial court decisions. The court merely needed to take a breath and reclaim its exercise of jurisprudence if not its sanity. The mob had again taken control of a case. Honestly, I don't recall how this aberration of justice got resolved by this judge but that it happened merely confirmed my belief that this judge was nuts and the court system was in dire need of new management.

I sent a letter to the court dated January 11, 2003, copied below, to again address the fruits of Judge Francis' administration of injustice for the benefit of my children:

The abbreviated hearing seeking justice for these children...produced little of the espoused and highly touted "justice for all" nor fruits of that ubiquitous court cliché "what is in the best interest of the child." What they did get was yet another delay of justice due, and the court's stated reference to limit any support by this mother, subject to appeal, of course. Of the little, this court decided in favor of these minor dependents it failed to reference in its order of the day's justice doled. Probably an oversight or perhaps considered hardly deserving of the written reference.

Specifically, the defendant-children requested access to their former residence, permanently vacated in June 2002, so they might be able to secure certain personal possessions still under the control of the mother, who interestingly enough lives rent-free while collecting child-support for these children who abandoned their court-sanctioned homestead. Since the mother acknowledged locking these defendant-children out of their 'court-sanctioned' residence, the only legitimate child support awarded them by this court of injustice, the court deemed it appropriate that the mother would allow the defendant-children limited access to collect their personal property with hopefully little interference to mother. And we thank you for that gracious gesture. But this award of justice for the benefit of these defendants was somehow lost in scripting the court's order of the day in this action.

Since these defendant-children get meager justice from this court, what is awarded for their benefit is rightly cherished. Please issue a revised order detailing this extended award of equity for their benefit, in this case, lest they be subject to the mother's charge of trespass. As she so eloquently stated, she was "entitled to her privacy" (to hell with the kids implied by the mother if not this court).

The court issued a revised Order dated January 27, 2003, that ordered "mother shall allow the children to have access to the marital home to obtain their things if need be. All other matters will remain as is until the scheduled hearing of February 14, 2003." The children were allowed access to the home to take possession of their personal belongings seven months after having fled their court-sanctioned residence.

So, we see the venerable Judge Francis in action, a champion of the Fourteenth Amendment that was seemingly embedded in his legal mind. This Fourteenth Amendment was crafted as a pillar of American justice born from the passions of those who believed, wanted to promote, guarantee, all citizens enjoyed equal protection under the law. Judge Francis went far afield, stretched, to insert his opinion that statistics alone acknowledged the state troopers' preference for stopping minorities who traveled the New Jersey turnpike. He did not seem impressed with New Jersey Family Court statistics that mothers were awarded custody of children in over 90 percent of its cases. He was not impressed by the court's statistics that might have prompted one to make the same observation as he did in the turnpike case; "the statistical disparities are indeed dark." Why not?

Judge Francis prosecuted the same court-sanctioned injustice in this case; he ordered the mother had no obligation to contribute to the college education of the children she claimed for ten years; that was the sole obligation of the father. Sounds fair if you deny the tenets of the Fourteenth Amendment. This honored guardian of the Fourteenth Amendment ordered this father was obligated to continue to pay child support to the mother after having given custody of these children to the father. But then there would be more, Judge Francis awarded the mother the financial benefit of claiming the two non-custodial children as tax dependents even as the record showed she did not provide any financial support for these children or even had them in her custody. Sounds fair if you deny the tenets of the Fourteenth Amendment. This court did not afford equal protection of the law to this father who supported his children in the absence of any such support by the mother. But this was New Jersey Family Court; the Fourteenth Amendment did not apply.

The Fourteenth Amendment to the U.S. Constitution was ratified on July 28, 1868. New Jersey Family Court just elected not to consider it in its rulings. These children absorbed all the abuse the mother and this court could mete out. The children finally claimed their rights and liberties when they walked away from this court's perverted sense of justice; it's injustice. Yes, they rode their school bus to freedom; they had escaped the mother's tentacles and those of the New Jersey Family Court.

In the fall of 2002, Paula dropped off to Katie a brown shopping bag full of college circulars, letters, brochures, and offers in one of her drive-by visits to the house-on-wheels. Based on her stellar results on both the PSAT and SATs taken through her sophomore year, her GPA, and class rank, this child was at the top of most colleges' list of candidates. That she planned to study Chemical Engineering and being a young woman highlighted her credentials. Receiving that bag full of mail, we all sat on the floor at the house-on-wheels that day for several hours sorting out schools from all four corners of the country by category: private, state, geographical locations, curriculum, etc.... Letters were read, offers noted, applications considered, schools eliminated for reasons of size, location, programs, etc.... It was fun, exciting to see all the future potential of this child. And she is just entering her junior year of high school. Eventually, many state universities from across the U.S. would offer her full paid tuition scholarships; most ranked national private universities solicited her consideration.

The potential was much to behold. Of the universities Katie expressed an interest in, several flew her to their campus for multiple visits. A Merit Scholar as well, she would eventually consider six top engineering schools of interest (Cornell; Rice; USC; Notre Dame; WashU; Texas A&M), and all accepted her and offered substantial scholarships that totaled some $700,000. Rutgers too offered her a scholarship as a participant in the State's Governor's School engineering program while she was also a touted New Jersey Bloustein Scholar. I asked if she wanted to plan a trip to visit Cornell University, just a five-hour drive away? She responded, "no, it was too close" to home. We did take a college "road-trip" of 1,500 miles one-way to her birthplace, Houston, to visit Rice University. We stopped at several other universities on the trip. Rice paid for Katie to visit the campus twice more and she earned their top scholarship. USC flew her out to visit and she earned their top engineering scholarship; she visited WashU three times. Texas A & M advised Katie all she need do is complete their application and she was the beneficiary of a full paid scholarship of tuition, and board. She eventually accepted a full paid scholarship for tuition and board to WashU for a five-year program that earned her BS and MS degrees in Chemical, Energy, and Environmental Engineering. She opted out of a Ph.D. offer and took a job with the Department of Energy in Washington, D.C. for four years.

I suggested Katie entertain a law degree as I thought that would complement her engineering background, perhaps as a patent attorney. She took a review course and sat once for the LSAT. She scored over 170, in the range of all the top-tier law schools. Electing not to apply to a law school, she chose to pursue an MBA and applied to the top five national programs: Stanford, Harvard, Penn-Wharton, U of Chicago, and MIT. Accepted at four of these schools, she went on to earn her MBA at Stanford in 2015. The applications required an essay answer to the prompt "what matters most to you and why?" Katie's essay answered "My dad."

Sometime in January Katie asked if I could drive her to the marital home to check for more college mail at the house. We had not seen nor heard from Paula in weeks. I answered I could not go to the house as I could not risk another violation of the FRO that excluded me from the property for anything other than to pick up or return the children for visitation. The children had vacated the home, I had no reason to be at that house. After some pestering, I said Ok but insisted she call the house to confirm the mother was not home; if no answer we would drive by to ensure the car was not in the driveway. No answer to the phone call, Katie, Molly, and I piled into the car and drove the mile to the marital home. The house was dark and no car was in the driveway. I turned the car around and approached the mailbox that was at the curb on this rural road. It was dark and we parked on the two-lane county road that had no shoulder and we faced any oncoming traffic on a hill. Little happening on this rural road at 7:30 PM, I reached into the mailbox and handed the contents to Katie who quickly sorted through looking for college material addressed to her. A car came over the hill approaching us slowly as we had the road blocked to some degree. As the car passed Molly said, "I think that was mommy." Hardly noticing the comment to expedite our sorting effort, a hand grabbed my wrist in the dark and screamed "I knew you were checking my mail." Startled, the kids and I jumped and noted we were only there to see if any other colleges had sent mailings to Katie. With that, we took what college mail we found, and left the scene, and returned to the house-on-wheels.

A half-hour later there was a knock on the door. I answered and there stood a local police officer. He stood in the foyer of the house-on-wheels and greeted the kids as they knew him from the local school. Paula signed a complaint alleging my violating the FRO. I explained the circumstances to the officer, and all confirmed we had not seen Paula for three weeks or more; Katie wanted to check for additional college mailings. Having checked by phone and a drive-by, believing Paula was not home, we approached the mailbox. We showed the officer all the mail Paula had dropped off some weeks ago. The officer understood and said he would return to Paula and explain the circumstances.

He returned a half-hour later to advise Paula refused to withdraw the complaint. I was taken into custody and driven to the local police station a mile away for booking. Fingerprinted and photographed at the station, for now, a fourth such arrest upon Paula's complaint, I almost knew where to stand and what to do. The officer contacted the judge on call and advised him I was in his custody, but my three children were at my home and unattended. The judge agreed to my release and ordered me to be in court for the scheduled hearing of the matter. Katie was devastated that her simple request ended with my arrest that night. I told her not to worry, we would handle it. It should be noted, of my four arrests in the duration of this case, I was returned home three times after having been "booked" as I had custody of the children each of those times at the house-on-wheels. The only time I was held in custody was at the local police station after the arrest at the office that post-Christmas morning in 1995.

Seeing the situation for what it was, and having custody of the children, I looked to solidify their residence at the house-on-wheels. Knowing the strained relationship between myself and Judge Francis, having seen him in court against other fathers, and best exemplified by his most recent ruling on child support and tax dependents in our case, I decided to again seek legal representation, for self-preservation in this court of the absurd. I seriously questioned Judge Francis's ability to handle this case with any sense of reason much less justice.

I interviewed a former County Prosecutor, Andy, about my situation. Andy was one of the three attorneys I had interviewed eleven years ago relative to the initial DV charge. Andy's opinion of that complaint ten years ago was "this is not domestic violence but an argument;" but I elected to go with Marty in those early days. I wonder to this day what might have been had I then decided to use Andy early in this case? But that was then and this is now. I explained to Andy I had full custody of the children who had left the mother's home eight months ago but was ordered to continue paying child support to Paula who now lived alone in the marital home. Andy questioned how such a situation was even possible? Something was wrong. I could not have agreed more with that assessment. It is called the New Jersey Family Court. Andy agreed to represent me at the hearing on February 14, 2003. Likewise, he told me not to come to court, that this judge had something personal against me to do what he had done in the hearings to date. And to think I believed the family court was all about justice, what was in the best interest of the children.

Andy arrived in court and announced his representation of me. The judge reportedly asked, "Where is he, is he in the hall? Get him in here; he always has something to say." Andy assured the judge that I was not in the building but at work. He then initiated the effort to convince Judge Francis his order of a change of custody of the dependent children with continued support payments to the mother was without merit. The judge agreed to rescind his order that I continue to pay child support to Paula. But remember, my child support was the obligation to pay the mortgage and property taxes on the marital home. And that home was to be home for the children until Molly turned 18 years old. Paula refused to vacate the property and the court did not order her to vacate. She was living rent-free off the child support due to the children she abandoned now nine months ago. I was given ten minutes to vacate this same home almost eleven years ago and ushered off the property by two police officers.

The court now had to determine Paula's child support obligation for the four children in my custody. Paula lived off the child support for these four children for ten years that typically averaged $18,000, tax-free to her. Judge Francis calculated Paula's child support to be $326, without any documentation as to incomes. He then arbitrarily reduced that support to a weekly total of $48; yes, $12 for each child. This for four children; aged 18, 16, 15, and 11 years of age; one in college for which this judge had previously absolved the mother of any responsibility to contribute to any higher education expenses for these children. In that Paula did not work in the summer months she was forever in arrears and the IRS would seize a $700 tax refund to pay her past-due support. This in addition to the family court having never executed its $2,000 judgment for the orthodontist bill awarded to me in 1999 and finally put to writing in 2000 as ordered by the appellate decision, but refused any effort to enforce collection. As for visitation with the children, Paula's only two visits in the last six weeks included her boyfriend. The girls refused to go with their mother.

This hearing also dismissed the complaint relative to my recent "mailbox" arrest. The court ordered the children, father, and mother to participate in psychological evaluations to be performed by Paula's counselor no less. "Purpose of the evaluation is to foster relationships with the mother." No such evaluations ever took place; I refused to participate. I had a very low opinion of those "professionals" who plied their psychology in and around this case and who feasted off the mentally ill who forever sought direction for her disheveled life. But I would have loved to have met any of Paula's psychologists to ask but a few relevant questions.

The court ordered the parties would work to choose a real estate appraiser to establish a fair value for the marital home to complete my effort to buy out Paula's equity in the property. Paula's home appraisal came from a real estate agent 30 miles away, and not from the resident county, and reportedly an acquaintance of a former male companion. That appraisal value was high by any standard and upon review brought to light several discrepancies, including incorrect dimensions of the home. I called this appraiser and asked if he had ever been on the property as there were several concerns with his appraised value. He assured me he had been at the property; his appraisal was accurate. Andy wrote a letter to this agent on February 20, 2003, advising him we considered his appraisal to border on fraud. The appraisal was withdrawn and we negotiated a sales price based on facts. I did not bother to file a complaint with the local real estate board as I assumed they would merely subscribe to any such discrepancies as a misunderstanding.

Paula looked for new legal representation, her sixth attorney, and was referred to a new, free legal service offered by the Diocese of Camden. This legal office now had its first client. The attorney, an old acquaintance for sure, was the same priest who was Paula's fourth attorney. He had represented Paula in 1995 relative to the change of custody of Adriana and my $400 buyout of Molly's education from the Camden public school system. He could not believe his misfortune.

A Consent Order was drafted that noted Paula agreed to vacate the marital home "on or before March 15, 2003." On April 25, 2003, I was approved for refinancing the marital property allowing for a settlement of the equity with Paula, who continued to press for a higher payout beyond what was fair value. But she had to vacate this homestead now.

Needing funds, and in dire financial distress, Paula settled on a payout of $40,000 less the $2,000 judgment I filed against her that dated to 1998. The same judgment the family, appellate and supreme courts of New Jersey refused to enforce for collection four years ago. The sales agreement signed; Andy sent me to the marital home several times over the next three months advising "the key was in the mailbox." It was not despite any agreements. Andy asked, "what is wrong with that woman?" She was living rent-free, period. Finally, opposing counsel got it done and we reclaimed possession and ownership of the marital home in mid-June 2003. The girls and I spent a month doing basic cleanup and repairs; painting the interior; replacing the rugs; cleaning out the garage; etc... The children and I vacated the house-on-wheels and took up residence in the marital home in July 2003. I was removed from the same property within minutes; Paula squatted there for twelve months rent-free.

Paula took her money, again not working the summer months, and spent seven weeks that summer touring Spain and France. Within eighteen months she had gone through the entire payout and was again financially broke. The marital home now ours, we continued to make improvements to the property; all the shrubs were replaced, and the lawn reseeded; a deck was added off the back doors; AC was installed; the kitchen upgraded; the basement was eventually finished after a drainage system was installed to address water issues. The girls invited their college friends' home.

In the summer of 2003, Paula offered to take the three older girls on a day trip to the Jersey shore. Molly would be with me for a day of softball. Katie refused to go when told Paula's boyfriend would accompany them. She went to the softball games with us. Michelle and Adriana went on that day-trip and questioned the two-hour long drive up the turnpike when the South Jersey beaches were just an hour away and to the south. They would soon have their answer as they walked over a dune to the beaches of Sandy Hook, the only nudist beach in the northeast region. The girls cowered on the beach as they were approached by nudists, singles, and couples, and eventually a busload of nudists up from Maryland for the day. Prodded to enjoy life, their freedom, strip, they were accosted in their only effort to put their feet into the surf. Paula's boyfriend begged to join in with the exposed crowd but Paula reminded him of their promise, not today. I could appreciate why the Mood Clinic decided years ago cognitive therapy did not work in Paula's case. I can only guess what Family Court would have thought of yet another foible of Paula's parenting skill. Having ignored all my complaints to date, Hamlet might best explain the court's opinion, "the (man) doth protests too much, methinks."

There were no court proceedings in 2004. I wonder who was best served, me and my children or this court, and its many flawed characters?

Paula filed a last motion with the family court in February 2005 that was subsequently postponed for a hearing on June 24, 2005. Assigned to Judge Testa, the fourth judge assigned to this case, he denied Paula's claim for the two non-custodial children as tax dependents; but he did terminate her obligation to pay the $12 weekly child support for each of the three oldest children. He calculated a new weekly child support obligation for Molly to be $44. Paula complained about why she was now obligated to pay weekly support of $44 for just one child when she was obligated to pay $48 weekly support for four children? The court advised the $44 weekly support was the minimum support mandated by the State's child support guidelines. And to think Judge Francis awarded me $12 a week in support for each child just eighteen months ago. Paula continued to be in arrears for these support payments as she did not work during the summer months. Her tax refunds and salary were garnished to collect this unpaid child support.

The court then denied my motion to withdraw the restraining order (FRO) imposed upon me at this former marital property that I now owned. A contradiction to say the least, but this was the New Jersey Family Court. I now owned and lived at the property where the FRO restricted my visits much less me living there. Under New Jersey case law, the restraining order could be released with agreement by Paula. Not having that, I would need to file a motion addressing eleven criteria as established under case law, Carfango vs Carfango. The court would then consider this motion to determine if there was "good cause" to release this FRO against me. I drafted such a motion but never pursued it in court. As crazy as the situation was, I had too many other things to do than waste any more time in this ridiculous court. Besides, the worst-case scenario was that a New Jersey Family Court judge might order me to vacate the house and property I now owned and again called home with my children. I decided not to risk such a filing in New Jersey Family Court.

As the movie *The Ox-Bow Incident* came to a close, and the posse informed they had hung three innocent men, a sense of guilt fell over those who just minutes ago were so sure of their deeds. I readily drew the analogy between my experience and that of my children in our thirteen-year search for justice in New Jersey Family Court to the injustice exposed at the Ox-Bow. This court, the posse, the mob as it was, laid waste to the laws in their demand for expedient justice for the mother. This "guilty" father was judged upon a dubious complaint such that he was found neither guilty nor not guilty of the charge. He was merely guilty of being the husband. That was sufficient evidence in this court to string me up and expose me and my children to all the injustice of the New Jersey Family Court. Judges, lawyers, professional evaluators, court clerks, prosecutors, Probation, DYFS, and the appellant courts were all members of the posse who rallied against me as they made my children watch their calculated lynching of not just me, their father, the one who provided for them, but justice itself. None of these hangmen said much; took a closer look for the facts, the truth; no, they just followed the mob's bias and the hanging of another innocent father was sufficient justice in New Jersey Family Court.

As victims of their justice, I tell this court now that my children and I survived despite your injustice, your laws, your hearings, your contempt for my demands for justice. The children and I survived despite all of you. It took us thirteen years; we paid the price you demanded; we suffered under your orders and processes, but still, we survived despite your ways and means. In the end, I huddled with my children and we went home, scared for sure, but we returned to our home as a family. We lost a piece of our belief in America's promised justice for all, a flawed system for sure. Don't ask the lawyers, the judges, the players in the dirty business of family law, ask the victims, the innocent fathers, and their children who are denied justice every day in this state-sanctioned family court of injustice. The closest this "family court" ever came to getting anything right was when I was warned in the December 1993 hearing that I was very close to being found in contempt of the court. No, I admit I was guilty of nothing but contempt of this court for the duration of this case, for the injustice it waged against my children and me, in its defense of the mother. Paula was not there to take care of the sick child that morning in March 1993, and she did not care for them for the next ten years. But this court defended her every day for the abuse and neglect she imposed on these children.

It is no coincidence that Judge Tomasello found me guilty of domestic violence in all of five minutes in his court merely on the word of the mother. When that same incident was prosecuted in municipal court, in front of a judge who did not have a gender-biased agenda, Paula's claim in the hands of the professional prosecutor, was easily defeated by myself by asking all of two questions about the facts. Surely guilty in family court, in another judicial venue, Paula's corrupted words were exposed to the light of truth. Could this family court of injustice have spared to ask two questions? Perhaps fathers should seek custody of their children in municipal court where they can escape the bias, and corrupt professionalism prosecuted in New Jersey Family Court.

Molly graduated high school in 2009 and was also a Merit Scholar and a New Jersey Bloustein Scholar and had many college opportunities offered from across the country. She thought she wanted to go to college in New England so we took a week-long road trip and visited several schools in and around Boston, Massachusetts, and Vermont. Not liking the prospect of such cold winters, we then took another college road trip into Virginia and North Carolina. Finally, I convinced her we should take a plane trip to visit the school I had attended in Arizona. Molly complained it was too hot in Arizona. We landed on campus and she fell in love with it. Molly's academic credentials qualified her for an Honor's College scholarship that paid her out-of-state tuition. I visited Molly a few times and we spent one Spring Break traveling around Arizona. Molly graduated in 2013 and returned home and again took up residence at home.

Molly was very active in her high school, serving as President of the Student Council, ran the annual blood drives, played softball, was a student manager for the boys' basketball team for four years, among many things. Upon landing on the Honor's College campus at the largest university in the United States, in her second year, she was selected as one of over 200 Resident Assistants that supported and assisted an on-campus resident student population of over 15,000. Coming from a South Jersey township of less than 3,000, Molly soon made her presence known in this large campus community. Molly interned in sports medicine for the Division 1 football team; she interned in a lab that worked to identify treatments to improve the cognitive abilities of young adults with Down's Syndrome, a population she knew well as her uncle, my brother, had Down's Syndrome. She volunteered for the campus blood drives among many efforts. The university nominated Molly, in her junior year, as their representative for the Resident Advisor of the Year at the Mid-Mountain conference of American Universities in Denver. In her senior year, Molly was one of four finalists of over two hundred nominees for the university's annual Spirit Award. The president of the Spirit Club won the award; Molly was not a member of the Spirit Club; she just did good things because that was who she was. My $400 investment in Molly's education in 1996 paid off handsomely.

Molly had several additional years living at the marital home as compared to the time the other girls enjoyed. Katie lived there for three years before she headed off to college. Adriana lived at home for a few more years while she pursued local job opportunities while attending a local college. Molly went with me to Arizona in 2015 when I purchased a retirement home. I sold our New Jersey home in 2017 and retired.

Molly and Adriana shared an apartment not far from the old homestead. Michelle met love at first sight and married her college sweetheart, an attorney, and they reside in the D.C. area with two beautiful children. Katie married her high school junior prom date who followed her to California while she attended Stanford. They are happily married and live in the foothills facing San Francisco Bay and the Golden Gate bridge.

The children went to great colleges from across the country. They garnered scholarships totaling $1.8 million. Paula, the court sanctioned custodial parent, contributed nothing, not a dime, to the success of these children as ordered by this family court.

Paula did show up for all their college graduations. The children graduated and have taken their place in society but with no thanks to the mother or family court. I, the father, was the one who ensured they survived, did not suffer more than the usual physical abuse the mother meted out, assured the girls' someone cared for them; ensured they got their deserved college educations. I was there to take them in when they fled their court-sanctioned home. I made sure the right things got done while the other players in this search for justice all chose to ignore such efforts for years. As Judge Francis expressed that day in court "and you can pay for it." By "you" I understood he meant the children and me. The children paid the price this court demanded of them. The exposed bias, fraud, committed against me and my children was as obvious as it was un-American. I know now what the minorities in this country endure every day at the hands of America's system of injustice.

The girls returned home from college and we gathered for holidays in years to come. I asked them to invite their mother to join them at the house and she spent nights sleeping over. I prepared the meals and provided the home setting for what were many good times in the home. When Paula was in the home I would retreat upstairs while they socialized downstairs. I just did not want to be in her presence.

Justice was not served in this case; the children and the father were victims of this court's blatant bias for the mother. The children received no consideration of justice from this court albeit Judge Herman's order that allowed Adriana to escape the mother's physical and emotional brutality. But he left the other three children to remain in such a deplorable environment and it did not end the mother's brutal assaults against Adriana. This court would rule years later it needed DYFS to substantiate such assaults. There was fraud exposed in this case at every level of the justice denied these children and their father. This New Jersey Family Court and its surrogates facilitated this fraud, turned a blind eye to it, denied its existence in its effort to deny justice to my children and me, as it sought to only protect the mother. The children, the father, justice, be damned!

The injustice we experienced was as pervasive in year thirteen as it was on day one, it didn't get better, sometimes worse, but it was persistent in duration and effect. This New Jersey Family Court never provided justice for these children, and the two youngest children simply fled the home years later, having been denied the constitutional promise due them. The court said nothing upon notice the last two children had fled the mother's domain. It merely continued the award of financial benefits to the mother for the support she had consistently denied these children for years. As I always stated, the children provided more for the mother than the mother ever provided for them. The benevolence presumed in this court's title was exposed for what it was, a court of fraud. Family court cared little for justice and even less for the welfare and best interest of my children.

I calculated my out-of-pocket expenses for this ten-plus year divorce and related child-custody efforts to total $125,000. These included fees paid to my lawyers and the expense the court imposed on me to pay Paula's lawyers, fees for the numerous court filings, fees paid for the two custody evaluations we never got, alimony and home equity payouts to Paula, and the expense of the family having to maintain a second household, etc... Not a dime of these family funds was spent on the care and welfare of my children. This amount does not include the lost opportunity costs of investing these funds and the disadvantage of not filing joint income tax returns. It also does not include any college expenses, or my child support payments paid to maintain Paula, or the many day-to-day expenses I incurred to meet the needs of the girls outside the child-support mandates. In the parlance of New Jersey Family Court, I was able to buy back my children's freedom for about $31,000 each. And I believed child trafficking was a crime. I put no price tag on the cost of the justice denied to my children and me by this court.

The Honorable John Philpot Curran, a staunch advocate for Ireland's freedom from England, is quoted to have said in 1790, "eternal vigilance is the price of liberty." Mr. Curran believed that ones' liberties are forever under assault and that one must always be vigilant of those efforts and be willing to fight to keep your freedoms. He argued our liberty was God-given, and to those who concede those liberties "servitude is at once the consequence of his crime and the punishment of his guilt." This fight for the custody of my children was the vigilance demanded for the liberties stolen from us by the New Jersey Family Court.

Just two weeks before my retirement, I was diagnosed with cancer. Molly was there when they wheeled me into the operation, and she was there when I woke five hours later. She took me home to the apartment she shared with Adriana and they nursed me back on my feet within a month. Molly drove with me out to my retirement home in Arizona for yet another great road trip.

President Lincoln said it best, and I cited his words to myself many times throughout this effort. The probability of continued failure in any struggle for justice must not deter us. During these thirteen years in the New Jersey Family Court, justice was neither considered nor delivered for these children. The children merely slipped out of the noose this court had strung around their necks, we cut the ropes that bound them to the mother, and we went home. We had finally escaped the mob's rule, we escaped New Jersey Family Court! My children were worth the fight and I'd do it again. In family court I was only a father; to these children, I was their father.

Katie, upon her graduation from Stanford University, noted, "Daddy, we are who we are today because of you."

# WHY THIS CASE? THE CHILDREN!

S o, what do you do with four little girls you only see on a visitation schedule as arranged through family court? Wednesday night visits were just about getting them a good dinner; doing homework and talking through so many concerns. I let the girls know I would always be there for them, to take care and provide for them, never doubt that! I sent them home with tomorrow's lunch in hand. Weekend visits alternated with me having the girls every Saturday and then alternating weekends of Friday night and Sundays. Favorite morning breakfast was easy. Then some morning TV shows they liked to watch; played Sega, and homework was always addressed to make sure it was done and reviewed. They asked me to sign their schoolwork if a signature was required.

Early on in the divorce, we hit all the local parks and playgrounds, weather considered. I bought the girls' bikes while Molly rode buckled into the seat behind me. We made many weekend trips to my sister's home in Washington D.C. and later Alexandria, VA. We rode our bikes all over the Capitol and Mall area, and the bike paths that flowed through the many local parks. We were chased off the steps of the Capitol on our bikes. We rode our bikes to Mount Vernon. We visited zoos in Philadelphia and D.C.; made a trip to the Baltimore aquarium. I bought four pairs of pink roller skates and we spent weekends at the Deptford skating rink learning the fine art of staying on your feet while wearing skates. We walked park paths along the Delaware River and rode bikes on the Kelly Parkway behind the Philadelphia Art Museum. We saw the most current Disney and other hit movies at the theatre. When we ran out of ideas or time, we went home to the apartment or the house-on-wheels and did homework, projects, or put on a Disney VHS, or just relaxed. When softball fever hit, we played catch in the adjoining field at the mobile home park or the local little league field. Then too, I always sent the girls home after having made one of their favorite dinners. God, I hated to see them go but assured them I was there for whatever they needed, just call me.

The latter custody evaluation report noted, almost complained, I pushed the girls to do their best; yes, these girls could do anything. When it came to the annual science fair projects in the later years of grade school, we thought long and hard for projects that taught the girls something and challenged them to learn. One involved a prism; another grew mold on vegetables and the school complained it stunk up the place. We did a project about magnets and another with plants and how they grew under various types of lights; another required testing water drawn from five local sources. We drove the hour to the shore one Saturday—the girls asleep for the drive. I ran nearly a hundred yards to traverse the beach to grab a bottle of ocean water and run back to the car hoping none had awoken to find me missing.

Then there was the project that topped them all. Katie loved doing math problems of any sort. Having bought the girls ten-speed bikes, I came up with the idea that asked, "Why do we change gears on a ten-speed bike?" Katie researched gears and calculated and grafted the distance traveled with each combination of gears that explained the circumstance of any gear. I mounted a bike pedal, chain, and rear sprocket on a piece of plywood for effect. The project earned Katie a second-place finish in the regional science fair for six grade students.

While the other girls were content to do their schoolwork, Katie had the drive to beat everything—be it a score, a time, a grade. In teaching the times tables, the third-grade teacher quizzed the class to complete sixty times-table calculations within a minute or less. Katie took this challenge to heart. The class soon realized Katie was fast approaching the teacher's timed results for these calculations. In fourth grade, I gave Katie one tip that allowed her to pick up needed seconds, and the teacher went down to Katie's time of 34 seconds. Seeing this child excel academically, I pressed the math teacher to let her go at her speed. Katie was able to test out of chapters before the subject matter was taught in class. By fifth grade, she sat in the back of math class working at her own pace and by sixth grade had taught herself algebra.

Upon arrival at the regional middle school, Katie complained to me that she was stuck doing seventh-grade math. I called the school counselor who questioned the merits of having any child skip ahead and perhaps face frustrations should they fail. I offered to pay for the test; asked him to call the grade school for input to no avail. The counselor denied my request to test Katie's abilities. I then called the school superintendent who also questioned my request. Finally, agreeing to test Katie, a week later, in early October, the counselor removed Katie from her seventh-grade math class. Katie was told she had done exceptionally well in the math test and was being placed in the top-level of the eighth-grade math class. Katie would eventually tutor calculus to engineering students for $15 an hour while she earned her degrees in chemical engineering. Never doubt the potential of your kids.

All the girls were involved in school and Michelle led the way. As Class Presidents, and with student council posts and the like, we were always searching for the next slogan to hang on a wall at school. Katie ran for class treasurer so I came up with the classic "Don't trust your buck to luck, vote Katie." There were others but I surely thought this was my best. When running for sixth-grade class president, I urged Molly to fly a banner from the school's gym rafters using helium-filled balloons. She was too afraid of getting in trouble for that stunt. I can still remember those great times many years later.

In the interim, I sat on the local school board for eight years.

We took a few memorable road trips in addition to the several college tours yet to be planned. The girls loved all our road trips. Our week-long trip to the Smokey Mountains and a pouring midnight rainstorm while camping in a tent rings a bell. We tried to keep ourselves dry on the air pillows as the water rose around us inside the tent. We went tubing on the local river. Then there was the big camping trip out west. We flew into Salt Lake City to visit another sister and her family before we headed out in a rental car packed with tents and other camping gear. We were not campers by any definition of the word and had never attempted to cook a campfire meal. Before this big trip, we took one night to hone our camping skills as we snuck out of my Deptford apartment, and set up the tent behind two big evergreen trees fifty yards behind the building. At dawn, we gathered the tent and our belongings and ran back into the apartment hoping no one would see us.

We headed out of Salt Lake City south to Mt. Zion National Park. We toured the park and in doing so lost track of time and had to set up our two tents in the dark and heat a can of stew when you could not see your hand in front of your face. We finally climbed into the tents only to awake the next morning feeling pretty lousy and quite disheveled. As we left Mt. Zion and having gained a better appreciation of the merits of the civilized world, I announced we would only camp out in hotel rooms for the rest of the trip. We rented a small cabin during our stay at the Grand Canyon. From the Grand Canyon, we headed west. The girls heard on the radio that the Backstreet Boys concert was on TV so we pulled into a motel in Barstow, California for the night. What a dive that was, just a notch above tent camping, but they had cable TV so they saw the concert. We left Barstow and made our way to San Diego to spend some time with my oldest sister and her family. The concert was again on replay in San Diego. We eventually headed north along the coast highway to San Francisco and all those wild, hilly streets and cable cars. Then on to Muir Woods, before we headed back to Salt Lake City and our flight back to New Jersey. Three thousand miles in twelve days with four kids was a trip we remember.

We did what we could to take our minds off the divorce and the home situation where the children lived. Weekends at my apartment and later at the house-on-wheels; quick visits or long weekends and holidays to Washington D.C. or Poughkeepsie; a trip to Niagara Falls; we kept ourselves occupied. During the summer months, we enjoyed many weekends in the apartment's pool. The mandatory return of the children to the marital home brought us all back to the reality of our lives and what I needed to do to take care of the girls. I was in a hostile environment at both the home and in court. Of what I remember of those many years, I remember the court efforts the most as that was the battlefield for the justice we sought only to be denied time and again. I hoped the girls could forget much of what they saw, heard, and lived in those years. For me, it was a time when I would remember everything that threatened my children. There are just some things you don't forget. This is the story I remember and can just now write about.

Good riddance, New Jersey Family Court!

# ACKNOWLEDGMENTS

All who find themselves in a very life-altering situation, must wonder how do you learn to cope and where do you find the energy and fortitude to face any challenge? I believe it starts with your genetics and for that, I am forever grateful to my mother and father. I never thought I could push myself to do what needed to be done until I found my children in such jeopardy. It became an issue of mind over matter.

There was just something about these four little girls in my life. We adopted the first two as infants, and I made a promise to them on sight that I would take care of them. They had already lost their parents once and I would not allow them to lose a second. And then the gift of our other two girls just added to the demands of my time and care. I just could not leave them in such a difficult circumstance in life and at such a young age. To this day, I maintain daily contact with them by phone or text.

I am forever grateful for the moral support provided by my large family of six sisters and two brothers. They knew and saw much of what my family lived in our home. After so many devastating setbacks in family court, my siblings always encouraged me in my search for justice.

I'm thankful to the editor who agreed there was a story here to be told. John worked with me to dig through my early efforts to script this saga. My early text was best defined as "thick" but with John's expertise and patience, I believe we have made a good effort to tell the story the children and I lived. I apologize for any remnants of such thickness, but I write what I feel.

I am also thankful for the cover design provided by Erin Ewasko Black. A great cover is the first page of any book.

I have lived my life with a stutter and always tried my best to hide it from everyone and every circumstance. The night I decided I had to assume the task to protect my children, my first thought was how I would get past the stutter that so controlled much of my life. I decided I had to take on this fight like nothing before in my life. What I am grateful for is that my speech impediment taught me to be quick on my feet. In any circumstance, I always found myself instantaneously searching for a word, or words, that I could convince myself I could say without getting caught in a stutter. Sometimes it worked, many times it did not, and I dreaded every possibility. I was always better and most comfortable ad-libbing a remark or an answer than delivering a prepared speech. The latter did not allow me to choose my words. Speaking is an acquired skill I will forever practice.

Last, but hardly least, I'm most grateful for the United States Constitution and specifically the Fifth and Fourteenth Amendments. These amendments were the bedrock of all my efforts seeking justice in this case, for these children. I believed in these amendments and almost dared anyone who challenged me. That New Jersey Family Court elected to ignore these amendments did not dissuade me from seeking justice where many agreed it did not exist. They took my children, they took me from my home, but they did not take my pen, and with that, I fought back and write this story today.

*The probability that we shall fail in the struggle ought not to deter us from the support of a cause we believe to be just.*

Abraham Lincoln

Made in the USA
Middletown, DE
02 March 2021

34698245R00139